HEART OF GLASS

a memoir

WENDY LAWLESS

GALLERY BOOKS

New York   London   Toronto   Sydney   New Delhi

Gallery Books
An Imprint of Simon & Schuster, Inc.
1230 Avenue of the Americas
New York, NY 10020

First Gallery Books hardcover edition March 2016

GALLERY BOOKS and colophon are registered trademarks of Simon & Schuster, Inc.

For information about special discounts for bulk purchases, please contact Simon & Schuster Special Sales at 1-866-506-1949 or business@simonandschuster.com.

The Simon & Schuster Speakers Bureau can bring authors to your live event. For more information or to book an event, contact the Simon & Schuster Speakers Bureau at 1-866-248-3049 or visit our website at www.simonspeakers.com.

Manufactured in the United States of America

10 9 8 7 6 5 4 3 2 1

Library of Congress Cataloging-in-Publication Data

Lawless, Wendy.
   Heart of glass : a memoir / Wendy Lawless.
      pages   cm
   1. Lawless, Wendy. 2. Motion picture actors and actresses—United States—Biography. 3. Actresses—United States—Biography. I. Title.
PN2287.L28555A3 2016
791.4302'8092—dc23
[B]
2015016465

ISBN 978-1-4767-4980-8
ISBN 978-1-4767-4984-6 (ebook)

To my husband

NEW YORK, 1980

chapter one

PUT YOUR HANDS UP!

I opened my eyes at five in the morning to see the flashing red lights from a fleet of NYPD cars swirling and bobbling across the ceiling of my tiny Eighth Street bedroom.

Some twenty-year-olds on their own for the first time might have been alarmed, but I thought they gave the spartan room a kind of festive whorehouse feel. They were a confirmation that I was no longer in Belmont, Massachusetts, under the same roof as my insane, increasingly violent mother—that I'd made my escape.

Then a belligerent voice squawked over a megaphone, crackling and beeping below my window: "This is the New York City Police Department! We have the building surrounded!"

Half-awake, I wondered who was getting busted, when someone's beefy fist started pounding on the front door of our apartment. My sixth sense for disaster, honed over years of sailing the emotional tsunami that was my home life, told me to run for the fire escape. Unfortunately I was pinned to the bed by the heavy arms and legs of my sleeping boyfriend.

"Wake up, Michael." I nudged him.

"Huh," he muttered into the pillow.

"I think the police are here."

"What?!" He bolted up.

"At the front door," I said resignedly, rolling off the futon and slipping on a cotton nightgown. "Here." I tossed him my oriental-print robe.

My roommate, Beth, a Parsons student fresh from Ohio, met us in the living room. She cowered next to the counter of the kitchenette, clutching the collar of her plaid bathrobe closed over her Lanz nightgown like the schoolmarm in a spaghetti western after the bad guys ride into town.

"Oh my God, what's happening, Wendy?" she whimpered as the reflected red lights played across her frightened face.

"Open up! This is the police!" a gruff voice bellowed from the hall.

"The police are here, Beth," I said calmly. She reminded me of the girls I'd gone to high school with in Boston—cherished princesses who had never had a big zit or a hair out of place or a cavity. I felt sorry for her. I'd had plenty of experience with the police but could tell this was her first time.

"It's probably just a mistake," I assured her. I was an expert at pretending nothing was wrong from the years I had gussied up the truth for my younger sister, Robin. "Some men came and took Mother away on a bed on wheels!" I'd explained after Mother had attempted suicide and was taken to Bellevue. "Heat wave!" I'd pronounced when we found the trousers of one of Mother's boyfriends draped across the wicker chair in Robin's bedroom.

"They probably have the wrong apartment, Beth," I said soothingly, shrugging my shoulders. I was so good at this.

"Are you gonna open the door or are we gonna break it in?!" the voice from the hall shouted.

I headed for the door. Bright light from the hallway glowed at the bottom like when the aliens come for the little boy in *Close Encounters of the Third Kind. I should be so lucky,* I thought.

I peeked through the peephole. A crusty-looking old guy in a crumpled fedora and a coffee-stained trench coat with a badge pinned to the lapel was standing in the hallway, flanked by a couple of uniforms.

"Come on, you gonna open up or what?" the guy barked, eyeing me through the peephole—its fish-eye lens exaggerating his nicotine-yellow teeth and pasty nose with clogged, enlarged pores, making him look like a giant feral rabbit with a skin condition.

I recoiled from the view and looked at Michael, who nodded at me to go ahead.

"Certainly, Officer," I chirped. Maybe because my last name is Lawless and my ancestors were sheep thieves, or because my mom had been arrested and liked to crank-call the cops to falsely report my sister for stealing from her, I had a perpetual feeling of guilt by association and so tended to be overly officious and polite with the police. "I'd be happy to open the door right now."

But as soon as I turned the lock, they shoved the door back—almost taking off my fingers—and barreled into the living room. In addition to crusty guy, there were four uniforms and two more plainclothesmen. Once they were in, they scattered, darting quickly, serpentine-style, through the apartment, checking our bedrooms and bathrooms with their guns drawn as if they expected to find a dozen naked Dominicans cutting cocaine with baby laxative. Unfortunately for them, there was just us: a terror-stricken princess, a bathrobe-wearing actor, and the recently liberated child of a crazy woman. I could hear drawers and closets opened, light switches flicked on, the shower curtain screeching along its rod, and the top of the toilet tank lifted up and down. Then, having found nothing, the cops regrouped in the center of the room, their SWAT-team dance coming to an end. Stone-faced, they all holstered their weapons and gave the three of us the once-over.

"There's nobody else here," said one of the uniforms who had searched Beth's bedroom.

"Are you Harvey Buchbinder?" the old cop asked Michael, eyeing the turquoise, flowered kimono that barely came down to his hairy thighs.

"No, I'm not. My name is Michael Pope," he replied somewhat righteously. Michael and I had been together for about six months. He was an actor, and I could tell from his overly dramatic delivery that he'd rehearsed the line in his head, going over various readings before finally settling on "indignant defiance," as if he were auditioning for the role of a perp on a police procedural show. The cop snorted, unimpressed.

Michael and I had met at the American Repertory Theater in Cambridge, where he was playing various small parts and I was working in wardrobe. Our first conversation had taken place in the dark backstage during a production of *A Midsummer Night's Dream*. He was playing one of the fairies and was wearing a celery-colored bodysuit that covered his face, making him look like a spring vegetable on steroids, so I didn't know until later that he was nine years older than me.

"I'm gonna have to see some identification," the cop said, unconvinced.

Michael retrieved his wallet from my bedroom and brandished his license at him.

"Are you Harvey?" he asked me.

Seriously? I thought. But, always the good girl, I answered sincerely, "No, Officer, I'm not."

"Call me Detective, Detective Stanley. They're officers, in the uniforms," he barked. "What about you?" he said to Beth.

"I'm from Ohio." Her voice quavered.

"No, she's not Harvey, either," I said before Beth had a heart attack. "Look, Harvey's not here. He went out for a pack of cigarettes—"

"When?" the detective said, showing a bit of liveliness for the first time. He pulled a small memo pad and a pen from his coat pocket—preparing to take down the details.

"A week ago. We haven't seen him since." I looked at Beth for backup.

She nodded eagerly. "He rented us these rooms." Her squeaky-clean tone seemed to express hope that the correct answer would end this hideous nightmare.

"There was an ad in *The Village Voice*," I said.

"Figures," Detective Stanley said sourly, "that's where all the sickos are."

I didn't like Detective Stanley, but I had to admit he was right. I had lived in New York when I was a little girl in the late sixties and early seventies. It had been the New York of Holly Golightly and Eloise, a clean, well-lit place where the only homeless person I saw sold pencils with his little dog on the carpet in front of the Bloomingdale's taxi stand. Nothing very bad could happen to you there. But now, in 1980, it seemed something bad could happen to you everywhere. It was very much the New York of Travis Bickel, Son of Sam, and Al Goldstein's *Screw* magazine—a city where the Guardian Angels rode broken-down, graffiti-covered subways when even the cops were intimidated, and drunk homeless people assaulted you for change every ten feet. Now I carried Mace in my purse and strode down the street with a "Don't fuck with me" attitude and my house key wedged between my thumb and forefinger in a fist in case

I had to fight off a mugger—or worse. I never got into an elevator alone with a strange man.

I'd seen a lot my first week in town as I looked for this "dream" apartment with its three flights of stairs, lack of closet space, cockroaches, and leaky faucets. The crusty radiator in my room blasted heat twenty-four/seven and emitted high-pitched screams like a troupe of teenage girls in a horror movie; I'd long since given up trying to open my window, which had been fused shut by coat after coat of slathered-on paint. I'd arrived, after a final fight with my mother, with one suitcase, an acceptance letter to NYU film school, and a couple of hundred dollars in cash. I stayed with Michael in his studio uptown while I looked for a place closer to school. I was wary of moving in with him—where I had once seen my boyfriend as my champion and defender, I now felt as if he had difficulty listening to me and seeing who I was. Maybe it was the age gap, but he tended to lecture me and tell me what to do. My frustration had led to some terrific arguments, and he'd pleaded with me a few times to give him another chance.

There wasn't enough NYU housing even for freshmen, so most of us were just tossed into the streets with the classifieds. Because of the city's bankruptcy, crime, and overall lack of services, a lot of people had fled to the suburbs, and it seemed as if every other residential building was filled with enormous rent-controlled apartments presided over by weird guys or lonely cat ladies who subsidized their "lifestyles" by renting out rooms. I must have looked at thirty shares or sublets. Some of the men were so creepy I worried that if I moved in, I'd wake up in a dog collar chained to the wall. The women were mostly loonies who'd been divorced and practiced chanting and incense burning or were fading actresses or dancers who were still waiting for their big break on Broadway and needed to be free for that last-minute audition.

Compared to them, Harvey Buchbinder seemed positively normal—a frizzy-haired hipster in his late forties who wore low-rise, bell-bottom jeans and an oversized belt buckle. There were no cats in the apartment, and Beth, with her entire girlhood room from Ohio—including skis, hair dryer, popcorn popper, and Kenny Loggins poster—was already ensconced. Harvey only asked me two questions: Do you do drugs? And do you have a steady boyfriend? I had answered no to the first question and yes to the second. I got the feeling the answers didn't matter, but he seemed nice and not likely to own a dog collar. So I gave him a deposit and moved in.

"Why are you looking for this guy?" Michael asked Detective Stanley.

"We believe he may be in danger. Do you know if he's armed?"

Harvey? Armed? I thought. *With what, soap on a rope?* I imagined Harvey wielding his long-ago Hanukkah present from a Hai Karate gift set, swinging it nunchakus style over his head. I smothered an impulse to laugh.

Apparently Harvey had embezzled money from a company owned by the Mafia, and he and his girlfriend had disappeared. The cops wanted to talk to him while his head was still attached to his body. It was a question, the detective explained to us as if we were children, of who got there first—the NYPD or the Gambino crime family.

I hadn't known Harvey long, but he had sort of grown on me. He always came home bearing gifts—like a middle-aged, denim-clad Santa with a Jewfro. One day he gave me the little, white, egg-shaped TV I had in my bedroom; another, a new, black vinyl Ciao! suitcase; and before he took off, a box of chocolate-covered cherries—perhaps, I thought now, as a farewell. It was only later that Robin revealed to me that during a visit she'd made to the apartment, Harvey had shown her his gun.

"What?! Why didn't you tell me?"

"I thought you knew, stupid." My sister shrugged at me.

I suspected he was trying to impress her by showing her he had a dangerous side. She was always getting hit on because she had big boobs.

"I'm going to have my colleagues Detectives Washington and Bernstein move in with you for a few days in case he comes back or calls." Detective Stanley waved his arm at the crowd of men, and two stepped forward.

Washington introduced himself as Stan. He was a dapper African American guy with a pencil mustache, a natty suit, and a knit tie. "And that's Lou," Washington added helpfully as Bernstein nodded at us, shoved his hands in his pockets, and aggressively chewed his gum. He was short, on the chunky side, with red hair and glasses. He seemed a little angry. Dressed in jeans and a denim jacket, he reminded me of a trigger-happy version of Richard Dreyfuss's character in *Jaws*.

Detective Stanley took the uniforms and left while Washington and Bernstein parked themselves on the sofa and played with their guns. Beth emitted a high-pitched squeal, ran to her room, and shut the door. I could hear the punched clacks and flat tones of the buttons on her baby-blue Princess phone as she frantically dialed her parents as Michael and I straggled back to bed.

After a few more fitful hours of sleep, we got up and said good morning to Washington and Bernstein, who'd already sent out for doughnuts and coffee. Beth was still holed up in her room even though I knew she had a morning class. I wasn't sure what she was still upset about; in a crime-filled city, we were the only apartment besides the mayor's with twenty-four-hour police protection. Michael left to go back to his apartment on the Upper West Side to prepare for a play audition, and I got ready for my Fellini/Antonioni class.

Starting with black tights, I dressed in the "Sheena Is a Punk Rocker" look that I'd adopted while hanging out in music clubs in Boston and Cambridge. Always short of cash, I shopped in the secondhand places a few blocks away on Second and Third Avenues, buying vintage dresses, men's jackets, and sequined sweaters from the 1950s. On top of the tights, I pulled on my favorite mini tube-skirt and a little, scruffy red-and-white-checkerboard-patterned sweater I'd picked up at Andy's Chee-Pees for three dollars. The East Village of 1980 may have been kind of a war zone, but I was thrilled to find a glut of cheap shoe stores on my street, where I had bought the cool pair of black ankle boots that completed any ensemble. I zipped myself into them, grabbed my book bag, and headed out the door.

Shopkeepers were hosing down the sidewalks, creating a putrid mist of trash and dog shit that wafted through the air as I headed for St. Mark's Place—a dilapidated hash of dive bars, hippie candle and incense joints, and record and book shops, interspersed with edgy leather- and spandex-filled clothing stores with names such as Search & Destroy and Trash and Vaudeville. The block was presided over by the ghosts of rock 'n' roll, living and dead, who haunted the now-boarded-up Electric Circus, a nightclub where the Grateful Dead, Nico, and the Velvet Underground had played in the sixties and seventies. On the other side of the street stood the St. Marks Baths, a gay all-hours playground for beautiful young men. The mysterious disease that would soon begin to kill many of them was then only just being whispered about, and the baths were still going strong. The corner of St. Mark's and Third Avenue seemed to belong to the Ramones—four hunched-over, pale guys dressed identically in white T's, jeans, leather jackets, and black high-top sneakers. They were there all the time that fall, their dark hair long over their eyes, which were hidden behind sunglasses—as if they were vampires shutting out the light of day.

I'd stopped at the Kiev, a grimy Ukrainian diner on Second Avenue, to pick up a bagel and a coffee to go for breakfast during the screening. I had already scoped out other inexpensive restaurants in the neighborhood. The Veselka, a Polish place a few blocks away, had huge bowls of borscht or chicken noodle soup that came with big buttered pieces of challah that would easily fill you up for the whole day. The Dojo, which I walked by on my way to school on Eighth Street, had a brown rice and vegetable plate that came with a delicious salmon-colored tahini dressing for a couple of dollars. I was a girl on a budget but quickly discovered I could eat well and cheaply on the Lower East Side. The simple food in heavy rotation became my version of a normal family's weekly menu, but instead of Meat Loaf Monday and Taco Tuesday, it was Tahini Thursday and Pickle Soup Sunday. The flavors and smells, chipped china, and fat-fingered waitresses were the grandparents' house and family dinner I'd never known growing up.

Crossing on Eighth Street over Lafayette and Broadway, I walked past the huge, black, metal cube sculpture in Astor Place that groaned as you spun it around on its axis. In the morning, the cube was surrounded by backpacking traveling kids in their sleeping bags, with a few homeless people strewn about snoozing. This encampment was usually broken up by the police midmorning, only to return later at night, after the drunk kids wandered home.

I cut down University Place. The theater where my class was held was on the far side of Washington Square

Park. Passing the elegant town houses with their gated stone staircases and shiny doors flanked by pristine window boxes of artfully arranged geraniums and ferns, I felt as if I were entering an Edith Wharton novel. But when I crossed the street and walked under the huge marble archway into the park, I left the genteel 1800s behind and entered a gritty, nefarious world straight out of *Serpico*. The lawns were bald and brown, trampled by stoned drug dealers and desperate addicts looking for a fix. Busking musicians, young couples making out, old men playing chess, and groups of black kids beating on upside-down white buckets for donations rounded out the park regulars. The rest of us—students, professors, and old Greenwich Village retirees—clutched our bags and moved swiftly across the sidewalks, trying not to stare. At night, we'd just walk around the park.

When I reached the south side of the square, I dashed up the stone steps to Vanderbilt Hall, where the movie theater was. I pushed the heavy swinging door open and felt an immediate calm. The familiar hush of the auditorium seemed to stop time. I settled into a shabby red-velvet seat in the back and waited for the lights to go down. It made me think of sitting in the audience with my sister when we were little, at Lincoln Center or the West End of London, or the Guthrie Theater in Minneapolis, squeezing hands until the moment darkness slowly fell and the show—*The Nutcracker* or *Mame* or a Shakespeare play our father was acting in—began.

"Keep your eyes peeled on the lights," we'd tell each other as we waited for Daddy to come onstage as Andrew Aguecheek in *Twelfth Night* or as Trinculo in *The Tempest.*

My parents had split up when I was seven. My father was an actor at the Guthrie Theater in Minneapolis, and my mother left him for one of the founders, a wealthy producer named Oliver Rea. We lived in the Dakota and on Park Avenue for the brief period of their marriage and its aftermath. Then, fleeing ghosts of boyfriends, husbands, and lovers past and present, my mother essentially kidnapped my sister and me and took us to London. I didn't see my father or hear from or of him for ten years. We'd had a brief reunion just before my final fight with my mother, where I'd learned of her deception. While I had a strong emotional connection with my father, I had only spent three days with him out of the last three thousand six hundred or so. His house and second family didn't at this point qualify as "home."

So for me, a theater, any theater, had become over the years a stand-in for home—a kind of sanctuary where I could invoke happier times. I had wound up in this one at NYU by accident, in a way, after my original career choice—acting—hadn't worked out.

I had wanted to go to theater school, but none of the schools I auditioned for would have me. Crushed, and lacking any kind of guidance, I spent a miserable year and a half at Boston University, studying whatever, just trying to get to my classes while what was left of my home life imploded: My little sister, Robin, became a runaway, my mother was arrested after drunkenly crashing Robin's high school graduation (literally, with her car), and I wrestled Mother into AA. When my sister escaped to college far away in the Midwest, I dropped out of BU and moved back home to babysit my crazy mom. I took a job working at a newsstand in Harvard Square, but missing the theater desperately, I lucked into a position at the American Rep, where I met Michael. He encouraged me to start taking photographs—even bought me a used Olympic SLR. Those pictures had gotten me into film school. The logic of it was loopy and half-assed, but, amazingly, it ended up being my ticket out of town and my mother's life.

I figured that if acting wasn't going to work out, perhaps I could find a way to be a filmmaker. Movies appealed to me the way the theater did—they were an escape, a journey to a different place where you could try on someone else's life for a few hours. But they also spoke to me in a language all their own—a collage of images, cuts, and focuses that I had always understood. My childhood had been a long series of changing locations, casts of characters, and dramatically shifting emotional levels. Movies gave me a way to see my world that made sense. When you grow up privy to conversations about infidelity, drugs, drinking, love, greed, and hatred in language you're too young to understand, it's the pictures that tell you the story. The packed suitcase in the foyer tells you all you need to know about the end of Mother's most recent fight with your stepfather.

The lights went down, and the musty-looking black curtains slowly creaked back, revealing the screen. In the dark, I heard the other students coughing, making hissing shush noises, and opening binder notebooks. The clacking whir of the projector started up in the booth. I popped the lid off my coffee and opened the wax paper wrapped around my still-warm bagel. The film was Antonioni's 1966 *Blow-Up*, the story of a bad-boy fashion photographer in London who discovers he has inadvertently taken pictures of a murder while strolling through a park. I liked the film's self-conscious beauty and expected it to be murder mystery, but then it evolved into a treatise on perception and reality. The hero, played by David Hemmings, has no concern or understanding for the world that surrounds him. Because he lives in a world of surfaces, where sex, love, and death are meaningless, he has difficulty discerning what's real and what isn't. It also has an amazing sound track by Herbie Hancock.

After school I walked home, thinking about how lost all the characters in the film were. They were numb with boredom and unhappiness, but at least they got to do it in Swinging Sixties London. It had been fun to see the city where I'd lived for five years, having teenage fun with my sister and our pack of friends while Mother partied and serial-dated, spending her divorce settlement. For years after we moved back to the States, I would draw diagrams of our flats so I would remember the places and times I missed so much. It had been a way to map my recent past, to remember where I had been.

I turned the key in the lock and opened my apartment

door to find Washington in full shooting stance, his gun pointed right at me.

"Shit!" I raised my book bag like a shield. Bernstein jumped out from behind the door. I was surrounded.

"You should have knocked," Washington replied matter-of-factly.

"But I live here!" I sputtered.

Bernstein shook his head and headed for the sofa, un-cocking his weapon. He seemed pissed off that he hadn't been able to use me for target practice. I looked around for Beth, but she was barricaded in her room.

"We have some forms we need you to sign; you'll most likely be subpoenaed after the suspect is apprehended and taken to trial." Washington motioned with his gun to a pile of papers on the dining table while I wondered how close they'd come to blowing my head off. He holstered his weapon, took a pen out of his breast pocket, and clicked it, handing it to me with a flourish. "Here." He pointed a thin, elegant finger to where he wanted me to sign my name. "And here." His nails were perfect.

I went to my room and put my bag down on a red-painted wooden chair that I had picked up on the street one day. White flight, rotating students, musicians, and artists had made the downtown sidewalks into a kind of pop-up Salvation Army or Goodwill. I had put a filmy piece of pale green, patterned fabric over my one window. My futon was covered by an Indian-print tablecloth that I had bought at Pier 1. I had decorated the bare white walls with a few postcards, photos, and some pictures I'd cut out of magazines. It was pretty sparse, but I hadn't been able to get much from my mother's house before I left. My last conversation with her had not gone well after I'd informed her that I was no longer planning to turn over my $50,000 college fund to her when I turned twenty-one. That money had been left to me by my grandfather, her father, who had obviously known there wouldn't be anything left to pay for college if she had access to it. So my records, clothes, winter coat, and all my other belongings were at her house, if she hadn't yet set fire to them in a fit of rage.

After doing some French homework and studying for a History of Film test, I jotted down some notes about *Blow-Up* to prepare for the paper I'd be writing. Michael was busy that evening, seeing a play he had an audition for to replace one of the actors. I didn't feel like spending the evening with Washington and Bernstein, so I decided to go to the movies. *The Man Who Fell to Earth* was playing at Cinema Village on East Twelfth Street, and as a big David Bowie fan, I didn't want to miss it. I'd always loved all the glitter-rock guys: Marc Bolan from T. Rex, Bryan Ferry from Roxy Music, and of course Bowie. Robin and I had even gone to his house in London, one day after school, and rung the doorbell, but ran away when the prospect of meeting our idol was too much for us to handle.

The movie theater was already dark when I slid into a seat with my dinner of fifty-cent popcorn. Only a few other people were in the audience. Bowie plays an alien who has traveled to Earth to find water for his planet, where everyone is dying. He loses his way and becomes addicted to television and alcohol. Everyone on his planet, including his wife and children, perish while he rides around drunk in a limo. The movie was trippy, with eerily haunting images, and Bowie looked both ethereal and fantastic in tailored suits, with a soft brown fedora angled over his flame-orange hair. When the lights came up, I enjoyed the afterglow, those moments after a movie is over but you're still in its world.

"Are you by any chance wearing Givenchy Gentleman?" a man's voice asked from behind me. Still a bit dazed, I turned to see a skinny young guy with hazel eyes and a dark blond punky haircut. He was wearing a mustard-colored jacket flecked with purple and a black skinny tie with a red gingham shirt. He looked like a super cute Tintin.

"Yes, I am." I had bought a small bottle of Givenchy Gentleman at the drugstore, after falling in love with its woodsy rose and leather scent. I smiled at him.

"Me, too." He smiled back. "Did you like the movie?"

"Oh, I love David Bowie, so, yeah."

"Do you wanna go get a cup of coffee?"

"Sure."

We walked down the street to the nearest diner and sat at the counter, drank coffee, and traded life stories. Ben was twenty-two and had just graduated from college. He had moved to New York from middle-of-nowhere Texas and was working in an office downtown as a proofreader, until he figured out what he wanted to do with the rest of his life. He lived in a tiny first-floor apartment with bars over its windows in Alphabet City, six blocks away.

I had this rushing, excited feeling as we talked, finishing each other's sentences and proclaiming a shared love for Blondie, Dashiell Hammett, French and Italian movies, and vintage clothing. I felt immediate kinship, an instant closeness that almost seemed as if we had met somewhere before, even though we hadn't.

My relationship with Michael was different, more straightforward and sexual. I looked up to him because he was older and wiser, and he'd opened up a world to me, buying me a camera and encouraging me to start my own life away from my mother. But because I had grown up without a father, and my mother was not just promiscuous but rapacious, going through lovers like a Chanel-clad, sex-crazed shark, I was somewhat unsure about the nature of relationships. Like David Hemmings's character in *Blow-Up*, my experiences of life were filtered. But instead of a camera lens it was my mother who had distorted my perceptions. What was love? Compatibility? Good sex? The ability to stay up all night talking? Or to be able to be together and not say a word? I wasn't sure.

"Have you ever been to the opera?" Ben asked. We were eating french fries and gravy that he had ordered. I confessed to him that I had not.

"Then you'll go with me, as my guest." He beamed at me over the glistening pile of potatoes.

"Really?" The opera made me think of powdered wigs and lorgnettes.

He told me that he had box seats for Mozart's *Don Giovanni* at the Met in two weeks. He said that the opera was such a pure expression of beauty and truth that I had to experience it. I looked at the clock on the wall. It was 4:00 a.m.

"Will you come?"

"Um . . ." My mind suddenly turned to Michael, who probably wouldn't want me to go to the opera with another man. Still, I felt drawn to Ben in an almost friendish, innocent way. "Can I call you?"

"No." He wrote down the date and time of when I was to meet him at Lincoln Center on a napkin and handed it to me. "Here. If you don't want to come, don't show up." He looked me in the eye.

He explained to me that he didn't have a phone, so we'd either meet in two weeks at the Met—or not.

"Okay." I nodded. It was kind of like a game, and it made me like him even more.

The sun was just peeking up behind the buildings when Ben walked me home. The garbage trucks had hit the streets, loudly whining and grinding up the trash as the men hurled it into the backs.

"Good night," he said at my building. He kissed my hand and walked back toward Alphabet City.

I took my key out and walked up the three flights to my front door. I was about to put the key in the lock when I stopped. "Washington, Bernstein, don't draw your guns, it's me, Wendy," I called out.

I let myself in and found them camped out on the couch.

"Where the hell have you been?" Washington asked. "We were worried about you, girl."

"I went to a movie, then out for coffee."

"Coffee?! Till dawn?!" Washington looked incredulous. "With that boyfriend of yours?"

"No, just with someone I met at the movies."

"There's just no one looking out for you, is there?" Bernstein chipped in, shaking his head.

"You are." I smiled.

"Well, we have good news and bad news," said Washington, getting up, stretching, and adjusting his cuff links.

The good news was that Harvey had been spotted in Florida at a gas station while he was filling up his rental car. The bad news was that today while the police were questioning the landlord, it came out that he didn't know Harvey had rented out rooms in the apartment. He told the cops that Beth and I were illegal tenants and we had to be out in twenty-four hours. I asked if Beth knew, and they said she did.

Now what? Clearly, I wouldn't be getting my deposit back from a man who was on the lam from the mob. My school tuition was covered by the money my grandfather had left me—just enough for a degree as long as I didn't switch schools again. My bank account had about $200 in it.

To cover my deposit for Harvey, I had already sold the monogrammed Louis Vuitton overnight bag my mother had bought me. I had taken it to a swanky leather shop on the

Upper East Side, but the owner had sniffed at me and said he wasn't interested. Luckily, a man from Texas who'd just broken loose from an executive retreat at the Waldorf had overheard our conversation and followed me out of the store.

"The little lady is going to love this!" Tex chuckled as his piggy fingers peeled off five twenties from a huge wad of cash.

The bag had my initials on it, and I wanted to ask what his wife's name was. Wanda? Wilhelmina? I wasn't sad to see it go. It matched my sister's and was very much the sort of thing Mother thought we should have. A status-symbol suitcase for those weekends in Paris. Those days were long over—along with the limo rides, the Broadway shows, the fancy hotels, and the posh addresses of my once-privileged girlhood.

Since it now looked as if I would be needing more money, I went back out to look for a place to sell a few items from my modest jewelry collection. I had considered calling the bank in Kansas City to ask for some cash from my college fund—but decided that my trust officer, the dour and disapproving Mr. Charno, would think that my story about the NYPD coming through my front door searching for a roommate running from the Mafia would sound too much like one of my mother's zany fabrications designed to suck the account dry.

WE BUY GOLD! the sign promised as I entered the grimy, little vestibule of the pawnshop, a few blocks from my apartment on lower Broadway. The greasy carpeting and smeared bulletproof glass created the ambience of an impending crime. I placed a gold chain and a gold bracelet with a little French-flag charm in the sliding tray in the wall to be tested and weighed by the sullen, doughy-faced man on the other side of the window. Both pieces had been gifts from my ex-stepdad. The necklace had been presented to me at Sardi's on my sixteenth birthday, and my ex-stepdad had purchased the bracelet at Cartier during a trip to Paris when I was twelve. My ex-stepdad, or Pop as my sister and I called him, was living comfortably somewhere on the Upper East Side, but after years of paying our private-school tuition and bailing my mother out of various jams long after they'd divorced, he had tired of her gold-digging shenanigans and had finally cut her off completely. He was just another in a long line of bridges Mother had burned. Ultimately, all her relationships turned toxic, and I thought that through guilt by association Pop wouldn't be happy to receive a plea for financial help from me.

The pawnshop man snatched up my jewelry. "You sure you want to sell these?" His dead eyes stared at me from behind the glass. I smiled and nodded, thinking that if I appeared cheerful and not desperate, he'd give me a better price. He just shrugged.

When I was younger and we needed money, my mother had often resorted to selling something—an emerald ring, the grand piano, or the Rodin sculpture she'd gotten in her divorce settlement from Pop. That way she wouldn't have to—heaven forbid—go out and get a job. She'd even once talked one of her boyfriends into buying us a new washing machine, though I never saw her do a load of laundry. She wasn't the domestic type.

"I'll give you seventy-five bucks."

"Each?" I was hoping that was what he meant.

"No, for both."

Deflated, I nodded and took the money. This and the two hundred in my bank account could get me a new room and maybe a month to find some kind of part-time job. I was sad to part with these fond little trinkets from my girlhood, but it seemed, in a way, Pop was still helping me.

That evening I was meeting Michael at McHale's, an actor hangout on Eighth Avenue in the theater district. I emerged from the Times Square subway station, breathing the familiar stench of a thousand uncleaned urinals. Trash whirled through the air like dirty confetti. All the taxis seemed to be honking in unison, while the hookers, autograph hounds, three-card monte hustlers, break-dancers, and the rest of the rabble competed for their share of the sidewalks. I walked up Eighth Avenue, past peep shows, the shoe-shine guys, bodegas, and stores selling sex toys and X-rated videos. A balding man with glasses in a shiny, cheap suit and scuffed Florsheim wing tips careened into me as he slipped out of a dirty-movie theater, clutching his briefcase and a giant pack of diapers, clearly in a hurry to get to Port Authority and the express bus back to New Jersey and his family.

With its frilly tartan curtains, old wooden bar, and Naugahyde booths, McHale's had a certain sad, crappy charm. You could imagine some poor bastard really crying into his beer here. It was always packed with up-and-coming actors, stage stars, has-beens, union set and prop guys, and local drunks. The food was middling but inexpensive, and the drinks were big and cheap. Michael was sitting at a table in the back, talking to a couple of other guys—actors, I guessed.

Before I met him at the theater in Cambridge, Michael had been in a successful Broadway play for three years, but times had been lean since then. He'd been working putting up drywall and had bought an apartment on the Upper West Side, fixing it up as an investment. His career had stalled, and he had been relying more on the construction work, which frustrated him. I approached the table and sat down, but they were busy talking shop: who was being seen for the new Arthur Miller play, how hard it was to get in to see a certain hot casting director, who was getting his or her teeth capped or a nose job, and what a prick Hal Prince was. I ordered a cheeseburger and waited for my turn to talk. I often felt, when out with Michael's friends, that I was invisible. Everyone else talked a lot, but I was afraid to open my mouth, in case it made me look stupid, so usually I didn't. Maybe because I was the youngest person by far at the party or the bar or the restaurant when we went out together, I lacked the courage and the confidence to join in the fray. I thought of *Manhattan*, a movie I'd seen in Boston the year before on a date, because I was the exact opposite of Mariel Hemingway's character, Tracy. Although Tracy is dramatically younger than her boyfriend, played by Woody Allen, and his crowd, she is enormously self-possessed and articulate, comfortable wherever she is. I wished I could be more like her, but lacking her assuredness and brio, I preferred to be a wallflower, hoping that I wouldn't be noticed or called upon.

After about fifteen minutes, Michael's actor pals patted him on the back and drifted away toward the bar. He told me how his auditions had gone and jokingly asked how Washington and Bernstein were. I filled him in about Harvey, the eviction, and my imminent homelessness. He didn't say anything, just nodded and stirred his scotch on the rocks with a little red plastic straw. I thought about telling him about Ben, but realized just in time that he would only be needlessly jealous. So I just told him about the movie, which he said sounded like a snooze. He didn't like David Bowie anyway.

Afterward, we strolled down Restaurant Row toward Times Square to look at the lights and do some people watching—something most actors love to do. Jazz music drifted out from the saloon doors along the street, scrawny trees rasped their branches together, and waiters on their breaks, dressed in black pants and white shirts, smoked cigarettes on the stoops. We turned the corner and, a few blocks down, ducked into Playland, so Michael could play *Space Invaders*.

The arcade was jammed with people, mostly young males, leather-clad street types with greased-back hair or disco-suited preeners in high-heeled boots with their shirts open to expose all their cheap gold chains. They were showing off to their drinking buddies or to their scantily clad, big-haired girlfriends. Pressed shoulder to shoulder hunched over the game cabinets, they jerked and flipped the buttons on the control panels, the screens throwing a ghoulish green glow over their faces. Loud beeping, buzzers, and bells all wailed simultaneously, and overhead speakers blared "Ladies' Night" by Kool and the Gang. There were whoops of victory or fist-pumping when someone made a big score or blew the most heads off. It smelled like old fry-pit oil and BO and made me feel dirty just standing there.

"I think you should move in with me!" Michael suddenly shouted toward me over the din, his hand smacking the firing button about a hundred times a minute as he killed electronic aliens.

"What?!" I wasn't sure I'd heard him correctly.

"You should move in with me!"

"Maybe!" I yelled back. The truth was I didn't want to move in with him. Having just escaped my mother's house, I wanted to be independent. But I was stuck and had less than a day to find another place to go.

"But I don't want you to feel like you have to ask me! I could probably crash on a couch somewhere until I figure something else out!" I had only two friends living in the city—women I'd met at BU—both of whom had transferred here. Jenny Ott was a native New Yorker who lived with her boyfriend, Pete Homer, and two roommates; and Julie was a vegetarian meatpacking heiress who was now studying painting at the School of Visual Arts.

Michael looked up at me from the popping, crablike images moving across the screen. "I want you to move in! I love you!" he practically screamed in my face.

"You do?!" I yelled back over the general cacophony. Suddenly I felt as if my throat were closing up. I cared about Michael, but wasn't sure I loved him—or even what that meant.

Michael leaned over, kissed me, and smiled. "Of course I do! Now cheer up and play some *Space Invaders!*" He shoved more coins into the slot.

"I'm terrible at stuff like this!" I said apologetically. The noise in the arcade was ear piercing, and I was starting to feel claustrophobic from all the bodies and the din. I just wanted to leave. I tried to play the game, but I was awful. I couldn't hit anything. "See?! I can't do it!" I looked at Michael and threw up my hands.

"Try again!"

"Really?!" I replied weakly, trying to think of a way to end this. I could pretend to faint—or vomit maybe.

"Wendy"—he shook his head at me, frowning slightly—"if you can't play a video game, how do you expect to play the game of life?!"

I couldn't believe he was serious, and my mouth dropped open a little. "It's just a stupid game, Michael! Can't we go?!"

I could tell he was irritated, but he took my hand and we left. I felt embarrassed at my clumsiness, but at the same time I wondered why he was treating me like a naughty little kid. Maybe because I was acting like one.

We walked out onto the smelly, crowded street on our way to the subway, past the transvestites, the break-dancers, and the Jesus freaks who wore REPENT signs—all the humanity lit up by the marquees of myriad porno theaters. Michael was going uptown, I was going downtown. After we went through the turnstile, I reached out and touched his arm.

"I'm sorry about the game." It seemed easier to apologize for myself and my failings at video games than to call him on his bullshit.

"Forget it." He gave me a peck on the cheek. "See you tomorrow. I'll get a key made for you." He smiled, then turned to descend to the uptown train platform. Watching him go down the steps, past a poster for *Don Giovanni* at the Met, I realized I hadn't told him that I loved him back.

The next morning I bade farewell to the frazzled Beth, whose baleful-looking parents were packing up her bedroom set, her bike, and area rugs to be shipped back to the heartland. Her experiment in Sodom was over. She'd decided to leave Parsons and find an art school closer to Cleveland.

No one was coming to pick me up and take me home. Luckily, I didn't have much to pack. Traveling light was my métier—a skill from a childhood spent on the move. I shoved my clothes into the now ironically named Ciao! suitcase

Harvey had given me and put everything else—my clock radio, a few books, and my toothbrush—in a Lamston's bag I'd found under the sink. I rolled up my futon and tied it with a pair of panty hose. Hoisting it all up on my shoulders, Sherpa-style, I walked down the stairs and out onto Eighth Street to hail a cab to Michael's apartment uptown.

Standing on the curb with my hand up in the air, I tried not to drop the futon on the filthy sidewalk. My first perch as a film student hadn't worked out. I had come to New York to escape my mother and to find a life for myself, but now I was moving in with my boyfriend. I couldn't help but feel that I had somehow failed, and that, like my mom, I was being saved by a man.

chapter two

MODERN LOVE

Leaving the jungle of downtown, traveling by taxi to the Upper West Side, I might as well have been aboard a steamship on an expedition to a foreign continent. This was the land of gourmet grocery stores like Zabar's and Fairway, yuppies, upscale watering holes and fern bars like Marvin Gardens and J.G. Melon, and enormous prewar apartment buildings: the Ansonia, the San Remo, the Beresford, with their uniformed doormen, high ceilings, and hardwood floors.

My cabdriver stopped at the light on Seventy-second Street and Central Park West, kitty-corner from the Dakota, another majestic building that had briefly been my childhood home during Mother's stormy second marriage to my now ex-stepfather. Lauren Bacall, Leonard Bernstein, and Rudolf Nureyev had all lived there or were living there still. Our doorman, if he hadn't retired, might be calling a taxi for John and Yoko. I looked up at the windows of the rooms where I used to play with my sister. Now I was an outsider, riding past a place I once called home.

Michael's apartment was not in one of those grand buildings but in a modest, narrow one wedged behind Broadway on Eighty-fifth Street. His place was basically a large studio with a tiny separate kitchen and bathroom. On the inside of the building with a view of the air shaft, the apartment was dark during the day, which lent it an atmosphere of limbo. I found the absence of light disorienting—you never knew what time it was or what the weather was like outside. If you wanted to see the sky, you had to stick your head all the way out the window and crane your neck acrobatically toward the top of the shaft.

Dragging my life behind me in a shopping bag and a suitcase, I paid the driver and emerged from the taxi futon-first. I trudged up the front steps, shedding a few wire hangers as I went, and pressed the button next to Michael's name. At the flat, harsh sound of the buzzer, I pushed myself against the door and into the foyer. I took the cramped elevator up to the fourth floor and knocked on Michael's door.

"You're here!" he said, opening the door, and grabbed at my largest bundle, the futon, which he stashed in a corner. A narrow hallway led to the main room of the apartment, which functioned as a bedroom/living room/dining room. "I cleared out a few drawers for you and made space in the bathroom," he said brightly. The apartment had no closets, but he had bought a few wheeled coatracks that lined one wall.

"Thanks." I forced a smile as I tried not to feel like some poor relative he was taking in. I hadn't even planned to unpack, just live out of my suitcase as if I were staying at a hotel. But I dutifully hung up my clothes and placed my stockings, underwear, and T-shirts in the drawers that were open and empty, waiting for me to arrive. The double bed was covered with a drab brown spread and hugged by a wooden, modular bed frame with built-in side tables. The room was barely illuminated by the dim track lighting that hung overhead. Everything felt, looked, very masculine. An awful cocktail of anxiety and fear began to wash over me—a mixture of the uneasiness I felt at being beholden to Michael and the realization that I was trapped in this gloomy space, expected to call it my own, too. It was as if I were giving away a piece of myself.

"I'm sorry, there's nothing in the fridge because I'm redoing the kitchen—but I thought we'd go out and celebrate your first night here."

I staved off a panicked urge to run out the front door. "Sure." I swallowed my feeling of impending doom. "That'd be nice. Let me just pop into the loo."

"I love that you call it that!"

I nodded weakly.

The bathroom was a few steps up, near the base of the bed. I walked in and closed the door, trying to take some deep breaths to calm down. I peed and splashed some cold water on my face. Looking at my reflection in the mirror surrounded by brown tile and speckled faux marble, I wondered if I'd made a really big mistake. Maybe I should have called my girlfriend Jenny to ask if I could crash on the couch.

Get a grip, I told myself, *don't think of it as "living together." It's just temporary, like I'm a houseguest, right?* Then why did I feel this heavy sense of dread? Oh, well, I sighed, it was too late now. I took a deep breath, plastered on my best fake smile, and walked to the door to meet Michael.

We went to a Peruvian Chinese place on Broadway called Flor de Mayo that was near Michael's apartment. We ate this killer rotisserie chicken that came with black beans and fried plantains, washing it down with Tsingtaos. The beer took some of the edge off my jitters.

"I do love you, you know." Michael grabbed my hands across the table.

"I know. I love you, too." I hoped it didn't sound like a reflexive response. I was still making up my mind about it myself but wanted to appear convincing.

"It's more than that, really . . . it's like I love the woman you're going to become." He smiled and looked at me dreamily.

"Um, thanks." This struck me as a curious thing to say. Did it mean that I wasn't a complete person, in some way? Was I watered-down, abbreviated? A *Reader's Digest* condensed version of a woman? I knew that I wasn't perfect, maybe even kind of a fuckup, but I thought I'd left my training wheels behind long ago.

Michael paid the check. He'd told me he wasn't going to make me pay rent, just my share of the phone and utilities.

Even though it was generous and decent of him, I couldn't help but feel like the oft-kept woman of my family—my mom.

During my childhood and teen years, she had been quite adept at finding some rich guy, usually an old boyfriend she'd kept waiting in the wings, to bankroll us. A new car, a fur coat, a weekend in Paris or Fort Lauderdale—just a few of the many perks she was able to scare up with her charm and frosty-blond good looks. When she wasn't suckering some guy out of cash, she was busy siphoning funds out of my trust account or my sister's. The only "job" she'd had in my lifetime was writing a novel, entitled *Somebody Turn Off the Wind Machine*, which she'd been at work on sporadically for seven or eight years now. It was a fictionalized account of a car trip we took across America to visit her father at her childhood home in Kansas City before he died. When she wasn't drinking massive amounts of white wine, chain-smoking, or trying to set fire to the house, she was typing her manuscript and planning how she would cope with the instant, overnight megasuccess her book—and the subsequent motion picture it would undoubtedly be made into—would bring her. She was convinced she was the next Erica Jong. I remained skeptical.

"Ready?" Michael looked at me adoringly across the table after the waiter had brought the change from the bill.

"Sure." I stood up and put on my coat. We went out onto Broadway, and Michael put his arm around me. I wondered if he would want to make love when we got back to the apartment. I tensed up, as our sex life had recently reached a roadblock, a development that I felt both responsible for and guilty about. I had had little experience with men, and Michael was older and certainly more knowledgeable than my two previous boyfriends—he had given me my first orgasm. But I still found it difficult to relax and sometimes struggled to climax. I could give one to myself, but it started to bother Michael that he couldn't always. I assured him that it was fine, that I enjoyed being held and touched, and that I didn't always have to "get off," but he would get annoyed and say things like "What's the point of having sex if I can't make you come?" I didn't know how to respond to this, except to apologize for my shortcomings, and reiterate that an orgasm wasn't always necessary to me. This way, it was all my fault, right? But his frustration had grown as our relationship moved out of the initial first-kiss crush stage, into the more everyday-life-of-a-couple kind. I'd even faked it a few times, thinking it would make him happy.

This time, instead of faking it, I decided to face the problem head-on . . . and lie to avoid having sex with him. "I'm super tired; I have a French test in the morning. Is it okay if I just do a little studying and go to bed?" It was my version of "Not tonight, Joséphine."

And it worked.

"Sure. I spent all day putting up drywall, so I'm beat." Michael was currently working on a crew, doing a renovation at a young, up-and-coming actress's place. She had made a few movies and was about to open in a play off-Broadway, a fact that pained him.

Back at the apartment, we retreated to our corners. Michael retired to the bed to watch the news, and I sat in the tiny kitchen at the Formica table, pretending to memorize irregular verbs.

I sat in the dark and sniffled, wiping my eyes as I watched Giulietta Masina in *La Strada*, playing Gelsomina—a simpleminded wastrel with a huge, round face, strawlike short hair, and black, pooling eyes. She loves this brute of a man, Zampanò, but he cannot bring himself to be even a little kind to her. The girl on the screen could have been me, I so identified with her search for love and her yearning for a place to belong. She always hoped and never gave up. Of course, she dies at the end of the movie of basically a broken heart, but it still felt romantic.

The lights came on, and we started filing out of the auditorium. I'd been at NYU a month but hadn't made any friends in any of my classes yet. I watched kids shuffle down the steps, lighting their cigarettes and talking excitedly about the film, not sure how to join them. I envied their confidence and surety about what they were doing here, especially considering I couldn't even bring myself to raise my hand to ask a question or venture an opinion. I felt an emotional relationship with films; my classmates seemed to know all the facts. I usually slunk out after the lights came up, more in touch with fiction than reality.

I came home that evening to find Michael, with plaster

dust in his hair, standing on a ladder painting the kitchen. The kitchen wasn't up and running yet, so we'd been eating takeout a lot—mostly Chinese and Indian food, with the occasional burger and fries from the coffee shop on Seventy-ninth Street for variety. Eating out of paper bags and cartons only added to my sense of being in limbo, as if my life were free-floating and I had nowhere to land. It reminded me too much of my childhood, living in hotels and scrounging the last Entenmann's doughnut from the box in the minifridge or leftover hors d'oeuvres from Mother's cocktail parties.

"How was your day?" he asked while applying white paint to the window ledges.

"Okay." I tossed my book bag on a chair.

Even though I disliked the unsettled nature of our arrangement, I also chafed at the forced "Honey, I'm home" domesticity. I couldn't help but wish that he'd just throw his paintbrush out the window and shout, "Let's go out clubbing all night long, baby!" It was as if I didn't live there and also as if we'd already been married for ten years, not that I would know how that looked. My understanding of a happy home life came from Doris Day movies—not from my life. But I resented having to be accountable to him—being asked where I was, whom was I with, made me feel angry at him, as if he were my husband or my mom. I swallowed these feelings, feeling guilty and ungrateful, and went to the fridge to get a Diet Pepsi.

"Hey, wanna go to Joe's house in Connecticut this weekend?"

Finally, some adventure. "Sure, I guess. I'll have to bring some homework." It would be fun to escape the city, *and the confines of this playing-house routine*, I thought.

Joe was an old friend of Michael's whose parents were well-known actors who'd been blacklisted in the 1950s for their support for liberal causes such as integration and labor unions. After the McCarthy era ended, they were able to return to show business and had a place in Connecticut that had been paid for by wildly successful TV commercials for Pepto-Bismol and Cracker Jack.

"Jesus, I'm living with a girl who does homework. I'll get the car on Friday, and we can drive up." Michael had an old yellow Dodge Dart with a black top and black upholstery he kept parked in a huge, barbed-wire-enclosed lot near the West Side Highway. He was proud of it, a car being a status symbol in Manhattan. It meant you could afford to keep a car in the city, you had a country house, or you could just have a little getaway when you wished to.

"Great." I smiled affably, and he went back to painting the window.

Michael picked me up after my last class on Friday around four, and we headed out of the city. As we turned off the Henry Hudson, onto the Saw Mill Parkway, we were instantly plunged onto a leafy, lugelike road that twisted through huge trees and by low stone walls and bridges. The Saw Mill was one of my favorite roads to drive down on the East Coast. I rolled down my window and took a deep breath as we drove past the sign for Chappaqua.

Newly landed back in the States, I had spent a happy summer in Chappaqua at the Saw Mill Summer Theater, doing a play, when I was sixteen. "There's the statue of Horace Greeley!" I pointed at the side of the parkway in front of the old barn where we had rehearsed the play four years ago. Now the red paint on the barn was peeling, the weeds had overtaken it, and a few boards had crumbled away. But it was still there. I smiled.

"Uh, yeah." Michael peeked quickly, probably wondering why I was so stoked about an old statue. "'Go west, young man,' right?"

The summer I was sixteen and Robin was fifteen, our mother had moved us suddenly—after five years in exciting, busy London—to a small, quaint commuter town in Connecticut called Ridgefield, away from our friends and our school. Reeling from culture shock and craving sophistication, we were lucky enough to get summer-theater jobs in the nearby town of Chappaqua, New York, about a thirty-minute drive away, in a production of Noël Coward's *Hay Fever*. I was in the play, cast as a bubble-brained flapper, and Robbie worked backstage on the props and sets. I had gotten my driver's license upon landing in the States, so if we had to live in this godforsaken hick town in the boonies, at least we could make our getaway—for a while—in a used car Pop had bought for us. I hadn't felt so free since London.

In the play, I got to wear a gold-lamé evening gown and got paid $12 per performance. Everyone in the cast was older than me by at least ten years, so I was the baby and a bit insecure about my ability to hold my own. One day in rehearsal, the director said, "You'll go far in this business, Wendy," but I thought he was teasing me, so I burst into tears and ran out of the room. I had a huge crush on a guy in the cast who came out at the end and played a medley of Noël Coward songs on the piano while the rest of us sang along. He was handsome, like a young Brando, with shining blond hair that swept up from his forehead and huge green eyes that matched the silk dressing gown he wore onstage. I would stand there, singing "Mad About the Boy," willing him to look my way, but he never did. I was so naïve, I didn't realize that he was gay—one of the first of many ill-fated crushes I had on men who were snappy dressers, good dancers, and sparkling conversationalists.

It had been a wonderful summer, driving back and forth to do the play, listening to the radio at night to stay awake. A few months later Robbie and I were immersed in the hell of being the resident freaks at our huge public high school by day and returning home to our dark house afterward, holding our breaths to see if there'd be dinner on the stove, or if our likely drunk mom was going to emerge from her room. But *Hay Fever* had been our refuge.

Michael and I pulled into Joe's folks' place a half an hour later. The house was a modest Cape Cod with a gray-shingled roof and black shutters. Some people were milling in the driveway, drinking beers and glasses of wine. Joe, with sandy-colored hair and an open but still interesting face, stood in front of a hibachi with a long fork, moving hot dogs and burgers around. Someone was cranking the Stones from inside the house—"Let It Bleed." Joe was the only friend of Michael's whom I didn't feel intimidated around. He was friendly and accepting and seemed genuinely interested in me. I felt like less of a Lolita in his presence. The rest of Michael's crowd either ignored me or gave me the once-over, as if to say, "Who's the schoolgirl?" Of course, they all wanted to know how old I was. Funnily, I looked even younger than I was—sometimes I thought of telling them I was jailbait just to see how they'd react. But I was always on my guard with this crowd. To be fair to them, I chose to remain separate and rarely uttered a peep. It seemed easier to skirt the edges. Years of being the new kid at school had trained me well. Instead of showing how ill at ease I was, I played mystery girl, believing that my aloofness would come across as sophistication and smarts.

"Hey, buddy!" Joe ran up to Michael and gave him a hug. "Someone get this guy a beer. Wendy, what can I get you?"

"Oh, hi . . . maybe some wine?" I kissed his cheek, standing in the driveway, the gravel playing havoc with my kitten heels. I took them off, let them dangle from my fingers, then slung them over my shoulder, the way I'd seen a lovely gamine do in the movies. Almost instantly, a large plastic goblet was shoved into my hand. I looked up to see Joe smiling at me winningly, then he returned to his grill. Michael melted into the crowd. There were about fifteen people, some of them I knew, most of them actors. I followed around behind Michael and stood at his side, smiling and trying to look interested in what everyone was talking about.

"Jesus, are you kidding me? I mean it's a perfect technical performance, but I'd rather see someone not so skilled play the part and actually feel something. Someone who doesn't have their head up their RADA ass," said Michael's friend Bill, who had studied to be a serious actor. Everyone laughed. Bill was blond and hunky and had recently played a doomed version of himself being impaled in a bunk bed while having sex in *Friday the 13th*. "That's why Tom Hulce is so amazing!" Bill spread his arms wide for emphasis, a beer in one hand, a cigarette in the other. "C'mon people!"

"Has anyone seen . . ."

"I loved her in . . ."

"Well, I've heard he's that crazy in real life . . ."

"She's a heroin addict . . ."

I walked around the patio, catching snippets of conversations in the growing dark. The food was set out on a long table next to the swimming pool; the underwater lights lit up swimmers, thanks to an Indian summer and Joe's having cranked up the heat in October.

Across the patio, Michael listened intently to his old friend Nick, a musician who worked in a record store during the day. At night, he was working with a rap artist in Bedford-Stuyvesant, sneaking up to meet him at his place in the projects in a zipped-up anorak so no one could see he was white. Michael nodded as Nick talked and shook his head, his long dark hair moving side to side as he stroked his beard. Between the hair and the beard, you could hardly see Nick. I only knew him a little bit—he had recently broken up with his girlfriend and was down over it. His dad was this eccentric painter who lived in the Westbeth, an artists' building on Bank Street where Dianne Arbus had killed herself. Michael told me Nick's dad hadn't been outside, not even to go to the store, in something like twenty years. I watched Michael put his hand on his friend's shoulder. Nick stared out across the lawn, looking miserable.

Helping myself to some steak and corn and sitting at one of the tables by the pool, I smiled at everyone who passed by, feeling a little like the nerd in the school cafeteria no one wants to sit with.

"Is this seat taken?" It was Bobby, an actor with a baby face and a twangy accent. Bobby was like someone from another time—a Southern gentleman with lovely manners and soft-spoken ways. I liked him and secretly wondered if he was gay.

"No, please, be my guest." I motioned to the three empty chairs at my table. My dance card was anything but full.

"'Be my guest'—what a quaint phrase that is! You sound like my mom. She's very homespun."

I wasn't sure if Bobby intended that as a compliment, so I just shrugged my shoulders and looked cheerful.

"Omigolly, look at this." He surveyed the crowd. "I just know what's going to happen next, don't you?" He picked up a drumstick gingerly and nibbled on it, then took a sophisticated sip of his three-olive martini.

"Um . . . they serve dessert?"

"No, my dear, I've been to a few of these, I can tell you—certainly more than you. In about ten minutes, everybody's going to take off their clothes and jump in the pool."

"Really?"

"Oh, heavens, yes—it'll be like Sodom and Gomorrah, right here in Litchfield County. Just you wait and see." He sighed deeply, clearly disappointed in all the other party-goers. Sure enough, Bobby's prediction came true, and in the allotted time frame no less. The first person to strip was Bill, who of course had nothing to lose since he had the body of an Adonis. Then a few women took the plunge, screaming and still holding their drink glasses. Then Joe dove in, followed by Michael—and then everyone else, in a charge en masse. Bobby and I sat in our deck chairs, trying not to peek at the bobbing breasts and penises, looking mostly at each other or down at our dinner plates.

"If you're worried that I'm going to get buck naked and go in there, don't."

"Oh, no . . . I won't go, either, I mean, I don't want to." I couldn't imagine anything more embarrassing, and apparently neither could Bobby. He was a prude, and I was just unwilling to expose my small breasts, big butt, and overall lack of muscle tone. The thought terrified me.

"Wendy! Come on in!" Michael hoisted himself up on the side of the pool and came running over. He started to drip onto my steak.

Bobby eyed him nervously, eyebrows raised.

"No, thanks. I'm going to sit here and keep Bobby company."

"We're having fun. I want you to come in." Michael reached to take my hand in his wet one.

Thankfully, Bobby came to my rescue, covering my hand in his. He looked up at Michael and said in a very courtly manner, "We are having a very intense, emotional discussion that we are in the middle of. I cannot possibly spare Wendy at this time."

"Okay," Michael said slowly, clearly turning it over in his head. Shrugging, he ran back to the pool, executing a perfect cannonball into the deep end.

"Thank you for saving me." I laughed and knocked back the rest of my wine.

"Think nothing of it—we girls need to stick together."

Maybe he is gay, I thought. In about twenty years time, after paying his dues big-time in the American theater, Bobby would come into his own and become a successful and in-demand character actor. But for now he was just my knight in shining armor.

"You're sweet." I smiled at him, grateful for the company.

At this precise moment, I recalled another charming man. Tonight had been the night I was supposed to meet Ben, the boy from the movie theater, at the Metropolitan Opera to see *Don Giovanni*. I had completely forgotten and now I would never see him again. With a buckling feeling in my stomach, I imagined him standing by the fountain at Lincoln Center, waiting for me, holding the tickets and checking his watch.

I had even taken the opera out of the library on cassette and listened to the score, dreaming of our romantic evening. I saw us drinking champagne in his box, him in a tux, me in some diaphanous, long dress, listening to the music as it floated up into the air. But now I'd blown it. With all the chaos of the past few weeks—the NYPD manhunt for Harvey, the swift relocation to my boyfriend's apartment, and the stress of school—I had simply forgotten the date. I would never get to walk home with Ben to his apartment in one of the most crime-ridden areas of the city. I wouldn't get to see the rats dash across the floor as he unlocked the door of his first-floor apartment and turned on the lights. I would never walk home the next morning in a fancy dress through the blocks of decimated, boarded-up buildings, empty lots, and bombed-out cars, fearing for my life and holding a paper cup of crummy coffee, like a downtown Holly Golightly in Dresden.

"Are you okay?" Bobby put his hand on my shoulder.

"Yes, yes, I just remembered—there was some place I was supposed to be . . . um, tonight."

"Oops," Bobby quipped. "You need a ride back to the city?"

I shook my head, feeling like an asshole, even though no one knew this except Ben and me.

I couldn't have gone anyway, even if I were in New York, now that I was living with Michael. I would have had to make up a story or tell him I was spending the night at Jenny's. *Oh, well. Maybe he can scalp the ticket.* I suddenly missed Ben keenly, pining for that connection I'd felt, that I knew he'd felt, too, the night we met. My face got flushed thinking about him, but luckily it was too dark for anyone to see. Watching the underwater lights cast fluttering shadows on the dark trees and listening to all the laughter and whooping, I was overwhelmed with the realization that I didn't belong here. Maybe my place was with Ben, whose last name I didn't even know.

The pool crowd straggled out, drunk and naked. Some paired up and went upstairs; others got in cars and went back to the city or to the motor lodge in town. I said good night to Bobby and Joe and went up to the guest room with Michael. He fell asleep right away, all tuckered out from swimming and a few too many Michelobs. I tried to sleep but lay awake next to him most of the night, staring at the ceiling, wondering how Ben had liked *Don Giovanni*, and whether he missed me, too. I would never know.

Back at film school, I began to feel even more alienated from my classmates. Suddenly, they seemed to me to be pretentious hipsters, with their neon-colored dyed hair and their full-time sunglasses, as if they were extras in a Fellini movie. The quick and easy answers and opinions they'd flung out that had intimidated me now seemed glib, superficial, and borrowed.

"Don'tcha see that Antonioni is just trying to shock us into a response, by, you know, painting the grass blue or making the trees red. Okay, I get it," declared a boy with purple hair.

But the problem wasn't them, not really—it was me. I'd thought film school was a good idea, but now it just seemed like a daft getaway plan. I had already dropped out of BU and, fleeing Boston and my mother, had fully expected my new life in New York to be not only academically and intellectually engaging but freewheeling, filled with friends, parties, fascinating conversation, and late nights at rock-'n'-roll clubs. But none of that had materialized. Everything was still the same. I was still just going along in my life, and I was suddenly filled with despair at the possibility that I wouldn't find a purpose here, in the city, or at school. I also wasn't having any fun. After each class, I limped to the subway to get the train uptown.

Going back to the apartment had become a monumental drag. I found myself going to coffee shops after school, or catching a movie, so that I didn't have to return to my current home. Michael hadn't worked as an actor in six months, his unemployment had run out, and he had not gotten a plum role he'd desperately wanted in a play at Lincoln Center. The atmosphere was so oppressive, like tiptoeing into a cage with a grumpy, sleeping animal and hoping it wouldn't wake up. I was afraid of his depression—of his anger and neediness. It was as if he was turning into another version of my mother, another person I'd had to watch carefully. He sometimes turned his negativity on me—which often manifested itself in criticisms. Suddenly, there didn't seem to be anything he liked about me. My clothes were too downtown scruffy, and my skirts were too short.

"Why can't you just wear jeans and a normal shirt?" he'd ask.

Because I'm not boring, like you, I was tempted to say. "Michael, I don't own a pair of jeans, and black is cool. I like it."

"I like your hair best when you wear it up in a bun," he said to me one day, making a sad puppy-dog face.

The next day after class, I went to the Astor Place Barbershop and told the hairdresser to chop it all off.

"Are ya sure? It's really gonna change the way you look."

I looked at her, tattoos covering her arms and the backs of her hands, a small cupcake with a cherry on her neck, and said, "I'm sure."

When Michael saw my new hairdo, he freaked.

"Jesus Christ! What the hell did you do?" He looked at my short, spiky pixie cut in dismay. "It's so . . . severe." He practically shuddered.

He hated it.

"I think I look like Jean Seberg in *Breathless*. It does make my neck feel cold, though." I ran my hand back and forth, savoring the feel of my newly shorn scalp.

The hairdo had been a fuck-you gesture, meant to horrify my boyfriend. But looking in the mirror, I saw a tough girl; it made me feel powerful and new. I wasn't going to change the way I dressed or styled my hair for him. I was going to rebel.

That weekend, we went to Boston to visit Michael's step-father, Robert Brustein, a revered intellectual man of the theater. He was a big celebrity in that world; he'd written plays and myriad books on the theater and run the Yale School of Drama before leaving to start the American Repertory Theater (ART) in Cambridge, Massachusetts. If that weren't enough to live up to, Michael's father was a hugely successful Broadway and television producer, and Michael's half sisters were all young, gorgeous supermodel/actresses. He was surrounded on all sides. I felt for him and saw the ways in which we were alike, with our broken families, even though that similarity didn't seem to bring us any closer.

I had only met Brustein once before, when Michael and I had first started seeing each other and we'd been invited to tea. Brustein had been married to Michael's mom, who had died suddenly at the age of fifty-one of a stroke the year before Michael and I met. I had been so immersed in my battles with my own mother, I had probably not been especially aware of the depth of my boyfriend's grief over the death of his mom. It had hit me that afternoon, during our visit to Brustein's grand house on Brattle Street, when I saw all the framed pictures on the walls and tables of the beautiful and beloved woman who had died so young. I was hugely intimidated in Brustein's presence. He was so imposing, intelligent, and effusive, holding forth on topics I knew nothing about—from politics to Jean Cocteau to gravlax—

he seemed to know everything or certainly acted as if he did. He terrified me, and I didn't utter a word that afternoon except to say please and thank you. While I may have been temporarily intimidated by the bluff of my pretentious film-school classmates and the bluster of Michael's young-turk actor friends, this was the real deal; I was convinced that if I opened my mouth to speak, he'd immediately see me as an insecure, inarticulate, silly girl.

We drove up Friday afternoon, and a big dinner party was in progress when we arrived. Michael and I were seated separately—most of the guests were actors and directors from the ART. Some of them I recognized from my time there working as a dresser; one of them had even pinched my ass at a party once. But it had been dark backstage, so no one seemed to recognize me. That was fine. I smiled at jokes when everyone else laughed, passed the food when it reached me, and tried to remember my best table manners from childhood. Coffee, brandy, and cigars were broken out after dinner. The smell of the smoke was horrible, and I wondered absently how I'd get it out of my clothes and hair.

When we went upstairs to our room, Michael looked at me quizzically.

"Why didn't you say anything?" He unbuttoned his shirt and threw it on a chair in the corner. I shrugged my shoulders. He took off his pants, tossing them aside, and riffled through his shaving kit in his boxer shorts. "You just clammed up. I mean, couldn't you find anyone to talk to, or something? You looked so . . . I dunno . . . bored."

"I didn't have anything to say, I guess." I chewed my nails, longing to just turn out the lights and go to sleep.

"Jesus, Wendy"—he looked at me and shook his head—"only children bite their nails."

I yanked my hand away from my mouth, instantly feeling the wave of shame I'd experienced as a little girl when my mother harshly commented on this bad habit of mine. I had started biting my nails around the age of nine and traced it back to being nervous while watching my father onstage, worried that something might happen to him. Maybe it was from the time I saw an épée scratch his cornea at a rehearsal for *Hamlet* when I was a kid—I would never know for sure. There didn't seem to be a way to make me stop. My mother had threatened to take away the little emerald ring she'd bought me when I was ten; she'd also threatened a few times to chop my fingers off with a kitchen knife, even chasing me around our Park Avenue apartment once with a pair of shears while I screamed and ran from her. Clearly, none of it worked.

Feeling like even more of a loser than I had during dinner, I quickly changed and slipped into bed, pretending to be asleep when Michael returned from the bathroom to turn off the light. I just felt sad and far away from everything— the theater glitterati at dinner and my boyfriend's painful attempts at the dinner table to show them he wasn't just another unemployed actor. I closed my eyes, wishing we could leave in the morning.

The following day, we hung out with Michael's younger

half brother, Tommy, in Harvard Square. A sweet kid in his early teens, he had red hair and freckles and was a little goofy in a cute way. We ate lunch at Mr. Bartley's, a burger place with an impossibly long menu of hamburgers named after celebrities. We browsed in the shops—the Coop, the Harvard Book Store—and Michael bought Tommy a cool Velvet Underground T-shirt at Urban Outfitters. By the time five o'clock came by, I had formulated a plan, complete with alibi, to escape another evening of hanging with all the geniuses at Brustein's. I told Michael I was going to catch up with some BU friends at a Boston bar. It was a complete lie, but even after a nice day with Tommy, I was restless and bored and still pissed at Michael for making that remark about my nail-biting.

It was beginning to dawn on me that, sure, I was messed up and adrift at this point in my life. But so was he. The difference was I was twenty. He seemed to look at me as if I were one of his projects—like his apartment. He was trying to fix me up. But it was a way to avoid his own problems, his own lack of success. It was easier to focus on me and my faults rather than turn and look at himself. Honestly, it was exhausting and making me kind of hate him. I even started to dislike the way he smelled; he gave off this peculiar cheap-plastic-toy odor from this dandruff shampoo he had started using. I couldn't stand it.

A little after five, we walked down to Out of Town News, where I briefly peddled magazines and newspapers before starting at the ART. Michael handed me the car keys, and I gave each of the boys a peck on the cheek. Tommy and Michael had a short and scenic walk back to Brustein's house on Brattle Street, and I went to get the car, parked on Mass Ave, behind the newsstand.

I fired up the Dodge Dart and started down Brattle Street, passing Michael and Tommy, who were trundling along the cobblestone sidewalk, talking too animatedly to notice me driving by. I was planning a return romp to all the scenes of the crimes of my teen years—a Wendy Lawless nostalgia tour. They weren't the happiest of memories, but they were mine. I turned right onto Mount Auburn Street, past the hospital where my mother had been rushed in an ambulance on Thanksgiving just three years before, hemorrhaging from an IUD she'd gotten when we lived in London—out-of-date and overworked, it had given out and attacked her insides.

I passed the sprawling Colonial we had lived in on Fresh Pond Parkway before being evicted for not being able to pay our rent, our situation made even more pathetic and ridiculous by Mother, who noisily accused the landlord of raping her, even brandishing her torn Pucci panties as proof to the moving men as they were carrying our belongings out.

There was the Howard Johnson where I once saw Pat Metheny and where my mother liked to befriend sad, drunk ladies, insisting later that I drive them home after she bought them martinis and cheeseburgers. Onto Belmont Street, past the public high school whose keg parties my sister and I had sometimes crashed in the summer. Then up the hill to our old house, on Ivy Road.

The house that the three of us had last lived in as a family was a stately brick two-story, with a sunporch and large rhododendron bushes flanking the windows. A narrow brick path led up to the front door, and terra-cotta tiles lay in scalloped rows on the roof. A year later, my mother had moved away—I didn't know where—and hated my guts. My sister was at Stephens College in Missouri, safe, for now, from our mother's fury. Even though most of my memories in that house were so hairy, I was still happy to see it. After all, it had been my home, or one of them anyway. The brick house looked ordinary and serene to me now; I no longer felt that impending sense of doom I used to experience pulling up to the curb on my way home from school. The past had somehow been defused, exorcised by the house's new owners or perhaps just from my few months away.

Switching off the engine, I got out of the car. I walked to the edge of the front lawn, looking into the lit windows of the house. I could see a woman and a man sitting at a dining table, a young girl clearing dishes. Outside in the dusk, the wind blew gently through the lone tree on the front lawn, which was thicker and taller than I remembered.

Then, from under a bush, there came a cat. It was a lilac-point Siamese, with the same pale blue, almond-shaped eyes, crooked tail, and trim, sinewy build as my cat Gus, who had lived in this house with us and had been such a comfort to me and who, I felt, knew me in a way only the two of us could understand. Meowing, the cat walked right up to me and rubbed against my legs, so I knelt down to pet this other

Gus. My cat now lived with my mother, and I would most likely never see him again. I looked up to see the young girl come out of the front door. She walked up to me and picked up the cat. Tall and dark, and startlingly pretty in a classic preppy way, she was wearing a Concord Academy sweatshirt and jeans, looking like the quintessential popular, lacrosse-playing high school sophomore.

"Hi, can I help you?" she asked politely. I could hear the cat purr and longed to hold him. His long legs stuck out straight, lining her elbow. He looked at me haughtily, as if to say, *Where the hell have you been?*

"Oh, well, I used to live here." I pointed at the windows of the bedroom where my mother used to hide. "About a year or so ago."

"Do you want to come in? I'm sure my parents wouldn't mind."

I had driven past streets and streets of houses filled with people like her and her mom and dad on my way to this house, wondering what it would be like to live in a home where all those routine, normal things occurred.

"Thanks, no." I didn't want to go inside. The house was beautiful all lit up and with happy people living in it. I looked at her Gus cat and wondered if he was a sign. I decided he was. *Nice to see you,* I thought.

"Well, good night." The strapping teen turned and took Gus the ghost up the pathway to the front door. I nodded and smiled.

Back at the car, I looked out at the view from Belmont

Hill over the city of Boston, starting to shine in the evening dark. I felt that same sense of freedom I remembered having in high school sitting on the hood of my boyfriend's car drinking Rolling Rocks and watching the city lights—I was alone and no one knew where I was. The night was mine.

I got in the car and turned on the ignition; the radio came to life. I turned the dial to my old favorite WBCN, the radio station where I used to hang out with my rock-'n'-roll pal Amy, and where we tried to get on guest lists at clubs to see Steel Pulse and Herman Brood & His Wild Romance.

Joy Division's "Love Will Tear Us Apart" was just ending, and Oedipus, the famous punk-rock DJ, came on, introducing the next song, by the Clash, "London Calling," as I drove though Belmont center, all the shops closed up and dark. Since I had nowhere to go, I decided to head down to the station to say hi to Oedi. I'd always thought that he might have a little thing for me—or maybe he just gave all the girls that hungry look. *It'll be fun to find out*, I thought.

I pulled onto Soldiers Field Road along the Charles River and continued onto Storrow Drive—the road my sister and I used to drag race on with anybody who'd chase us after Robbie flipped them the bird. As I passed my old college, BU, I thought of all the nights I'd spent at WBCN with Amy, answering an occasional telephone to take a request and getting to meet some of the musicians from local Boston bands. It was also where I'd met my friend Lee Thompson, who played the sax in Madness and passed in and out of my life periodically.

WBCN had moved a year before from its original location in a penthouse in the Prudential Tower to a subter-
ranean, bunkerlike building five minutes farther away on
Boylston Street in the shadow of Fenway Park. I turned into
the lot in front of the building and saw a lightbulb screwed
into the wall above the door—there was no sign.

I pushed the door open and walked down a sloped,
brightly lit corridor that led to a large, dark-carpeted, win-
dowless room with a low ceiling. Some scruffy club kids
milled around, talking on the listener-line phones at a table
pushed up against the back wall. Behind them I could see
Oedi, seated at the board on the other side of the glass parti-
tion, headphones on. He looked up and gave me one of his
wicked smiles.

"Can I help you?" a skinny, pimply guy in a pilled,
stretched-out, olive-green sweater asked.

"Um, no . . . I just came to say hello to Oedipus."

Oedi motioned with one thin, white arm for me to come
on in.

"Oh, go ahead."

I went through the double, soundproofed doors into
the room. I had never actually been inside the booth. Oedi,
dressed in a tight, sleeveless, black T-shirt and jeans, was
putting what looked like eight-tracks into a machine next
to him. He turned and looked at me. Perhaps eight or nine
years older than I was, Oedi was not handsome or tall, was
a kind of a runt-of-the-litter type. But in a true revenge-of-
the-nerds move, he had transformed himself into this sexy,

ice-cold dude who dressed like a rock star and oozed power and cool. He was a Boston celebrity—the first punk-rock DJ—and he knew it.

"Hey, it's Wendy. What are you doing here? I'd heard you were living in New York."

"Just visiting for the weekend. Yeah, I'm going to NYU—film school."

"Impressive. I'll be finished here in about fifteen minutes. Wanna wait?"

"Sure." I wandered around the room, which was a maze of shelves filled with LPs. There had to have been thousands. I ran my finger along them, reading the titles on the spines—B-52s, Bad Brains, the Beat, Black Uhuru, Blondie, Buzzcocks. I was back in a corner when suddenly I felt hands on me. I turned around, and Oedi pushed me against the wall of records, planting a kiss on my lips. It was slightly savage, deep and abrupt—as I hadn't known it was coming—his teeth biting into my lip. I knew we were blocked from being seen by anyone outside the booth, but the suddenness and ferocity of the kiss made me feel as if I might be a little out of my element. Of course, I didn't want him to know that or to see it on my face.

"Almost done," he murmured into my ear, biting my lobe so hard I nearly let out a yelp. I was nervous, excited, and frightened all at once. I was being a bad girl—for the first time in my life—and there was something thrilling about it.

In the Dart, I followed him back to his apartment, where he offered me a beer. Then, before I even took off my coat, he walked back into what I assumed was his bedroom. I watched him light a candle next to the bed and put on music.

Really? No sweet talk? No foreplay on the sofa first? Just, *Here's a beer and let's fuck?* But I wanted him to think I had done this sort of thing before, so I tossed my coat on a chair and walked nonchalantly into his bedroom.

By the time I got there, he was undressed and under the covers. Some kind of slow, throbbing make-out music was playing. I took off my clothes and slid in beside him. The sex was mechanical, very little touching besides the necessary parts. It was over quickly, and he rolled off me unceremoniously. After the dangerous thrill and promise of the kiss in the record stacks, I felt the letdown of mild shock and disappointment—from the image of how I'd thought it would happen, sleeping with a kind of famous person, instead of the way it had gone down. I had been expecting it to be more passionate, maybe even wilder and with more of a connection. Not that I was such a sexpert. I guessed this was how guys like him did this. He probably had women throwing themselves at him all the time, because of his job and connections. I was just another lay.

"You should probably go," he said. "I have a big day tomorrow."

"Sure. Me, too."

I dressed and picked up my coat on my way out of the apartment. In stereotypical ungentlemanly fashion, he didn't even walk me to the door. Driving home in the dark, I felt foolish and ashamed of myself. I'd been flattered thinking that Oedi wanted me, but now realized that it had meant nothing to him. I could have been any girl. And I'd betrayed Michael.

I was back at the house on Brattle by one in the morning and crept around to the back door, knowing it would be unlocked. Years of experience sneaking home without Mother's hearing had taught me how to be cat-burglar quiet. I took off my shoes, padding through the kitchen to the stairs. Slowly, step by step, I tiptoed up to the second floor like a partially paralyzed ballet dancer, slowly turned the doorknob to the room where Michael slept, slipped in, stripped off my clothes, and carefully slid into bed without making a sound. Not only was I a sneak, I thought, I was also a total whore. Okay, maybe not a whore, since I hadn't gotten paid, but definitely a slut.

The next morning, we had breakfast with Michael's stepdad and half brother before heading back to New York. Sleep deprived and filled with fear that everyone could see the blazing-red Hester Prynne *A* on my forehead, I almost barfed from the smell of the cigar smoke mixed with onions and smoked salmon. I wasn't a sophisticated eater and had hoped for French toast or pancakes.

In the car on the way back to New York, while Michael chattered away and fiddled with the radio stations, I occupied myself with feeling horribly guilty about being a cheater. I hadn't planned to sleep with Oedi; I thought I'd just sort of flirt and maybe make out with him on the sofa. I was also freaking out about not having brought my diaphragm with me.

I'd felt older and even a bit nostalgic looking at the old house in Belmont—as if I'd moved on, grown up. But in truth I'd only moved out. Intimidated by and disenchanted with film school, experienced yet unsophisticated, resentful of Michael but nevertheless clinging to him, I was weighed down by a lot more baggage than just my Ciao! suitcase. I was older now, yes, but no more mature than the lovely teenage girl standing in front of our old house, clutching the cat that used to be mine.

chapter three

MOMMIE NEAREST

When we got back to Michael's apartment, his answering machine was blinking. He was excited, expecting to hear about a callback for a David Rabe play supposedly heading to Broadway. But it wasn't his agent; it was my mother. She'd found me. I stood there in the dark, wondering how she'd gotten Michael's phone number.

"Hello, Wendy." She paused and took a theatrical drag on her cigarette. The sound of her voice, slightly nasal, with its sneeringly arch tone barely masking her fury at me, made me want to puke with fear. "I thought perhaps I'd inform you as to my plans for the remainder of your possessions."

I had basically walked out of our house in Belmont with a suitcase and the clothes I was wearing. Everything else, the contents of my bedroom, I had left behind. That was three months ago, which until this moment had seemed like light-years in the past.

"I am now living in a lovely condominium in Ridgefield, Connecticut. Your things are here. I, of course, paid to have them shipped."

I couldn't believe she had returned to Ridgefield, where, as a family, we had spent a torturous year with our mother becoming first the town nymphomaniac before devolving into a perpetually-nightgown-wearing drunk. I was also surprised that the State of Connecticut had let her back in. I thought that when she had tried to return her Volkswagen Dasher because "it was a lemon" to the governor, Ella Grasso, by driving it up onto the poor woman's front lawn and leaving it there, she'd been banned for life from returning. Apparently I was wrong, and she was now a half an hour away by car.

"I am willing to sell you your yearbooks, clothes, and records. Oh, and do you want your portrait?" She took another suck on her Merit.

Charcoal drawings of me and my sister had been done by Pedro Menocal, who had painted Mother's portrait when she married my stepfather in the Dakota. Pedro had done ours later, while we were living in London—when I was eleven and my sister was ten—and they hung in pretty gold, oval frames.

"Uhhhh," I croaked, bending over and clutching my stomach as the razor-winged butterflies escaped from their cage inside me.

"I can sell them with or without the frames—that's entirely up to you."

I could see her, sitting in her little flat, perched on the olive-green velvet chair with the pretty ornate carved legs, flicking her ash into a cloisonné ashtray on the marble-topped side table next to her.

"I'll telephone you later in the week, so we can negotiate a price. Good-bye."

She had such a talent for making me feel small, unloved, and unimportant. God, I hated her.

Michael pushed the erase button, Mother's message sounded like the high-speed voice of a chipmunk while it played backward, before disappearing.

"Jesus, your mom is a fucking nutcase. What's she going to do? Burn your stuff on the front lawn?"

"Well, yeah . . . I mean, that's probably on her list of options." I suddenly imagined driving the Dart up to Ridgefield and staking out Mother's condo. Maybe if I waited for her to go out, I could break in through a window or a back door and get some of my things. Or maybe I could hire someone to break in? Where did thugs for hire hang out in cutesy, little commuter towns? I mentioned this to Michael.

He shook his head. "Not a good idea."

Rats, I thought. Of course he was right. I didn't care so much about my stuff, just that she was using it as a way to get to me in a way that only she could. She still made me doubt myself, wonder if I really was the ungrateful child she'd told me I was when I was growing up. Walking away from her hadn't resolved the feelings that she brought up in me. Those emotions weren't just going to disappear overnight now that

I had left her behind. In a way, I was still there, still in the relationship with her. Somehow wishing it were different, wishing I had a mother who could love me. I thought I'd made my getaway—but I was still in the shit.

Mother didn't call back that week or the next. Maybe she was dancing around a pile of my burning books and clothes or sticking pins in a voodoo doll of me—I didn't care—I was glad for the reprieve, however temporary. Since her call, I had been having nightmares and tremendous anxiety. Taking advantage of my student health plan, I went to see a shrink named Lopez at the NYU clinic a few times. She was tall and thin, with dark, lustrous hair and café-au-lait skin. She dressed elegantly, exclusively in camel and black. Always wearing two-tone-colored clothes struck me as odd, but she consistently looked fabulous, and she was a shrink, right? We all had our little quirks. She lived in an airy, light-filled apartment with windows that looked out on Washington Square Park. She'd sit in an Eames chair while I blathered on about my problems.

I told her about my recent hideous nightmares, which were always about being trapped at night in a glass case or being lost in a room full of taxidermic animals, like a sort of freaky natural-history museum with all the lights out. It was dark, and sinister, with terrifying, twisted faces surrounding me like the opening-credit sequence from Rod Serling's seventies TV show *Night Gallery*.

"Well," Dr. Lopez said in her calm, low voice, "you're clearly under a great deal of stress—the dreams are a manifestation of your fears. Your mother is a trigger. The next time she calls you and you pick up the phone, try instructing her to be civil. If that doesn't work, simply inform her you are ending the conversation. Then put the receiver down." Dr. Lopez recrossed her legs and pulled gently at the hem of her beige wool skirt.

"You mean hang up on her?" I realized that as I was saying this, my eyes were bugging out.

"But, you see, you are not hanging up on her. You're giving her the opportunity to behave properly. And you are telling her that if she doesn't, you will end the conversation."

"Wow." It had never occurred to me to hang up on Mother. She was the one who hung up on me, generally after delivering a blistering critique of my character or her latest list of demands.

Dr. Lopez put her hands up in a "Stop! In the Name of Love" position. "You need to learn to lay down some ground rules and protect yourself. Especially when dealing with such an irrational person."

"Okay, I'll try." I smiled weakly.

I walked back through the park in the dusky, cold air under the fuzzy glow of the streetlamps, struggling with the mind-boggling notion of attempting to set boundaries with my mother. She had always run the show and had defined the limits, not me. How would I ever be able to defuse her? To not feel a slap across my face at the sound of her voice? I descended into the West Fourth Street subway station and shoved my token into the turnstile. In the overheated train car, I felt a trickle of sweat run down my back as I stared at the graffiti-covered walls, every space filled with a spray-painted obscenity, initials, or savage curlicue designs. I was so used to seeing it, I hardly noticed it anymore. But now it looked like the sound track of my mind, a terrifying roar, a vomit of confusion.

Michael had almost finished his renovation of the kitchen. He told me I could choose the paint color from a fan of shades. Barely thinking, I picked a pinkish lavender that might have been passable in a discount department store ladies' lounge but that looked out of place and rinky-dink in a kitchen. Something about seeing that kitchen painted such a horrible color convinced me that it was over between us. I shouldn't have chosen it, he shouldn't have let me. It was like our relationship—wrong.

I was sitting on the living-room sofa, trying to do homework, staring at the cream-of-kidney wall when Michael came home.

"Hi, sorry it took me forever, the subway was packed." He took off his peacoat and draped it over a chair. "Should we just order? Chinese maybe?"

I nodded and chewed on my pen.

He started riffling through a drawer next to the phone where he kept all the take-out menus. "Whatcha working on?"

"A paper on *Citizen Kane*." We had watched it twice in class; my professor had seen it more than eighty times.

"Oh, I love that film. Do you want me to help—look at what you've got so far?"

He looked all eager-beaver, and I was annoyed that he seemed to think I couldn't write a simple paper without his assistance. I loved the film and had been doing fine until now.

"Um, no, thanks."

"You know that Welles didn't actually write the movie script, don't you? Herman Mankiewicz did, and Welles took all the credit."

"Well, that's not in my textbook."

"But it's true. He also tried to take credit for the cinematography that James Wong Howe created."

"Really?" I started leafing through the chapter of the book dedicated to the movie.

"Absolutely. James Wong Howe invented deep focus and used it in *Citizen Kane*, but again Welles said he invented it."

"But Gregg Toland was the cinematographer."

"No, that's wrong. It was James Wong Howe."

"Michael, it's here in my textbook—see?" I got up off the couch and walked over to him to show him, using my finger to point to the paragraph about Toland's groundbreaking techniques in the film.

"That's wrong!" Michael became agitated.

"No, Michael, look—right here. It's in my book. You're wrong." I chuckled smugly, relishing proving him incorrect.

"I'm not!" He slapped me across the face.

No one—besides my mother, of course—had ever hit me before.

He immediately tried to take it back, but I was struck blind with rage.

"You asshole!" I screamed, throwing the book at his head.

"Wendy, stop! I—"

In a furious rush of adrenaline, I grabbed him and pushed him as hard as I could across the room. "I fucking hate you!"

He hit the wall with a thump. I dragged him along the wall toward the window and tried to throw him out, mushing his face against the glass. Holding his T-shirt in my clenched fists, I realized that what I actually wanted to do was push him out of my life.

Letting him go, I grabbed my coat and walked out the door into the December evening. I started walking up Broadway to Jenny's, stopping at every phone booth to try to let her know I was coming. The line was always busy because her Korean roomie was always on the phone to his girlfriend in Queens. When I made it to the building, I rang the buzzer, and she let me in. I was shaking and crying and fell into her arms when she met me at the elevator. When I raised my eyes to her face, I saw that it was covered in tears.

"What is it? What's wrong?"

She started to sob and took my hand as we entered the apartment. Her boyfriend, Pete, sat in the dining room with a bottle of Jack Daniel's and a shot glass on the table in front of him. He looked the saddest I'd ever seen him.

"Some psycho just murdered John Lennon in front of the Dakota."

I crashed on the couch in the living room for a few days, refusing to talk to Michael each time he called. Jenny had never said that she didn't like Michael, but ever since he'd called her feet "flippers" once when we were all out to dinner, she had cooled a bit on him. In his defense, she wore a size 11 shoe.

I had met Jenny in my huge anthropology lecture class at BU two years before when the teacher, who was discussing taboos in society, mentioned the taboo of the student-teacher love affair. A handsome, reedy type, he wore a safari jacket and an ascot, like a faux David Attenborough. He clearly fancied himself quite a bit and suggested that it was almost always the student who was the aggressor in these forbidden relationships.

A cream-skinned hand shot up about ten rows ahead of me, the nails impeccably painted Jungle Red.

"Yes?" the professor called on the girl who belonged to the hand, and she stood up, tossing her butt-length, light blond hair behind her shoulders and sticking the beautiful manicured hand on her hip. She had the pretty, clean good looks of a model you'd see in a fashion magazine or a Sea Breeze commercial and dressed in the quintessential preppy style—clogs, jeans, and a Fair Isle sweater, with a white turtleneck peeking out at the neck. I noticed her makeup was perfect. She was a typical shiksa goddess type, but with an edge, a snark factor that made her stand out.

"It takes two to tango," she declared emphatically, raising her chin defiantly.

"I beg your pardon?"

She put both her hands on her hips now. "I said, it takes two to tango." She delivered this line with a flourish, like a prized athlete delivering the final thrust or executing the perfect smash over the net.

The class erupted in applause. Jenny flashed a winning smile and sat down. *Wow*, I thought, *I want to be friends with her.* I followed her out of class and back to her dorm, which was right next to mine in a little row of town houses off Commonwealth Avenue. We sat on the floor in her room, trading life stories, smoking Marlboro Reds, and eating Nestlé Crunch bars. She left for Barnard soon after, but we'd been friends ever since. Whenever we went to a party or even just walked down the street, all the guys looked at her, not me, but that was just the way it was. It never bothered me that she was the beauty and I was "the friend."

Although Jenny's place was only ten blocks from Michael's apartment, the neighborhood where she and Pete lived was quite different, more sketchy and run-down. Her building was between West End Avenue and Riverside Drive, with a single-room-occupancy hotel across the street. With the ongoing economic crisis of the city, thousands of mental patients had been turned out onto the street as the city scrambled to find shelter for them, and the homeless population grew visibly. The SROs were a Band-Aid for the problem, but created new ones: many people living on the fringes of society in close quarters, with easy access to drugs and alcohol. People constantly hung out the windows, shouting out to someone in the street, playing loud music, partying. One man hung around on the sidewalk all day, wearing paint-encrusted clothes and a potato sack over his face. We called him Potato Man; he seemed harmless.

Jenny's apartment was prewar, with high ceilings and wood floors—but the walls were coated in layers of paint and grime, and continuous wear had scuffed the floor. The furniture had been salvaged from the street mostly or left behind by the prior tenants. The tatty, white-gray foldout sofa, where I was currently sleeping, we dubbed "the golf course" for its lumpiness and bulging springs. A few sad armchairs and a wooden-crate coffee table accompanied it, and a big desk sat in the corner where Pete did his studying and cramming for exams. One wall held bookshelves sagging under the weight of all the books former tenants, mostly Columbia and Barnard students, had read while they lived there. Three or four copies of *The Powers That Be*, *The Prince*, *The Awakening*, *Jane Eyre*, and the condensed version of the *OED* they used to give away with a subscription to the *New York Review of Books* formed a veritable in-house syllabus. The stereo rested on the bottom shelf, and records lined the wall below along the floor. Even though it was a trifle dilapidated, with its scruffy furniture and a major cockroach problem, I loved that apartment on Ninety-seventh Street because Jenny and Pete lived there. It was a place I was always welcome, where I felt safe and accepted for just being myself.

There was one bathroom, a kitchen, a dining room, and two small bedrooms besides Jenny and Pete's, where their roommates lived. A Korean American kid named Hee-Jon lived in the back bedroom—I had never seen him actually— and a guy named Anthony lived in the room behind the kitchen when he wasn't at Juilliard studying to be an actor.

I came home from class one evening to find Jenny putting groceries away in the kitchen. "Ugh—Michael just called, sounding all hangdog. You're gonna have to talk to him sometime, Vend."

"What's for dinner, honey?" I asked, ignoring her advice.

"I'm making fish for supper, with green beans and rice. I hope that's okay?"

"Great, thanks—I'll clean up."

Jenny pulled a gallon bottle of cheapie white wine from the fridge and poured us each a glass. Daintily unwrapping a piece of Saint André, she put it on a wooden cutting board, with a little dish of shiny olives. She sliced a baguette and placed the pieces elegantly around the cheese. Jenny was a foodie before there were any. Per her instructions, Pete would take the butter out in the morning before he left so it would be room temperature and easier to spread on her croissant when she got up and had her breakfast.

I heard the front door slam—Pete was home. He came barreling into the kitchen, dropping his heavy book bag on the floor with a loud thump, and took Jenny in his arms. They had a mad make-out session right there by the stove.

"Must you suck face with such zeal?" I rolled my eyes.

It was kind of embarrassing—as if they were going to drop and do it on the scuffed-up linoleum floor. They had been together for two years but still couldn't keep their hands off each other. Theirs was the kind of deep, true love I dreamed of having, but I didn't really need the floor show.

"Sorry." Pete leaned over and gave me a peck on the cheek. He was over six feet, with brown hair and little, brown, nubby teeth that Jenny called his "Indian corn." He laughed a lot and was the kind of person who could do a lot of different things really well: speak French or Spanish, draw, tell jokes, pick up any instrument and play "Turkey in the Straw" on it immediately. Five years older than me, Pete was incredibly sweet, book smart, and kind. I was very much in awe of and had a sort of little-sister crush on him.

After we ate the fish and everything else, I helped out with the dishes while Pete went to study in the living room. He was trying to get through Columbia's premed program in two years instead of three, so he was constantly hitting the books.

Just as Jenny and I finished the dishes, the kitchen wall phone rang.

Jenny lit up a cigarette, blowing expert smoke rings at the dingy overhead light fixture. "Oh, boy." She looked at me. "Why don't you answer it?"

I reached over and picked up the receiver. It was Michael.

"Look, Wendy, I know you hate me right now."

"I don't hate you. There's a room opening up here, so I think I'll come get my stuff, if that's okay."

Hee-Jon's parents were swooping in to take him home—they'd discovered he was seeing a white girl—so his room would soon be conveniently empty.

After a long pause Michael replied, "All right, if that's what you want. Sometime tomorrow?"

The next day, I packed up my few possessions and clothes while Michael pleaded with me to give him another chance. He was sorry about slapping me, and I believed him. But the fight had just been a bad end to a bad idea.

"What if we get married?"

"I just think that it's over." I put my small collection of books in a milk crate I'd picked up on my way down Broadway.

"I'll go to my safety-deposit box tomorrow. There's a diamond ring that belonged to my mother. I want you to have it. Actually, all her jewelry is in there. I'll give it to you."

My first marriage proposal felt like a desperate bribe. It reminded me of when my mom had offered to buy me a car if I lived at home while attending BU. It hadn't worked then, either.

"No, Michael. It just isn't going to work out. C'mon, we're really unhappy together."

"But I love you. Don't you love me? I mean, it was a stupid fight, and I wish more than anything I could take it back, what I did." His eyes looked shiny, and he tried to smile but couldn't.

"I'm sorry, but I don't love you. Maybe I did, but I don't anymore."

His face fell. He looked down and nodded. "I see."

He walked me downstairs and helped me get my stuff into a cab. I turned to say good-bye before getting in and giving the driver my new address.

"I guess I can't make you love me," Michael said plaintively.

But he could have made me love him. If he had been kinder, less concerned with turning me into someone he thought I should be. Now there was nothing left to say. I wanted what Jenny and Pete had, and I wasn't going to find it here.

"Good-bye. Take care."

I slid into the backseat—with the Ciao! bag, the milk crate, and the futon—and closed the door. I didn't turn around to see if he was watching the taxi head up Broadway.

A week later, I realized that my period was late. I had felt sort of queasy the last few days, and my boobs were sore. Terrified, I made an appointment with a doctor I found in the phone book.

Dr. Anna Manska was an elderly Russian doctor who wore support stockings and what appeared to be Soviet-issued beige orthopedic shoes. She walked hunched over, had a mustache, and looked as if she lived on a diet of cigarettes and strong coffee. Perhaps because her examination room had the bleak astringency of an outpost in the gulag, Dr. Manska only charged $35 per visit. I peed into a cup and crawled onto the examining table, my heart pounding in my ears. I couldn't breathe as I watched her stick a little piece of paper into my urine and flick it, holding it up to the institutional-looking overhead lights. Then she shuffled over to the table and gave me a pelvic exam, moving her hands around inside me.

"You are pregnant—maybe four weeks or so." Her hands left my body, and she snapped off her rubber gloves.

I started to cry. She looked at me as if I were a moron.

"Do not cry," she said disdainfully. "You are a young woman. You have your whole life ahead of you." She walked to the little sink in the corner of the room and started washing her hands. "You can get it taken care of."

Drying my eyes, I wrote her a check and squeaked a thank-you. I walked out onto the icy streets, knowing that it was Oedi's baby, and also knowing that he probably wouldn't care and that I didn't want to have it.

I went home and told Jenny.

"Holy shit!" She lit a Marlboro Red. "What are you going to do? Have you told Michael?"

"It's not his. It's this guy in Boston, he's . . . kind of an asshole."

"Well, be that as it may—you should call him and ask him to pay half." Jenny was a feminist and a women's studies major. Of course she was right. Besides, I needed the money.

When I finally got up the nerve to call Oedi and tell him I was pregnant, there was a long silence on the other end of the line. I stood in my bedroom, eyes screwed shut, gripping the receiver and feeling ill with despair and utterly vulnerable. Asking a man for money was something my mother did all the time—but this was a first for me.

It sounded like there was no one on the other end of the line. "Hello?"

Only then did he speak. "Yes? And? What does that have to do with me?" His tone was glacial.

"Well, it's yours." My hands started to shake, and I tried to keep my voice from trembling.

"So what do you want?"

I plowed on, trying not to notice the deadness in his voice. "I'm planning to have an abortion. I was hoping you could, you know, contribute to the cost. Just, like, half. That's all."

"Wendy, I assumed that when you came to my apartment, you were on the Pill. I'm certainly not responsible for you making a stupid mistake. That's your fault, not mine."

"Oh, all right." I was so flustered by his superior tone, all I could think about was getting off the phone. There was another icy pause, and then he spoke.

"So give me your address."

I managed to jabber it out. "Well, uh . . . good-bye." I quickly pressed down on the button with a click.

A few days later, I received a check in the mail from him for $25. In his scrawled note he said it was for me to take a cab home from the abortion clinic. It was so nasty and seemed calculated to make me feel small, like giving me a tip. I couldn't believe I'd had blah sex with this creep and now I had to literally pay for my mistake.

I called to borrow the $300 for the procedure from my friend Julie, the art student, who had rich parents and therefore was the only person I knew who had that much money in her checking account. It was awkward for me to ask; I could tell she was nervous about loaning me the money. Julie was the kind of person who would bring a bottle of wine to a party, then take it back home with her later even if it had been opened. No matter her instinct or inclination, she came through for me.

Jenny went with me. We sat in the waiting room of the Manhattan Women's Medical Clinic on Park Avenue South in the thirties. Other couples in the room were holding hands; some of the men had their arms around their wives or girlfriends, who were crying softly into Kleenex, their makeup running. A girl who couldn't have been more than fourteen sat with her mom. I just felt numb. Jenny was leafing through a magazine when I heard my name called.

"It'll be okay, Vend. I'll be here when you're done." She gave my hand a tight squeeze, and I stood to walk through the buzz-in door into the back of the clinic. I sat in a small room and talked to a nurse at a desk about the choice I'd made.

"And have you decided that the abortion is what you want to do?" she asked, her face open, no judgment in her tone. It was as if she were asking me if I wanted to drop a class.

I nodded and said that I was sure. She had me sign some forms, and I was sent to another room, where I sat with a group of about ten women. We watched a film strip in which another nurse explained what was going to happen once we were in with the doctor; a series of increasingly thick steel rods would be used to open the cervix, then a handheld vacuum device would empty the uterus. This was called an aspiration abortion, which I thought was weird—it seemed like somebody's idea of a sick joke. *Aspiration* meant "hope" or "desire"; it didn't seem to go along with what we were all about to do. After the movie, we all shuffled to another counter in the hall, where we were supposed to pay.

In the procedure room, I lay on the table in a cotton hospital gown. Two nurses moved around the room, getting it ready for the doctor. When he came in, he looked at my chart. He was probably ten years older than me and reminded me of the boys I'd gone to high school with who would grow up to be lawyers or doctors. He looked at my chart, then to me and smiled.

"Miss Lawless?"

I nodded.

"I'm Dr. Cohen, and this is Nancy and Greta—they'll be your nurses today."

The nurses also smiled at me. We were all smiling and I was about to kill a baby.

"It says here that you don't want to be put to sleep."

"No, I don't." It seemed fair that I should be awake, to pay for what I was about to do. I deserved it.

"Let me just tell you that if you were my girlfriend, I wouldn't want you to feel this."

I turned to Greta and Nancy for backup.

"It's quite painful, even when we numb the cervix. If I

were you, I'd go for the drugs," Nancy said, and Greta nodded in agreement.

"Oh. Okay." Suddenly I was afraid.

Nancy put the tube in my arm and asked me to start counting backward from ten. Greta held my hand and said, smiling, "It'll all be over in five minutes, sweetie."

Ten, nine, eight, six . . . I laughed as I saw myself flying over an antique map of Spain, and then I went to sleep.

I came to in a brightly lit, narrow room that was lined with beds. Women, covered with thin cotton blankets, lay in mounds in various stages of waking. It made me think of *Madeline*, the children's book set in a French convent—twelve little girls in two straight lines, except we weren't getting up to have breakfast and brush our teeth; we were emerging from the ether after having our fetuses erased.

Afterward, Jenny and I went to a café, one of the ones that dot Columbus Avenue across the street from the Natural History Museum, with an outdoor, glassed-in patio that looked out onto the sidewalk. She ordered a glass of wine. I picked at my salad.

I spent a week shuffling around the apartment in my bathrobe, crying, unable to sleep or eat or go to class. I felt weighted down by all the shit and the agony I was carrying around with me, as if someone were standing next to me and tugging on my clothes, but I also felt empty inside, stripped—physically aching for a way to understand how I'd been so stupid as to allow myself to get knocked up.

One morning four or five days later, Jenny came into my

room. She sat on the edge of the bed, handed me a cup of coffee, and reached over to gently stroke my hair. "So, Vend, this is your best friend speaking. I know it's been hard, but, you know, that's enough. You have to pull yourself together—you've had time to recover."

I knew she was right. I nodded and sipped the coffee. Tough love with a warm beverage.

"It'll get easier—you'll see."

I went down to NYU to speak to my adviser. When I explained to him that I had missed so much class and final exams because I'd become pregnant and had an abortion, he looked at me skeptically. I wondered how many times he'd heard this story and how many times it had actually been true. I couldn't help but cry a little, which embarrassed him. He grimaced slightly, as if in fear that I was about to launch into a monologue about my lady parts.

"Hmm, I see," he said instead.

He offered to reschedule my finals for the end of the week.

The Friday before Christmas, I walked into a classroom and filled out the blue exam booklets. I knew the material cold and was confident I'd ace it. As I scribbled away, I felt a sense of triumph as well as an understanding that, although I adored the cinema, I no longer wanted to study it. I finished the essay question about Fritz Lang's film *Metropolis*, closed the booklet, and handed it to the TA sitting at the desk by the door.

Then I dropped out of NYU.

chapter four

HOUSES IN MOTION

My modest room at Ninety-seventh Street couldn't have been more than forty feet square. The single bed was pushed up against the wall where a padlocked black metal gate stretched across the one window, looking out on the air shaft. The apartment was on the seventh floor of the eight-story building, so I could just catch a glimpse of the sky. In a less glamorous version of Hitchcock's movie *Rear Window*, I had views inside other people's kitchens and bathrooms, accompanied by the teeming noises of crying kids, loud Spanish-speaking radio stations, hacking, phlegmy coughs, and flushing toilets. I regularly heard the couple above me having sex at night.

"*Sí, sí,*" the man would begin to groan as he approached climax. After usually three or four more *sí*'s, it all came to a thumping, metal-bed-frame-squeaking end.

A battered dresser leaned against my wall next to the

bed, and homemade two-by-four bookshelves stuck out halfway up the opposite wall and reached the ceiling. The tiny closet contained more shelves, so I hung my clothes on nails pounded into the back of the door. Cramped, yes, but I was so happy to have my own room, where I could shut the door, be by myself, and not feel that someone—Michael or the NYPD—was watching me. While living with my mother, a closed door had often been an invitation for her to barge in—drunk or sober. Privacy then had not been an option. In a way, this little phone booth of a room was the first place I'd ever been able to call my own.

Since everyone else was in school, and I was now a college dropout for the second time, I took it upon myself to cook supper, pick up the milk and the mail, and to lug our laundry to the Chinese laundry on Broadway, where they put your huge bag of dirty clothes on a scale and charged you by the pound to wash it. I was always mystified by the meticulously folded and perfectly square block of clothes that they handed back to me, after I gave them our tickets. After the chaos of constantly moving and the emotional turmoil of Michael, it was fun playing house, and I relished each domestic chore except, of course, cleaning.

We were all about to take off for the Christmas holiday. Jenny and Pete would be going to her grandmother's house in Connecticut, before swinging up to visit Pete's family in upstate New York. Anthony, the Juilliard acting student, would be flying home to San Francisco.

That Christmas I was joining my sister and we were flying to spend the holiday with our father, stepmother, and stepsisters in Minneapolis. I had visited Daddy that summer, but Robin had only seen him briefly, at Logan Airport in Boston, when he was between planes. Neither of us had seen our stepmom, Sarah, or her kids since we were little girls, before Sarah and Daddy had even been married.

Robbie and I arrived in the Twin Cities, where the temperature was below freezing, a few days before the holiday. My stepsister Jules was living in the guest room at the house, so we were booked into a nearby motel. The place was kind of a dump, with red shag carpeting and pilled pink chenille spreads on the twin beds. Paint-by-numbers landscapes of mountains and snow-covered pine trees hung on the walls. Because of the Minnesota cold, the floor of our room was heated, which led to a rather fantastic explosion of condensation and steam whenever we opened the door to enter our room or exit into the outside parking lot. We looked like a magic act appearing in a cloud of smoke or rock stars with smoke bombs going off around us.

Although our relationship had been strained at times, fraught with anger and recriminations in our teen years, my sister and I were the only constant in each other's life. We had been in touch, mostly by telephone and the occasional letter, while she was at college, sharing the PTSD fallout symptoms of our childhood—the anxiety, sleepless nights, weight loss and gain, and the overarching sadness we both grappled with. And so I was glad Robin was with me; it promised to be a surreal experience for both of us—but at least we would be together. Our childhood Christmases were always punctuated by high drama (one year Mother had collected all our toys and presents in a rage and thrown them away in black trash bags because she deemed us ungrateful) or stony silence (sitting at the table eating gray, overcooked roast beef while Mother guzzled Chablis and chain-smoked). Most people approached the season expecting love, warmth, happiness, and familial harmony, but our Christmases seemed to be more about what you *didn't* receive, not getting what you wanted with all your heart. So Robin and I both pretty much hated the holidays.

Compared to our dreary yules of the past, Christmas at Daddy and Sarah's was like the Little Princess's (before she loses all her money and gets sent to the attic). Presents galore spilled from underneath a tinseled tree—my stepmother was a buyer for Dayton's department store in Minneapolis and had a knack for picking out the perfect gift. For me she'd chosen a snazzy pair of tan leather boots with corduroy sides and a trendy winter coat that was olive colored and had big pockets. Robin got a pair of pretty ruby earrings and was touched that Sarah had remembered her birthstone. After opening presents, we feasted on eggs Benedict washed down with Bloody Marys. It was a little disorienting for my sister and me, a totally new experience—this constant jovial feting of food, toasts, and treats. I'd catch Robbie's eye from across the room and smile, as if to say, *Well, this isn't so bad, is it?* And it wasn't, although it was also a bittersweet taste of all that we had missed out on.

My stepsisters, Jules and Mary, were just a few years older than Robbie and me. They were both caustic, wisecracking types and had inherited their mother's tall, handsome looks and her low, throaty laugh. The last time we'd seen them had been ten years ago, on the front steps of Daddy's apartment building on Humboldt Avenue, where we had stayed with him during the summer. We'd all sat on the steps and discussed our parents' romance.

"It looks like your dad is gonna marry our mom," Jules, the older and more serious sister, informed us.

"Yeah, that'll be good." I figured that now Daddy would have someone to look after him and not be on his own anymore. And we'd have sisters to play with in the summers. It would be like a real family.

"And I can babysit!" Jules smiled.

I laughed, thinking of all the fun we would have making tents out of blankets and chairs in the living room and having slumber parties, telling scary stories by flashlight.

But Mother had whisked us away before that dream could become reality—kidnapped us, really, furious that our father had found happiness—and our stepsisters, not us, had grown up with our dad. A part of me couldn't help feeling jealous of them, of the years we had lost, of not being a part of what seemed like a normal family. Especially compared to our twisted home life with Mother.

The table was set for Christmas dinner; instead of china, my stepmother preferred funky pottery dishes in vibrant colors of orange and blue that brought to mind New Mexico, one of her favorite places, where she and my father tried to spend time during the brutal Minnesota winters. Steaming side dishes of potatoes and green beans were strewn about the table in mismatched bowls, and squat, fat candles burned in curly iron holders, casting the room in a golden haze. The standing rib roast sat on the table in front of my father, looking like the severed antlered crown of a mythical beast. We all took our places, and my dad raised his glass.

"A very merry Christmas to all," he announced gaily.

"Merry Christmas!" we all sang.

"And I must say that I am especially overjoyed this year to have Wendy and Robin with us." His eyes shone in the candlelight.

"Thank you, Daddy," my sister and I replied in unison, just like the little girls we used to be.

My father carved the roast, and everyone dug in.

I looked at Robbie across the table and knew she was thinking the same thing: it just wasn't fair. It made me even more furious at Mother. Also, I desperately wanted to know why Daddy had chosen not to rescue us, or at least why he didn't show himself when he found out where we were. But our first Christmas together in ten years didn't seem like the time to bring it up.

Although our stepfamily did everything to make us feel wanted and welcome, everything was, for me and for my sister, tinged with sadness and a melancholy sense of loss. I was woefully aware of just how much we stuck out as the strangers in the room that evening when Robbie and I sat at the dining table listening to stories about vacations, parties with wacky friends and relatives, and my stepsisters' kooky teen escapades, in which our dad sometimes figured as the savior and sometimes an accomplice. They were marvelous stories, and Robbie and I laughed out loud with the others at many of them, but a lot of the time we didn't know whom they were talking about because we simply hadn't been around. It was like watching somebody else's home movies. Robbie and I exchanged forced cheerful looks, putting up a front so as not to show how weird this all was to us. In a way, the sting of meeting our new family was worse than never having known them before. Like rescraping a badly skinned knee or the way a healed broken arm throbs when it rains, the pain had always been there, dormant, and was now being brought to life. Maybe it would ease over time—but for now it felt fresh and raw on the surface of my skin.

We went to the movies and out to lunch at restaurants where the maître d' always knew Daddy and Sarah by name, made a fuss over them, and gave us a great table. You'd think we were the royal family of Minneapolis or something. Sarah took all of us girls clothes shopping—something I could never remember doing with my own mother. We played games—poker and Trivial Pursuit—laughing into the night.

After one evening of playing cards at their house, Robbie and I went back to our motel, flopped down on the ugly bed-spreads, and cried.

"This is so hard!" Robbie sobbed into her pillow.

"I know!" It was exhausting doing our sister act, feeling awkward and guilty about pretending we'd immediately bonded with our new family, and I had a headache from all the bourbon I'd drunk trying to keep up with everybody else. They were a tough crowd to match drink for drink.

"Who's that guy they kept talking about?" Robbie blew her nose loudly.

"I don't know."

We finished our little crying jag, and I turned on the radio to see if anything cheery was on. The "Russian Dance" from *The Nutcracker* burst from the speaker. We had seen the ballet a few times at Lincoln Center during our privileged Manhattan early childhood. I turned it up and looked at her, smiling. Within seconds we were up on our feet, dancing to the music in our shabby little room, laughing and spinning each other around, doing our best Cossack imitation, and trying to forget that we had spent all day feeling like newly adopted orphans. I imagined people out on the snow-covered street looking into the window of our room and seeing two crazy girls, arms raised, giddily hopping up and down, screeching with laughter. We would have to make our own happy memories—and it was a start.

Back in New York, I settled into the domesticity of life at the apartment, in the bosom of my chosen family, Pete and Jenny. I happily helped with the cooking, making stews and curries from inexpensive cuts of meat I bought at the shady, smelly grocery store nearby. Completely different from the spotless and fancy Gristedes from which my mother used to order over the telephone on the Upper East Side, the Red Apple, on Ninety-sixth Street, reeked of mouse droppings and freezer burn. Rat-catching cats who lived in the store pounced on the cockroaches skittering across the floor. The linoleum, missing tiles, was cracked and uneven, so that pushing your tiny cart through the narrow aisles was more of a strength exercise than a leisurely stroll through the dairy or meat section. The produce was droopy, cans of tuna and soup were past their expiration date, and only one checkout lane was ever open. But it was cheap and only a block away.

In a sort of zany American take on *Jules and Jim*, Jenny, Pete, and I were like a love triangle sans the sex, in my mind anyway. Cheap rent was an added benefit—I paid $175 a month and my share of the telephone. Even better—my insane mother didn't know where I was. I was off the grid.

I got a job working in the textbook department of the Barnes & Noble on Fifth Avenue and Seventeenth Street. My boss was a thirtyish, whippet-thin gay guy named Rodney. He was like a skinny African American Paul Lynde, with a nasal, whiny voice and a lit Benson & Hedges menthol always sticking out of one corner of his mouth. He had a shaved head, favored earth tones, and wore oversized Swifty Lazar glasses with Coke-bottle lenses.

The job was easy: all you had to do was sit at a communal desk in the textbook department, wait for the telephone to ring from a school or a student, and take the order. Because the work was fairly mindless and Rodney was a pushover, we could pretty much do whatever we wanted when the phone wasn't ringing—read, take frequent breaks to smoke in the loo, eat, or drink coffee—as long as we picked up the phone.

Another girl my age, Annie, worked there, too. A punk Snow White dressed in black, she had porcelain skin and dyed-jet hair and wore bright red lipstick. She had the mien I'd always dreamed of having: exotic and dark with a kind of mystery and edge. We were the youngest people working there by far; everyone else was sort of faded and middle-aged and had been there for years. Losers who had once had dreams of fame and fortune in New York but now were stuck in a crap job. Of course, Annie and I were just passing through and would be moving on to bigger things any day now.

She and I bonded over music and books and these sandwiches we adored at a nearby restaurant, Patsy's, called Steak Bunnies. She was from Maine and had a boyfriend and a second job as a salesgirl at the ultraposh department store Barneys a few blocks away. When I'd swing by to visit her there so she could sneak me some samples, she reminded me of the model Esme, whom I used to see working behind the counter at the Urban Outfitters in Harvard Square before she was discovered; they both had the same smoky looks.

At the bookstore, Rodney sort of doted on us in his own way. I think he liked our youth and thrift-store style.

"Love that skirt, Wendy. And, Annie, well, that leather jacket is divinely you."

"Thanks, Rodney," we chirped in unison. We had just

gotten back from lunch fifteen minutes late, but he didn't seem to care because we were so flash.

Rodney placed a skeletal arm around my shoulders one morning and rasped into my ear, the smoke from his Benson & Hedges stinging my eyes, "Don't tell anyone, Wendy, but you and Annie are my favorite ones."

"Gee, thanks, Rodney."

"It'll be our little secret." He pretended to lock his lips and throw the key away. I nodded solemnly to show I understood. Sometimes I felt that he wasn't so much our boss but our babysitter.

I worked at the B&N during the week, and on the weekends I had a gig that Pete had found me, modeling for an artist friend of his, Dan. They'd grown up together in a small town in upstate New York. Dan was a talented painter and printmaker; his work had been bought by the Metropolitan Museum of Art in New York, the Walker in Minneapolis, and by private collectors. Even with these impressive credentials, he was still a starving artist, barely able to pay the rent on his share way uptown in Washington Heights. He drove a dilapidated, rusted-out, yellow Volkswagen Rabbit, which always seemed to be in need of a jump. He was tall and softly bearish in build, with dark blond, scraggly hair and an unkempt beard. He had a chipped front tooth, which made him look kind of sweet and defenseless, which he actually was, like a little boy. He wore plaid shirts and worn corduroys and looked as if he slept in his car. He was the kind of nice guy whom women shunned and generally mistreated.

He wanted to do a series of large portraits, four in all, and needed a model. Pete had volunteered me—and I was excited. It would be fun and fairly easy work—after all, how hard was it to stand around? The job also had a hint of glamour, à la Dora Maar, Picasso's famous muse and mistress. Just as important, Dan was paying $10 an hour, more than I had ever made doing anything else. Pete had mentioned that I might have to pose nude, and I thought it might be cool to have a picture of me, naked, hanging in someone's living room. What the hell, right? It's not as if anybody who saw the paintings would know me. I was psyched—it was almost like having someone write a song about you, something I'd fantasized about my friend Lee Thompson doing, though he hadn't yet.

Passing by the tatty mélange of cheap restaurants with their stink of rancid fried food, and bargain clothing and housewares stores—the kind of places where you could buy a giant pack of tube socks for a dollar or an oversized suitcase to mail your grandmother back to Mexico in for ten bucks—I walked down Fourteenth Street between Seventh and Eighth Avenues, where Dan's studio was. Below the studio was a great Cuban place, where I picked up a café con leche before traipsing up the rickety stairs.

Dan's studio was basically an empty room with a low tin ceiling and grimy windows overlooking Fourteenth Street. A huge easel stood in one corner, and at a spattered worktable crowded with coffee cans stuffed with brushes, he would furiously squeeze tubes of paint. The air smelled of turpentine and mold even though it was drafty. A banged-up boom box sat on the window ledge, playing staticky music from a classical station. One chair perched atop a wooden box against the opposite wall, with a shadeless floor lamp casting a flat, white light across the room. The chair was for the model—me. We didn't talk much—I knew he had to concentrate on what he was doing. Surprisingly, I wasn't bored. Sitting for Dan gave me all this time to think, like being on a train and looking out the window—it was like mental floss. I would think about what I was going to make Jenny and Pete for dinner, how my sister was doing back in Boston after opting not to return to college, and what the hell I was going to do with my life.

In the first painting, I wore my street clothes—a white-collared shirt underneath a black crewneck sweater. After a few sittings, Dan finished it.

"Can I take a look?" I hadn't wanted to crowd him by asking to see it before it was done, even though I was dying of curiosity.

"Sure."

I walked around to his side of the easel. It was beautiful. I looked ethereal, even ghostly, as if you could see right through me. Maybe trying to forge your own identity was like a painting, layers and layers applied until people could see you, and you could become your own person. Looking at myself on the canvas, I could see I wasn't quite there yet.

"You look like an angel," he said, showing his snaggle-tooth smile as he wiped a brush on a rag.

I didn't think I looked like an angel, but I loved the way my eyes looked in the painting—they had a fierceness that I wanted to believe showed in my real life. I yearned for something— I didn't quite know what—and he had captured that. It was a little window into my soul.

As we moved on to the next portrait, I asked Dan if he wanted me to take my clothes off. I wanted to try on being that tough chick who strips not giving a damn who sees her. I also wanted to see if I could shock him with my brazenness. Before he could answer, I popped my sweater off over my head and started to unbutton my shirt.

"No, Wendy! Stop!" Raising his arms and practically making the sign of the cross, he seemed mortified. I realized that I had embarrassed him, so much so that he was acting as if I'd asked him to take off his clothes. It seemed like the opposite of the artist-model relationship to me, and I was a bit offended.

As I slowly got to know him better, I began to realize that Dan was quite religious. He was completely unlike Pete's other friends from childhood I'd met, like crazy Colin, Pete's flamboyantly gay chum who wore leather, shot heroin in the closet of the apartment, and got into bar fights regularly. Or the guy who once arrived for dinner at our door stark naked. Dan was like a monk compared to them.

I finally convinced him to let me wear a camisole for the last two paintings—I didn't own a bra because I was so flat-chested. These portraits had a more brutal, confrontational feeling to them—my mouth was an angry red smear and my eyes looked empty. Something had clearly changed between us. Whether I'd upset or frightened him I would never know. The first, more innocent, portrait remained my favorite— the phantom girl. She seemed full of possibility, and I looked forward to filling in her blanks.

Back at the Barnes & Noble, I was answering the phones with Annie and taking orders as usual. Rodney spent the days talking to his boyfriend on the phone and smoking. He always looked tired and hungover. I imagined him voguing until dawn in some gay club in the Meatpacking District.

I'd dragged Annie to a B-52s concert the previous night. The band came out in these crazy neon-colored suits and dresses. The women wore towering beehive wigs in purple and hot pink, leopard-print minidresses, go-go boots, and huge dangly earrings. We danced to songs about going to outer space, dance parties, poodles, and ancient Egypt. The B-52s were all about having a great time and looking outrageous while you did it.

But Annie had a lukewarm response to the band; she liked the Talking Heads more because, she said, they were intellectuals, in addition to being artists. Because I liked Prince, she accused me of having frivolous taste in music.

I'd seen the Talking Heads a few years before in Boston at the Berklee College of Music. All dressed in black, looking like actors in a modern dress play or beat poets, and barely acknowledging the audience, they'd picked up their instruments, unsmilingly, and began to play. After each song, they said nothing, not even introducing the songs. At the end of their set, the lead singer, David Byrne, said, "Thank you," into the microphone, and that was it—they walked off the stage. Maybe they had lightened up since then.

"The Talking Heads are serious thinkers with a super deep message, don't you see?" Annie sucked on the straw in her Diet Rite, her heavily kohled eyes looking at me as if I were an idiot. "They don't have to put on a show for you— they're doing it for themselves. And fuck what you think."

"But they acted like assholes. It was like they hated us." I shrugged. She was so intense sometimes. It was just rock 'n' roll, for Christ sakes.

After work we walked together across Eighteenth Street and turned down Seventh Avenue to find a bar and ducked into the Riviera Café, a joint in a brick building across from Sheridan Square on West Fourth Street. It had once been a hipster hangout in the late sixties and seventies, but was now just a place where you got a cheap drink after work. We were playing the jukebox, drinking rum and Cokes, and bumming a few cigarettes from the bartender when this wraithlike man walked in with a young boy, about ten years old or so. The man looked familiar to me, but Annie ID'd him right away.

"Jesus H. Christ, Wendy! It's Iggy Pop!" she hissed to me behind her hand, her black-rimmed eyes opened wide. I knew he hadn't heard her, but somehow his radar picked it up, and he made a beeline for our table.

"Are these seats taken?" Iggy Pop was asking if he could sit at our table. With us.

After a sizable pause, I answered, "No," because Annie had been struck dumb.

Iggy and the boy sat down. He introduced the kid as his son, Eric. Eric played waiter and asked us what we were drinking, then he went to the bar and ordered drinks for all of us.

Everything about Iggy looked cadaverous, except for one thing: his eyes. They were the only part of him that looked alive. His face and body looked leathery, and his skin hung from his frame, clearly having turned on him, but those blue eyes burned in his face, searing into you. I was terrified; it was like seeing someone who'd come back from the dead.

"What's this?" He snatched up from the sticky bar table a copy of Oscar Wilde's play *The Importance of Being Earnest*, which I had been carrying around. At Christmas in Minneapolis, I'd done my audition pieces for the artistic director of a small summer theater in the mountains of Colorado. It wasn't much pay, but my dad had encouraged me to try out, and I'd gotten a job as an apprentice mostly, but I'd get a chance to act in the Wilde play, as Cecily, a sort of madcap schoolgirl who doesn't like to do her homework.

"Just something I'm reading," I stammered as the drinks arrived, including Eric's Dr Pepper. I didn't want to tell Iggy Pop that I was going to act in the boonies.

Annie was still unable to speak, but I could tell that it

was her he was interested in. She had that Siouxsie and the Banshees thing going on. I was just the friend, which suited me fine.

Iggy asked Eric for a pen, and the boy went to get one from someone at the bar. When he returned, Iggy started drawing on the inside cover of my play. I thought about stopping him but didn't. He drew a little cartoon head, bald with bulbous eyes and a sagging mouth. Underneath the picture he scrawled, *Cancer can be cured.*

"For you," he growled.

"Um, thanks," I said—not knowing what else to say. I was sure I'd be the only girl on the block with an Iggy Pop autographed Oscar Wilde play. Maybe I could sell it?

"Hey, do you girls wanna stick around? Bowie's picking me up in a limo real soon. Maybe we could all go someplace." Iggy looked straight at Annie, but it was nice of him to include me.

"Wow, that's really . . . tempting. Bowie? You mean David Bowie?" I tittered nervously and looked hard at Annie, wondering how much more talking I was going to have to do. Eric shoved a toothpick in his mouth and leaned back in his chair like the badass boy in math class who always sits in the back row and gets sent to the principal a lot. He looked bored; I was fairly certain he'd seen this all before. It must have been tough being the only kid in the limo.

"Yeah, he's coming here. We could drive around for a while—then check out the Mudd Club?"

The Mudd Club was one of the hottest spots in town—

an underground, hip cabaret with Keith Haring's art gallery on the second floor, fashion shows, gender-neutral loos, and a bar and a dance floor. Blondie and the Talking Heads had performed there once, and Lou Reed and Nico chilled there with Andy Warhol.

"Cool," I said.

"We're supposed to meet up with Bill Burroughs there. You should see that old geezer dance, he's smooth." Iggy cackled.

I looked at Annie and nodded. No help. "Mudd Club," I said coaxingly, trying to tantalize her as if cake and ice cream would be waiting for us when we arrived.

"I have a boyfriend," Annie sputtered, nodding her head like Iggy should have known.

Iggy just looked at her as if she were a juicy lamb chop.

Suddenly she grabbed my hand. "We need to go!" Annie squealed in fear as if we were running away from the Mummy, or Dracula, which we sort of were. I was surprised that Annie was so afraid of a middle-aged rock star. I guessed her tough-chick appearance made me think that she could take care of herself, get rid of him or drink him under the table.

We bolted up and ran like hell through the front door, booking it along West Fourth Street.

We ran down into the subway and collapsed onto a bench on the platform, the book he'd signed clenched in my hand. The familiar steel-grinding sound almost drowned out our voices.

"Oh my God! That was so freaky!" Annie squealed, and grabbed my arm, squeezing it.

"He was so into you," I gasped, still trying to catch my breath as we stumbled onto the uptown train.

"Really? Do you think he was telling the truth? About Bowie and all?"

"I dunno."

She kissed me on the cheek and got off at her stop. I rode home looking at the strange doodle creature in my script.

A week later, Annie disappeared from the bookstore, not showing up one morning or ever again. Looking for her, I cruised Barneys and the restaurant where we'd eaten the Steak Bunnies together on our lunch breaks. I stopped by her apartment a few days later—the landlady told me Annie had moved back to Maine but had left no forwarding address.

We all came to New York to try on new selves, new ideas, maybe even make new homes. But if things didn't work out, most kids could go back to where they came from and who they used to be with doors held wide-open for them by their families. Their days in the city would become memories, stories of mystery and excitement told from a safe haven. No door was being held open for me, except the one at Jenny and Pete's at Ninety-seventh Street. And I was glad to have it.

I'd miss Annie and wonder how things had worked out for her—if she ever told her friends or family about the Steak Bunnies or Iggy Pop or me.

It was easy to lose people in the city—it seemed that if you let go of someone's hands for a moment, they were gone, slipped away. And all you could do was close your eyes and try to remember what they looked like, the sound of their voice, or what their last name had been.

chapter five

ALL THE YOUNG DUDES

That May, I flew to Minneapolis to visit with my dad and Sarah before heading to Steamboat Springs, Colorado. I'd inherited my trust money on my twenty-first birthday, so I felt emboldened when I called the trust officer Mr. Charno on the phone and asked him for $1,500 to buy a car. Daddy took me shopping at various used-car lots, although his only criteria for a good deal seemed to be a working radio and a cigarette lighter. The minuscule chocolate-brown Honda Civic I chose resembled a clown car, but it was in my price range. It would just about fit me inside, along with my giant, battered, white Samsonite suitcase that I had bought to supplement the Ciao! bag and named Moby, purchased at the Salvation Army in New York right before I left. I had crammed it with my possessions and just hoped it would survive the baggage handlers at LaGuardia.

"Take care, sweetheart—those roads can be treacherous.

I'll make it up there once you're into the run." Daddy hugged me good-bye.

I wedged myself into my car. "Bye-bye." It was still weird to say good-bye to him, to voluntarily leave my father. A part of me thought I might lose him again, that he might not be there when I came back.

"And remember"—he leaned down and spoke through the open window—"the mountains of Colorado are a place where men are men and sheep are nervous."

I had no idea what he meant, but I laughed anyway; he had great delivery. I headed south through Iowa, with its rolling hills and cornfields and entered startlingly flat Nebraska—where the speed limit shot up to seventy-five miles an hour. Outside of Omaha, I shoved my David Byrne and Brian Eno cassette, *My Life in the Bush of Ghosts*, into the tape player. The screaming evangelists, droning melodies, and thumping drum loops seemed an apropos sound track for this monotonous moonscape terrain—the home of the Strategic Air Command, Boys Town, and a seemingly endless stream of billboards that said JESUS LOVES YOU, HALLELUJAH! and DON'T KILL YOUR BABY. Feeling sleepy later that night, even after a drive-through McDonald's cheeseburger and coffee, I pulled into a Best Western off the highway in Kearney to get a room for the night. Dad had given me an Amoco credit card before I left, in case I got stranded somewhere. I could buy gas, snacks, and even put a hotel room on it.

I walked through the dark motel parking lot, which had

huge fields on either side and smelled faintly of cow poo. In the too-bright lobby, deserted at midnight, I asked the skinny, pasty guy working the overnight shift—his name tag said RAY—for a room. I signed the book and plonked down my credit card.

He smiled and slid a key on the counter to me. "Sweet dreams, ma'am."

Once in my room, too tired to undress, I pulled back the thick, floral polyester bedspread and collapsed, facedown. In the pitch black, I suddenly heard an odd, throbbing noise from somewhere inside the room. I got up and turned on the lights, checked the bathroom—nothing. But when I returned to the bed, I saw that it was covered in crickets, sawing away. I shrieked, grabbed my bag, and ran downstairs to tell the clerk.

"My room is filled with bugs!"

"Yes, ma'am." Ray nodded apologetically. "Crickets, ma'am."

"Well, can I have a room that isn't filled with crickets?" Freaked-out, I was about to tell him that I was even willing to pay extra.

"All the rooms have them this time of year. They come in through the windows from the fields across the way. We just can't stop 'em." He shrugged.

"Okay, thanks. I guess." It wasn't Ray's fault; he was doing his best.

I trudged back upstairs, swept as many of the crickets off the bed as I could, stuffed my ears with Kleenex, and pulled the bedspread over my head.

The next day, still sleep deprived, I drove out of town, dipped into Wyoming, and reached the mountains. The scenery was gorgeous—buttes capped with snow, craggy rock formations, forests of towering pine trees—but as I was a city kid, it all kind of scared me. I didn't know how to respond; it was so picture-perfect, so vast, it looked like a mural or the opening scene of *The Sound of Music*. I could practically see Fräulein Maria skipping around in her ugly novice uniform, singing to the trees.

When I stopped at a gas station to fill up in Cheyenne, dressed in my black jumpsuit and red Keds, a menacing-looking man in a cowboy hat and boots looked me over, scowled at my pixie haircut, and spit on the ground at my feet. I ran inside to pay and bought a cup of coffee and a candy bar, receiving more hairy eyeballs from flannel-clad, bearded truckers and the big-haired gal at the register. Walking out of the store, I felt their stares follow me; I jumped in my car and fled. I drove into Colorado, through little mountain towns on narrow, twisting roads punctuated with hairpin turns. I passed through Kremmling and Granby, which looked to me like Mayberry from *The Andy Griffith Show*. All the people, especially the guys, seemed bigger, taller, louder. Maybe it was all the fresh air; maybe it was the bolo ties and over-sized belt buckles. I guessed that's why they were referred to as mountain men. I drove by ghost towns that had sprung up during the silver boom and were now deserted, crumbling, and roadhouse bars in the middle of nowhere. I even saw some buffalo grazing on a hillside. I'd only ever seen them dead and stuffed at the Natural History Museum.

I drove through Rabbit Ears Pass, my ears popping from the nine thousand plus feet of altitude, and descended into Steamboat Springs. When I reached the town, I marveled at how dinky it was. There was basically one street, home to a Western-wear store, a gas station, a clapboard restaurant advertising a chicken-fried-steak dinner on a handmade sign in the window, and a convenience store. That was it. I was in the sticks. Expecting to see tumbleweeds blowing across the road at any moment, I walked down the main drag, feeling completely out of place—like a female David Bowie in my own version of the girl who fell to Earth. Since arriving, I had raised quite a few eyebrows and had felt anxious when the cashier at the minimart had asked me if I had gel in my hair with a tone implying gel was a felony in Colorado. My runaway friend, Annie, had turned me on to Tenax, a French hair product that came in a green-and-black tube. It was essential for eighties hair, Annie had told me, and I used it religiously. I didn't explain that to the cashier, merely nodding.

When I got to the address where the theater was, using a map I'd picked up at the chamber of commerce, I pulled over to the side of the road and looked around. All I saw was a big white tent in a field with a dilapidated trailer and a few trucks parked nearby. Where was the theater? I walked over to the tent, figuring someone inside might be able to direct me. Drawing back the heavy duck flap, I saw two men inside, hammering.

"Excuse me," I yelled over the din. "Do you know where

the Steamboat Repertory Theater is? It's supposed to be around here somewhere."

They looked up from their work. One looked like a Deadhead, in a rumpled tie-dyed T-shirt and a droopy mustache. The other one looked like the Marlboro Man come to life.

"You're standin' in it, little feller," said the Marlboro Man. I guessed it was the hair. And the jumpsuit.

"Really? You mean, it's in a tent?" Then I noticed some of the workmen were setting up folding chairs in rows and saw the large lighting instruments on the ground waiting to be hung. It had a dirt floor, the grass tamped down by many pairs of work boots.

The Steamboat Springs Repertory Theater had been founded by Richard Geer—not to be mistaken for the movie star—during a bleak winter with little snow in the resort town. He was affable, liked to wear Hawaiian shirts, and saw himself as a visionary bringing culture to the five thousand people who lived in town year-round. We'd be putting up three plays. Although the theater ended up going broke a few years later, we were all invigorated that summer by Richard's enthusiasm and his unshakable belief that we were making the world safe for the arts.

My housing was in a college dorm that was empty for the summer: cinder block with a thin single-mattress bed, overhead lighting, blah-colored curtains, and a communal bathroom down the hall. I had a roomie—a young African American woman named Bernadette who had a job in the costumes department. She must have weighed about two hundred and fifty pounds, was really into purple, and had a huge stash of M&M's under her bed. She was always scribbling in a diary in French—perhaps because she was afraid I might read it, which she was right to be because I did once when she'd left it lying around. There was only one reference to me—she called me *le papillon*—the butterfly. I don't think she was comparing me to the Steve McQueen character in the prisoner movie of the same name. More likely, it was a condescending description of my size. I was kind of small, five feet three and three-quarters, and barely hit a hundred pounds. When I was eight, the kids at school had teased me, calling me a dwarf. When I ran home to tell my mother, she took a drag on her cigarette and said, "Darling, you're not a dwarf—you're petite." Then she went back to her *Cosmo* quiz. Twelve years later, I was neither a dwarf nor petite; I was a butterfly.

Bernadette snored horribly, her enormous body a sound chamber that rattled and creaked with her every breath all night long. I had to go the drugstore and buy earplugs. This helped me sleep better at night but backfired when I couldn't hear my alarm clock in the morning—Bernadette having gotten up and gone, not bothering to wake me. I couldn't help but think she did it on purpose; she had taken an instant dislike to me. She claimed to have never heard the song "Bernadette" by the Four Tops, which simply couldn't be true. She looked at me blankly when I started singing it to her one day at rehearsal, using my comb as a pretend microphone. In the end, our tenuous relationship didn't matter because she moved in with the hippie lighting guy who lived in the fetid, crusty trailer next to the theater. I don't think he knew what was happening—one day she cleaned it from top to bottom, miraculously removing the stench that emanated from it, and set up house with him. She would pad around in an apron, screaming at him, and he'd try to smoke a joint behind the trailer without her seeing him or smelling it. They were like a Rocky Mountain take on Ma and Pa Kettle. Bernadette didn't think much of me, clearly, but I was slightly in awe of—and impressed by—her ability to take what she wanted; even if what she wanted was to shack up with a stoner dude. She got her man. I was still in the planning stages of figuring out what and who I wanted.

My next-door neighbor in the dorm was the other apprentice—a twenty-three-year-old business major from Virginia named Stanley, who would be working in the box office. He was a Mormon. I had never met a Mormon before. He was gangly and blond, with a receding hairline. He looked exactly like Clint Eastwood. Some days I could make him squint like Clint and say "Well, do ya, punk?"—which sent me into hysterics. He was a sweet guy with a girlfriend back home, whom he called Old Valerie; he said they'd probably get married. Even though they'd been going out for a year, I doubted they'd even seen each other's kneecaps. Shortly after Bernadette moved out, I got altitude sickness, and Stanley stayed by my side the entire time. I had a fever of 102 and genuinely thought I was going to die. Delirious,

I promised to leave him all the mixtapes my friend Amy had made me as well as my Grace Jones cassettes. We talked about his religion—or, rather, he talked while I shook with chills and perspired. I learned that Mormons couldn't drink alcohol or caffeine, couldn't smoke, couldn't have sex out of wedlock, and weren't allowed to masturbate. Even swearing was verboten. "Graham crackers!" Stanley would holler endearingly after he'd slammed his finger with a hammer. As he explained the teachings of the Mormon Church, it became clear to me that it had a lot of rules. Having grown up with few, I wondered if it made life harder or easier. Either way, from what he told me, I was pretty sure that in Stanley's world I would totally be going to hell big-time.

The first show of the season was *The Rainmaker*, a somewhat corny and dated play about a spinster named Lizzie living on a ranch in Oklahoma during the Depression. There's a terrible drought, and a charismatic con man named Starbuck comes to town and claims to be able to make it rain for a price. Lizzie and Starbuck have a one-night stand (demurely depicted in a play from the 1950s), and he tries to convince her to run off with him. But having learned something from him about herself—that she is beautiful in her own way—she stays on the ranch, and he's run out of town.

My job on *The Rainmaker* was to sober up one of the actors before the play's first—and his only—scene. No actor, really, he was a disc jockey at the radio station in town. He drove a pickup and usually arrived at the theater drunk, so I was in charge of getting him cups of coffee, and if he was really shit faced, I ran him around in circles in the field next to the tent. I'm sure we looked odd together, like a turbo-charged comedy act—him stumbling a bit and little me working hard to keep up with his long legs. Then, when I got him settled in his chair in the dressing room, I went to help Stanley at the box office, passed out programs before the show, and served coffee during the intermission on a folding table at the back of the tent.

For about two weeks of the run, it rained torrentially during the performances. Since the play's set on a farm during a severe dry spell, this led to some hilarious moments on-stage for the actors and the audience. An actor would stick his hands in pockets, look up, and drawl, "I sure do wish it would rain!"—while water poured down the backdrop and leaked into buckets on folding chairs placed around the theater, and the company tried to keep a straight face.

Although Stanley and I were buddies and spent so much time together just sitting around the tent, I couldn't confide too much in him because of his religion. Sharing my recent sordid past with him—sex, abortion, smoking, drinking—seemed inappropriate, and I feared that if he knew the truth about me, he'd judge me in some way or shun me. He wouldn't have done either, but I felt embarrassed about my wanton behavior and found that I often edited myself when I was talking to him. In many ways he was the perfect guy: thoughtful, kind, funny, sweet, and nice looking. But I knew I'd never cut it as a Mormon. *Too bad*, I thought.

The next show was the musical *Camelot*, which Richard

Geer would be directing. I was playing young Wart, pulling the sword out of the stone, and would be in the chorus as a lady-in-waiting, dancing around in a long dress and a wimple. I found a bestie in Barbie, who was playing Guinevere. She was about five years older than me, slender, with flaming-red hair and a wicked sense of humor. She was a badass and didn't take any shit from anyone, especially the men in the cast. She hated the guy who played Lancelot so much (he was a pompous windbag and not a great actor) that she took her contacts out before the show so she couldn't see him. Barbie adopted me in a big-sister way, and I was grateful to have a gal pal to hang out with.

One night after *Camelot* had opened, Richard came backstage, again, to give notes in the dressing room. Barbie was tired of his barging in every night, so she just stripped down to her panties—she didn't wear a bra—while he stood there blushing and stuttering. I thought she was awesome. She had a boyfriend who was off somewhere working as an actor. She showed me his picture, a glossy eight-by-ten of him naked except for his mustache and a bow tie. He had one leg up on a chair and was striking a defiant pose for the camera.

She had grown up in Boulder and had a condo in a complex there. We started driving down there on our days off and spending the night and next day there. Since she knew the way well and drove way too fast, we always made good time. We'd whip down the two-lane roads, blasting Grace Jones singing "Pull Up to the Bumper" with windows down and an open, cold bottle of Moët champagne stuck between

my legs for sustenance. A Steamboat Springs eccentric, a
zaftig lesbian lingerie heiress who insisted that we call her
S.O.B.—we never knew why—lavished each of the actors
with a case of Moët on every opening night, so we were always well stocked.

Barbie and I arrived at the apartment, took a late-night
swim in the pool, and flopped into bed. Boulder was a
crunchy place, full of Deadheads, flower children, and fol-
lowers of Jack Kerouac. The Naropa Institute clung to
a mountain overlooking the town; an Oxford-educated
Buddhist had founded it, and Allen Ginsberg taught poetry
there. The town had a grungy, groovy vibe, which normally
held no appeal for me, but at least you could buy the *New
York Times*, browse at bookstores, and get a decent cup of
coffee. Civilization!

I had recently received a summons for my former roommate Harvey's trial, forwarded to me through the mail by
Jenny. I called the court from Barbie's apartment, as I had no
phone number of my own—Barbie saved me from taking a
roll of quarters to a phone booth. The trial was set for late
August in New York. I was able to convince the clerk that
I didn't know anything about Harvey personally. We didn't
hang out—I just rented a room from him, and he gave me a
suitcase and a TV. Since I was now in Colorado and wasn't
a strong enough witness to be flown in by the government,
they released me. It was a relief—I had been worried about
testifying against Harvey and seeing him being dragged

away in handcuffs. Also, I had simply nothing to wear on the stand.

Finally, the show in which I had an actual speaking role, *The Importance of Being Earnest*, opened. It was directed by the smart young guy who'd hired me in Minneapolis. Playing the peculiarly charming Cecily was a blast; I wore a blond Gibson-girl wig that made me look like Carol Channing and skipped around frivolously with a paddle-ball toy. Barbie was playing Gwendolen, and we had such fun sparring during the tea scene that we had difficulty keeping our composure.

Robin arrived in Steamboat a few days after our *Earnest* premiere in the wee hours on a bus from the Denver airport, looking a little green and dazed from her long trip from Boston.

"Thanks for schlepping all the way out here!" I hugged her and grabbed her cotton Gap duffel bag.

"You're welcome," she slurred, zombielike. "Where the hell am I?"

"The Rocky Mountains, girl." I made a sweeping tour-guide arm gesture, even though it was dark and we were in a bus station parking lot.

"East Jesus is more like it. Why are you doing theater on the prairie, for God's sake?"

I shrugged. "It's a start, right?"

As it was around four thirty in the morning and eleven thirty in London, we drove over to watch Prince Charles and

Lady Di get married on the little, crappy black-and-white telly in the theater office. We watched in the dark, the TV casting a nearly lunar glow on us as the future princess got out of the coach in front of St. Paul's Cathedral and floated up the red-carpeted aisle, swathed in a cloud of taffeta and lace.

"Wow, that dress looks like it might swallow her up," Robin said.

"Yeah." I sighed. "She's the same age as me."

"And the similarities end there. Jeez, look at that ring! Nice rock."

We were two girls in the middle of nowhere watching a fairy-tale wedding taking place in a glittering city that we had once called home. It was like everything you'd ever dreamed about in the movies: a shy, lovely young woman plucked from obscurity to marry one of the world's most eligible bachelors. Pure fantasy. The faces of the men we would marry were still a blank. Maybe those guys were out there somewhere, but who knew if we'd ever find them.

My sister took in the play that evening, after we had both had power naps. I could hear her laughter from the audience; she was enjoying herself. Afterward, she sneaked back to the dressing-room tent.

"You were great! What a kooky play." She smiled at me.

"Thanks. It's fun." Robbie's support of my acting never wavered. She came to see me wherever I managed to work, and it meant a lot.

I drove her down to the Denver airport, and we popped into a place that looked like a HoJo's, called Denny's, for dinner before she got on the plane. We sat in a booth, eating club sandwiches and sipping on enormous iced teas loaded with crushed ice, and talked about the future, the fall specifically. She was planning to take some classes at UMass Boston—maybe study the classics or film—she wasn't sure. I guessed I'd head back to New York when the play ended. I told her that Daddy was coming to Steamboat soon.

"That's nice," she replied.

"It's too bad you'll just miss him."

"Yeah."

There was an awkward silence. A wave of guilt swept over me as it dawned on me that perhaps I had Pollyannaishly dragged my sister into reuniting with our father and maybe she hadn't been ready at Christmas. I had been focused on how I'd feel better having her with me. Perhaps I'd unwittingly pushed her into something she didn't want. I had forced my way into Daddy's life, carving out my own space; my sister was different—maybe she didn't feel the connection I'd grabbed on to and embraced. I realized in that moment that whatever relationship Daddy and Robin forged, it would have to be achieved between the two of them, without me. I searched for a way to tell her this, apologize maybe.

But suddenly Robin leaned over the table and said in a low voice, "Don't look up right away, but I think there are policemen outside."

Out of the corner of my eye, I could see little black flecks darting around, popping up and down, like in one of those shooting-gallery carnival games. "Um, I guess we should get the check?"

"Yeah, maybe, before we get taken hostage."

"Let's just do this." I pulled a twenty out of my purse and put it on the table.

We rose stealthily and slowly ambled out of the restaurant past about ten cops squatting in the low bushes outside with their guns drawn. Losing our nerve, we squealed and made a break for the parking lot. The officers ignored us, storming into the restaurant. Screams and shouts erupted from the Denny's dining room, followed by silence. Hiding behind my car, I turned to ask a guy crouched down behind a tree next to us what was happening. Apparently an armed gunman had been inside, planning to rob the place, but someone had tipped off the cops. Police and thieves were seemingly never far away from the Lawless sisters. We got into my Honda and drove away.

"Close call," Robin said as she lit up a cigarette.

My father came to visit and see the show, causing a bit of a stir, as he was a sort of regional-theater celebrity. As everyone crowded around him—the director and some of the other actors—I felt like Jimmy Lawless's daughter for only the second or third time in my life. I wondered if people thought I had some special advantage because of who my father was. No one in the company knew that we'd only recently reunited or that I'd had a crazy-train childhood, instead of growing up with him. Unexpectedly, I didn't feel nervous at all knowing he was out in the audience. It gave me a feeling of security—as if he was rooting for me—and made me want to do my best.

At dinner after the show, he told me how relieved he was when I made my entrance and said my first lines. "You can't teach that, you know. You've definitely got 'it,' kid."

"Thanks, Daddy," I gushed.

He told me he had been worried that if I wasn't good, he wouldn't know what to say to me, regaling me with funny stories about going to see friends in shows who were terrible and having to go backstage and say something nice. He'd say, "That was the most amazing thing I've ever seen!" or "Do you do that every night? Incredible!"—not wanting to lie.

"Soon, I'll be known as Wendy Lawless's father!" He laughed, and so did I. I was thrilled that he liked my performance. I had lived up to his expectations and gained his respect as a fellow actor. I was giddy with happiness. He drove off in his big black Buick LeSabre the next day to play Falstaff in *Henry IV, Part 1* in Denver. Someday, I hoped, it might be me going off for a big role somewhere. For now I was happy with his encouragement and just to be working.

At the end of the summer the tent came down, and we all dispersed. Being in a theater company was intense yet fleeting. You quickly became a family with your coworkers, then it was over—and you never knew if you'd see each other again. Some people I'd never want to see again, but others wrote down their contact information on the clipboard that was passed around on that last day and I promised to write letters or call. Many actors went back to Denver. Barbie returned to her condo in Boulder, where she said I'd always be welcome. Stanley and I caravanned in a torrential rainstorm, following each other's car as far as Kansas City, where we spent the night at a hotel in the Plaza section of town. I remembered staying in this same hotel with my mother and sister while visiting my dying grandfather eight years previously. Stanley and I shared a room, sleeping in separate double beds. The air-conditioning in our room was broken and couldn't be turned off.

"Can I get in with you?" I asked after failing to fall asleep for what felt like ages. "I'm freezing!"

"Sure, Wendell."

We cuddled spoon-style for warmth beneath the covers, not speaking. I could feel his breath on the back of my neck and a hardness that pressed into my lower back. Politely ignoring the latter, I said good night. We got up before dawn the next morning—he was headed to DC to work at the Arena Stage in the box office, and I was headed back to New York.

"Well, little ole Wendy, you take care."

"You, too." I embraced him.

"Let me know where you finally end up."

"I will. Good luck with your job."

"Oh, and thanks for the English Beat cassette."

"Sure, Stanley."

We got into our cars and drove off on our separate journeys. Watching him in my rearview mirror, I saw Stanley riding toward his new job, his marriage to Old Valerie, and four or five perfectly blond Mormon kids. He had it all figured out: a map of the future. I was driving into the unknown—but at least the sun was starting to come up.

chapter six

SPRING AWAKENING

After my stint in Wild West theater, I returned to Manhattan, not knowing where else to go. I moved back into my room at Ninety-seventh Street; it was almost as if Pete and Jenny had it waiting for me. After turning heads in a tiny town in Colorado with my personal style, I needed to work a bit harder to get noticed and stand out in the city. To go along with my spiky do, I took it up a notch by wearing suits and ties. A pair of white Keds high-tops completed the androgynous look that I fancied made me look like little David Bowie.

Some people, though, seemed threatened by my macho style.

"What are you? Some kind of Nazi?" a male friend of Pete's asked me one night at dinner.

I was about to open my mouth when Pete stepped in and quipped, "No, Wend's just feminine—in a butch sort of way."

Rodney, my old boss from Barnes & Noble, had vanished, and my job had been filled by some new kid fresh off the bus. Since I couldn't type and acting jobs weren't falling from the skies, I capitalized on my skill set—talking on the phone. I got a job at an Italian deli on Lexington in the Forties, Piatti Pronti. This lunch place catered to office workers in Midtown, and I took the orders for delivery. I thought I could probably make a killing teaching most of the people I talked to how to speak properly. Many were simply unintelligible, squawking into my ear in a thick Queens or Brooklyn accent. Sometimes I had to ask them to repeat or—if it was especially garbled—spell their orders, addresses, and names. It was crazy busy from noon to three, the phone ringing and everyone yelling, and then I was back out on the street, heading home by four.

After work on an especially gorgeous November afternoon, I thought I'd take a nostalgic stroll up Fifth Avenue and maybe take the crosstown bus at Eighty-sixth Street, walking the eleven blocks home. Along the way, I dreamed of my million-dollar idea of teaching speech classes to accent-challenged New Yorkers. I headed west along Forty-second Street past Grand Central Terminal, and turned up Fifth at the stately New York Public Library, with its imposing marble lions, Patience and Fortitude, keeping sentry at the steps. I peered through the glass front of Scribner's bookstore, with its ornate beaux arts ironwork and vaulted ceilings, looking like a place far too serious for me to go inside. Just past Saks Fifth Avenue, I could see the opulent neo-Gothic spires of St. Patrick's Cathedral, where my sister and I had once watched on television our mother, swathed in her mink and sporting a dramatic fluttery, black chiffon head scarf and Persol sunglasses, mount the steps to attend Senator Robert Kennedy's memorial service. I was looking in the windows of Saks, contemplating going inside to breathe in the high-end-department-store smell of leather and fresh lipstick, when I ran into Nina Franco, who was on her way out, clutching one of the store's classy taupe shopping bags with the curly script.

I had met Nina the summer I was seventeen, at a small theater in New Hampshire, the Peterborough Players, where we were both apprentices. I had been very much in awe of her; she was outspoken and accomplished and had a serious boyfriend, who was the youngest actor in the Equity company. Nina was a few years older than me and had recently graduated from NYU undergrad. She was brainy, spoke at least two languages besides English, and was well connected in the New York theater world.

"Omigod! Hi, Wendy Lawless!" Nina gave me a big hug. She was about five feet tall, in heels, with perfectly streaked, long brunette hair, and her nose was just a little too big for her face, which kept her from looking like any other pretty girl from the Upper East Side. She had a lovely smile and perfect teeth.

"Hi, Nina!"

"I just got out of Georgette Klinger on Madison and was doing a little shopping. How are you?"

Nina was the first person I'd ever known who claimed to go regularly to get her blackheads sucked out at Georgette Klinger, the first fancy facial spa in Manhattan, opened by a Czech beauty queen who'd fled the Nazis and who used to make beauty creams in her kitchen before she opened her first salon. Nina dressed well, and dramatically, all in black, making her look like a chic imp. If I was thrift shop, Nina was definitely Saks.

"I still remember how amazing you were in that Tennessee Williams play."

Nina was referring to the apprentice production at the end of the summer where I got to be in *This Property Is Condemned*, the story of a young girl walking down some railroad tracks, haunted by the death of her beautiful older sister. It was a great part, and I had gotten some compliments from the actors in the company who had attended the show.

"Thanks, Nina. Gosh, what are you up to?" I noticed her face looked all dewy and blemish-free.

"I'm directing an Equity showcase, and I'm casting it right now. I can't believe I ran into you because you'd be perfect for it. Are you available?"

I was almost always available. I nodded at Nina.

"This is amazing. Come the day after tomorrow, say around six p.m.—here's the address." She scribbled on a scrap of paper from her purse.

"Wow, really? Thanks! Oh, what's the play?"

"It's *Spring Awakening*. Wedekind. Do you know it?"

I nodded eagerly. Nina was an intellectual, so of course

I had never heard of the play. But I didn't want her to know that.

"I can't believe I ran into you today. It's like it was meant to be! See you soon." And she was gone, clicking away down the street in her black, high-heeled boots surrounded by a swirl of orange fall leaves as they flew off the trees.

I ran past St. Patrick's and Cartier to Fifty-third Street, jumped on the E train, and got off at Port Authority. I booked it across Forty-second Street praying that the Drama Book Shop in Times Square would still be open and have a copy of the play. I raced up the narrow staircase to the second floor and breathlessly asked the oily-haired clerk at the register which section Wedekind's *Spring Awakening* would be in.

"That's gonna be in German expressionism. All the way in the back," he said without even looking up from his copy of *Backstage*.

I found the play, bought it, and started to read it on my way back to Jenny and Pete's on the train. The play was dark, incredibly sad, and filled with all kinds of taboo stuff—rape, masturbation, flagellation, abortion, homosexuality, and suicide. It was about this group of German teenagers living in a small village in the 1800s whose parents keep them completely ignorant about sex, with disastrous results. The kids are also under huge pressure at school, where they have to be at the top of their class or be expelled or become garbage collectors. I could see the appeal for Nina—it was out there. The play was scary and weird and had a heightened quality of theatricality

and otherworldliness. I wondered what part I'd be reading for.

Two days later, I sat in a dingy basement hallway on Tenth
Avenue outside the rehearsal room where the auditions were
taking place. I was reading for the part of Wendla—the
lead—but I was sure that all the young women were reading
that part. There were four girls, school friends, in the play—
I figured Nina was considering casting me in one of those
roles, if I got lucky. There were some older actors there, too,
in their late twenties maybe, and I wondered if any of her
Yalie pals were here; I probably didn't have a chance of getting in the show.

I briefly thought about just fleeing, running out the door.
I was super nervous; this seemed so much more serious than
performing in a tent in a small mountain town, which I now
felt almost embarrassed about. But I desperately wanted to
impress Nina. They called my name and I went in and hoped
they wouldn't notice my hands were trembling. The actor
who'd already been cast as the leading boy, Melchior, was
reading with me.

"Let's do Wendla and Melchior's first scene together."
Nina nodded at us. "Start when you feel ready."

We did the scene; Wendla is very trusting and innocent.
She has a crush on Melchior, but in a schoolgirl way—she's
only fourteen. It seemed to be going well when Nina stopped
us about halfway through.

"Good. Now, I'd like you to improvise the rest of the
scene. Just put your scripts down and use your own words."

I was terrified—I'd never improvised anything before, except my own life. I looked at the other actor, hoping he would say or do something first. Wendla, I realized, wants to know what it's like to suffer—something she's never experienced in her happy, placid, sheltered childhood. Then, I had an impulse; I picked a script up off the floor and smacked myself across my legs with it.

"Hit me!" I felt as if this weird energy had taken me over. I slapped him on the chest with the script.

He grabbed the script away and then gingerly tapped me.

"That didn't hurt at all. Hit me harder, Melchior." I beat on his chest with my hands. I shouted, "Harder!" Then I pushed him.

He brought his hand high above his head, as if he were going to strike me hard. Then he froze. He looked at Nina and smiled as I held my breath.

"That was great, guys!" Nina beamed. "Wendy, I want you to play Wendla."

"Really?" I couldn't believe it—I had faked my way through the audition, and it had worked.

"Yes—what do you say?"

I stood there for a minute, dumbfounded, then managed to squeeze out, "Uh . . . sure."

"Fantastic! We'll start next week."

We would be rehearsing at night, so people could go to their day jobs or make their other auditions. We were to rehearse for about four weeks, then perform for two weeks at a church on the Lower East Side Nina had snagged. She'd called in favors all over town so we'd have sets, costumes, lighting—just like a professional production. It would even have original music, scored by one of Nina's composer friends. There was no pay, but we'd be given subway tokens to go back and forth and an occasional dinner-break delivery from the corner deli on late nights. I ran home to tell Pete and Jenny.

"Yeah for you, sweetie! You did it!" Jenny gave me a big hug and a kiss.

"Awesome, Wend," said Pete with the sweet smile that displayed his Indian-corn teeth. Their love and support was palpable and meant the world to me, and I felt so fortunate to have my little family in my corner, cheering for me. They assured me that they would be there opening night. Jenny and Pete were the best.

The cast and crew of *Spring Awakening* started rehearsals— I felt a little intimidated by the other actors, all of whom had some kind of formal training, which I did not. I was playing a tragic, sexually confused, insecure young girl. So I pranced around onstage scantily clad in my underwear, playing a version of myself. I found my last scene, before I die of a botched abortion offstage, especially painful to perform. I cried every time we did it, thinking of the baby I'd aborted the year before and whom I would never know. It may have looked like acting, but that pain was real and never far from the surface. I couldn't stop those tears.

Usually after rehearsals, the cast and crew went to a dive blues bar called Dan Lynch's nearby on Thirteenth Street for a few drinks. Sometimes, Earl and Clyde, two African American janitors in their late sixties, came along with us to throw back a couple of beers after they closed up the church for the night.

One night, a group of us straggled into the bar through its beaten-up wooden saloon doors, the only light inside coming from the neon beer signs that hung in the window. The air was moist with sweat and smelled like cat pee and watered-down drinks. I was dancing by myself to a guitar player named, improbably, B. B. King Jr., and his band, while the cast and crew hung out at the bar. B.B. was ripping his guts out on the stage and singing in a guttural howl through the wall of cigarette smoke. Clyde sauntered up and started dancing with me. I turned toward him—he was an amazing dancer.

"You can't dance by yourself, girl," he shouted in my ear. I turned to him and we became a couple. He had so much style and cool; his moves were fluid and matched the music. I was sort of pogoing, the popular club dance of the moment. I was such a white girl.

"You're an incredible dancer, Clyde," I yelled back. He smiled, mopping his face with a crumpled bar napkin.

"You want to know my secret?"

I nodded, running my hand over my scalp and wiping it on my skirt.

"Listen to the music and dance to one instrument at a time." I watched him do it—he switched from following the guitar, to the bass, to the drums—stepping around the floor like a man less than half his age. I tried to copy him, but he felt the music in his body in a way I just didn't.

From the dance floor, I saw Nina's brother, Lincoln—an artist who was doing the sets—sitting at one of the tables, looking at me intently. I had noticed him before, but he was usually immersed in painting and hammering. He was a big guy, barrel-chested, with a strong face that was handsome, but you could tell he couldn't care less about shit like that. That he didn't care made him seem sexy to me. He had a rumpled Julian Schnabel–esque aura about him, a kind of bad-boy thing. It was real—he wasn't pretending to be a hard-drinking, wild-haired, paint-spattered artist—he really was. I'd heard he had a live-in girlfriend and that sometimes he got so drunk he fell down. All that just made him more alluring to me. He had never looked my way—until now.

The set ended, I thanked Clyde for the dance—he nodded and smiled, moving off to where he'd left his beer—and I went over to the bar to order a bourbon. Lincoln sauntered over and stood next to me. He ground out his cigarette in the ashtray and lit another, exhaling the smoke from his nostrils in a heavy plume.

"Hi," I said. I climbed onto a barstool and sipped my drink, trying to play it cool.

"Hi."

I recrossed my legs, showing off my black tights, short, black tube skirt, and the baggy, long, emerald-green sweater I'd bought in a Boston thrift store. He studied my legs, and then, seeing a hole in my tights, put his finger there, rubbing it around on my bare skin. He just kept looking at me, with no expression. His actions did the talking.

He took the cigarette out of his mouth. "Do you wanna dance?"

"Sure."

Hand in hand, we strolled out onto the floor. It was a fast number, but he pulled me into him and held me close, looking right at my face, inches away from his. I could smell bourbon and cigarettes on his breath. As we moved slowly around, he took one of my hands in his and placed it against his chest, the other gripping me strongly across my waist. We were still looking into each other's eyes as the song ended around us.

"Wanna get outta here?" He didn't let go of me but moved his hand from my waist, up under the back of my sweater, and made my bare skin shiver.

I swallowed. "Okay," I croaked.

"You got a place?"

I nodded. Once we began having rehearsals that ran especially late, Nina had kindly given me the keys to an empty studio apartment nearby so I wouldn't have to take the subway home after eleven or twelve o'clock at night—when the creeps, muggers, and jack-offs rode the trains, which often stopped in the tunnels inexplicably or were plunged into darkness when the lights cut out. The studio belonged to a friend of hers, an older character actor who was out on the road touring in a show. I had crashed there a few nights already and even kept some clothes there so I could change for work at the deli the next morning.

"Just give me a minute," Lincoln said.

He released me and went over to a booth to pick up his cigarettes and down the rest of his Jack Daniel's. He looked over at me and cocked his head in the direction of the door. I grabbed my stuff and followed him out, glancing quickly at his sister, who was immersed in a conversation with her current boyfriend, a successful actor named Paul who had the blond good looks of a California surfer.

Out on the street, I saw that it had rained and gotten cold while we were inside Dan Lynch's. I had a coat, but Lincoln didn't. He put his arms around me, burying his hands along with mine in the pockets of my coat, our breath fogging the air. We walked wordlessly over the metal doors in the sidewalks, banging past all the closed shops along Second Avenue. When we reached the building on Sixteenth Street, I ran up the steps and unlocked the outside door, then the inside door. Inside the first-floor apartment, I turned on a lamp, which cast a yellow glow on the threadbare Persian rug in front of the sofa. The place was minimally furnished by someone who didn't have a lot of money, but it was clean and tidy, with theater posters on the walls, an old, wooden rolltop desk, and plenty of books lining the shelves.

"So, have you brought other guys here?"

"Just you." I took off my coat and tossed it nonchalantly on the sofa in my best woman-of-the-world manner.

"So I guess I'm lucky."

"Well, that depends on how you look at it."

Before anything happened and—I thought—much to his credit, he told me about his girlfriend. I'd seen her at rehearsals. Tall and pale, with red hair and glasses, she looked fragile, like a crushed flower. He loved her, didn't want to hurt her, he explained, but felt trapped and bored. I guessed this is where I was going to come in.

"It's fine with me," I said, attempting to sound cavalier. I wasn't eager to have a serious relationship, I lied—telling him what I thought he wanted to hear—just so he would stay. I didn't tell him I was lonely, and that I fancied him, and that his interest made me feel wanted.

That night we drank a bottle of red wine we found and invented a new game, Strip Bongos. One person played the bongos, and one person took off an article of clothing. Then we switched. He left around three in the morning, heading back to Brooklyn to sneak in without being noticed. I could tell he felt guilty, but my dizzy logic told me that no one was getting hurt as long as his girlfriend didn't find out. His not being truly available made it easier in a way—knowing that whatever happened between us had a shelf life. I wouldn't have to give all of myself, to fall in love, with all the vulnerability that implied. I could keep a part of me hidden.

The show opened the following weekend, and because Nina was so well connected, a lot of important people came to see it—hot young actors she'd worked with or whom her actor boyfriend, Paul, knew, directors, and casting agents—some of whom asked me after the show if I was interested in reading for film and television. I said yes, thrilled at all the attention. Being in *Spring Awakening* felt big-time to me, as if I were actually getting a taste of being a successful, in-demand actor. I liked the way it felt and yearned for more.

I called my dad after opening night to thank him for the telegram he'd sent me—it had read, hilariously, given the text of the play—"Break a hymen." He was still playing Falstaff in *Henry IV, Part 1* at the Denver Center Theatre Company and wouldn't be able to see the show, and I was disappointed but understood; actors are not like regular people. You show up for every performance, and your understudy only goes on if you're dead.

When I got Dad on the phone, he said, "You're finally in a position where a lot of people will see how talented you are, sweetheart."

"I hope so."

"Just go out there every night and fuck 'em in the heart."

Determined to do just that, I got an answering service—just like all the other serious New York actors—called Bells Are Ringing, to take my phone messages in case any of the muckety-mucks who saw the show tried to contact me. I regularly dashed into a phone booth to check if anyone had called. I was flattered by all the people who told me how good I was in the show, but how did I know they meant it? Maybe it was just my ability to cry on cue. The part felt so close to me, it was more like I was *being* this lost girl rather than *acting* her.

Nina had already been asked to assistant-direct a play on

Broadway the following month. I was happy for her, grateful to her for giving me this chance to be seen. Other actors in the *Spring Awakening* cast were booking jobs in regional theater and small films.

One casting agent, Meg Simon, was especially enthusiastic about my work in the play. She had this cascading mane of black ringlets and thick-framed glasses, and she always wore boldly colored retro dresses and chunky jewelry. Meg believed in me and was warm and funny, and I was drawn to her like a big sister.

She asked me to come to her office and told me she had me in mind for a few projects. "You remind of a young Katharine Hepburn. How old do you think you play on TV or film?"

I mumbled that I didn't know as I ogled all the posters on her office walls from the Broadway, Second Stage, and Lincoln Center shows she had cast.

She laughed. "Well, I'm looking for a young actress for a soap opera I cast. I'll send you there first."

I thanked her, and she gave me a big hug.

A few days later, I read for the producers of *Ryan's Hope*, an ABC daytime show about a large Catholic, Irish American family who run a bar and live in Washington Heights. I knew the audition had gone well when I had a message on my service from Meg.

"They want to test you!" She was ebullient, as was I. "But first, you need an agent."

Meg sent me out on meetings with agents who might

possibly be interested in negotiating my soap contract, in case I got the role. With an agreement in place, I would be locked in and couldn't back out or ask for more money. It seemed crazy to me that I'd be signing on for three years on the show before I even knew if I had the job, but I didn't have anything else going for me.

The first agent Meg sent me to was an incredibly odd woman. Probably in her forties, she resembled a wizened tortoise and reminded me of an old, lesbian babysitter of mine from long ago. During our meeting she said strange things and seemed obsessed with my glove size. She called that night to tell me she was just thinking about me when she was in the shower. I told her thanks, but Meg wanted me to meet a few other people.

Another agent, David Guc, took me out to dinner after the show one night. He invited me back to his house; he was sort of oily, sexless, and overweight. A powerful agent, he had many celebrity clients, so I went—I didn't get the feeling he was that into me. He kept going on and on about his newest client, a famous actress named Kathleen Turner, who he claimed was also his lover, something I found hard to believe looking at him.

He wanted to know if I had ever read Chekhov; I told him that I hadn't. He plucked a copy of *Three Sisters* out of his bookcase and gave it to me. "You should read this play. You were born to play Masha—you have her soul—but you probably will never play the part."

When I asked him why not, he told me I was too sweet

looking, too cherubic, to be considered for "heavier" roles. I thought he was an arrogant prick.

My first appointment the next day was with someone named Didi Rea at the Susan Smith Agency. As I sat in the waiting room in my blue pin-striped suit, baby-blue shirt, and red-and-navy-striped skinny tie, I turned that name around in my brain, thinking that it sounded vaguely familiar, perhaps someone I'd met at a party. I dismissed the feeling and flipped through a magazine.

Then, when the assistant led me back to the office, I was face-to-face with my ex-stepsister Didi, the daughter my mother's second husband, Oliver Rea. I had not seen Didi, who was nine years older than me, since 1974, when I got drunk at El Morocco one night, danced with her older brother, Peter, to "Midnight at the Oasis," and passed out in a cab. I'd been fourteen.

"Jesus Christ!" Didi stood bolt upright behind her desk.

"Omigod!" I couldn't believe I hadn't put it together that Didi Rea was her.

We hugged and laughed, and she sent the assistant out for a bottle of champagne to celebrate our reunion. While the girl was out getting the wine, we caught up. It had been seven years; she was married now and had a little girl. Her husband was a photographer, and they lived on West End Avenue in the Eighties near Fairway.

I didn't have that much in the way of news, except for the show and my upcoming screen test. Didi asked about my mother. I felt my face flush—it pained me to think of how my mother had caused her parents to split up. "We're not really speaking right now," I said. "She's living in Connecticut."

I still felt, in a kind of guilt by association, that just being my mother's child made me somehow partially responsible for all the havoc she had created in other people's lives. I also knew that my mother was one of Didi's least favorite people. In fact, they had loathed each other openly. I couldn't say I blamed Didi—who would be happy about some young, pretty thing coming along and busting up your family?

The summer of 1967, the only one we all spent together as a family, we lived in Southampton. After the two divorces and our parents' marriage, Pop rented a huge house that belonged to Andy Warhol. The enormous, two-story, barnlike structure with an open floor plan had an entire wall of windows that moved on a track like a massive sliding glass door. Tall shrubbery enclosed a huge lawn in which stood plenty of good climbing trees. This cozy enclave was where we were supposed to get to know one another and blend as a family.

That summer, Pop spent the weekdays in the city at our apartment in the Dakota. I was never sure what he did for a job exactly, but the husbands stayed in town and sent their wives and children out to the Hamptons or Connecticut; that was just what people did then. On Friday evenings, while it was still light out, my mother would pick him up at the train station, sometimes with me, Robbie, and our youngest stepsister, Maggie—who was two years older than me—in tow in our nighties, already dressed for bed. We'd wait for the train and put pennies on the tracks to pick up after they'd been squished into flat ovals by the train's steel wheels.

By the time Pop made his weekly appearance, the tension at the house that had been building all week was as thick as kudzu. My mother had enough trouble being a parent to Robbie and me—but throwing three more kids she barely knew into the mix, two of whom were opinionated teenagers, pushed her limits of patience. Maggie, only nine, was our playmate. We'd put the sound track to *Exodus* on the stereo and perform big dance numbers or play tag out on the immense lawn. Didi, who was sixteen and had a summer job at a pie shop in town, clashed the most with Mother, who incessantly nagged Didi about her smoking, her diet of Bazooka bubble gum and Jack Daniel's, and the general indifference and annoyance that Didi didn't bother to hide. Then Friday would come, and my mother would say icily to my stepsister, who had just changed out of her pink pie-shop uniform, "When your father gets here, everything will be fine." Didi would merely smirk at her; I suspected she was saving up points to exact her revenge on Mother at a later date.

My stepbrother, Peter, was a whole different story. First, and most important to Mother, he was a man—so Mother set out to charm him. He seemed taken with her—one reason might have been that there was only an eleven-year difference in their ages. She was closer to his age than Pop's and she enjoyed the attention. Peter's girlfriend was pretty, coltish, without much going on between her ears—or so Mother claimed.

Further complicating Didi's and my potboiler summer was the drama of our now dismissed au pair, Michelle. Mother had hired her to watch us so she could go to Elizabeth Arden whenever she liked and to lunch and cocktail parties at the country club. Unfortunately, homely Michelle, who wore old-lady glasses and a mousy Dorothy Hamill hairdo, promptly fell in love with my stepbrother and, a few weeks later, ran into the ocean trying to kill herself because Peter didn't return her feelings. Luckily, she failed, but Mother fired her on the spot and called a taxi to take her away while she cried on her bed in the spare room.

Left with no help and severe limitations cramping her social life on the island, Mother fumed in the kitchen, turning out bland Midwestern dishes that Didi blatantly turned her nose up at and the rest of us listlessly pushed around on our plates.

Then Pop would zoom in for the weekend and cook us all gourmet meals. Mother had married someone who was sophisticated and well traveled—whose kids were, too. Suddenly Robbie and I were expected to eat fancy foods we had never tried—smelly asparagus, spiky artichokes, monsterlike lobster, and stinky fish. Pop had even brought live eels home, which he energetically clubbed to death on the patio before throwing them on the grill, horrifying us. We would sit at the dinner table for hours, not eating, begging to be excused—Mother was infuriated. Eventually, we'd be dismissed and sent directly to bed, tummies rumbling.

At the end of the summer, Pop, who had a weird sense of

humor, thought it would be fun to have a whipped-cream-and-pie fight in the yard. Peter and Didi drove into town and cleaned every store out of Reddi-wip and all the pie they could stuff into the station wagon. No room was left in the fridge by the time the big day came.

The fight started out fun—Maggie, Robbie, and I each threw a pie but missed because we were the smallest and everyone else could run much faster than we could. A lot of people threw stuff at Peter's girlfriend, whom no one liked, so she was completely coated in seconds. Then before our eyes the whole thing morphed from a simple game to a food-fight rugby match. A frenzied aggression sprang from all the chaos, ratcheting up to a point where it became a big person's game, and Maggie, Robbie, and I were too little to play or to protect ourselves. So the three of us climbed up into a tree and cried, waiting for it to be over. No one on the ground noticed.

The shadows lengthened while we sat up in the branches watching Mother, Pop, and the big kids scream and grind pies into one another's faces and shoot whipped cream into one another's hair. When they ran out of ammo, they dashed through the huge sliding glass doors into the house to grab anything they could find in the refrigerator. Eggs flew through the air at people's heads and cracked open against tree trunks. Didi emerged from the house with a container of ice cream and a scoop and started pelting my mother with gobs of rocky road. Peter ran out with a jar of peanut but-ter and smeared it all over his sister's face with his hand.

Finally, the grown-ups collapsed, spent and laughing, on a lawn littered with lumps of peanut butter that looked like dog turds, smashed pie crusts, and empty Reddi-wip cans. The air smelled like sour milk; Maggie and I climbed down, helping Robin, and, holding hands, snuck into the house and to bed.

A few days later, we were back in our apartment in the Dakota—Maggie having returned to her mother's apartment on the Upper East Side, and Peter and Didi were dispatched to their respective boarding schools in Massachusetts. I had seen them only once since then—the night at El Morocco.

The assistant returned with the champagne, and Didi and I drank a toast. We agreed that she would negotiate the contract for me, she even offered to loan me a suitable skirt and blouse to wear for it, as my Bowie style wasn't going to work on daytime television.

"What do you call that look?" She gave me the up and down as she pointed at my clothes.

I shrugged and laughed, sipping the fizzy wine.

"We always wondered what was going to happen to you poor girls." She looked at me wistfully, shook her head, and filled my paper cup with more champagne. I was touched by her concern and by her acknowledgment that Robin and I had been handed a train wreck of a childhood.

I didn't have a response, so I just said, "Cheers!," and tapped my cup against hers, sealing the deal.

The test was later in the week. In the meantime, I was seeing Lincoln when he could get away from his girlfriend, which sometimes meant he called me from a phone booth close by. "She thinks I'm out buying cigarettes," his voice rasped into the phone. Lincoln told her he was getting milk, picking up the newspaper, or grabbing a beer with a friend. He was running out of reasons to go out in the middle of the night.

"Unless I get a dog!" he joked.

Eventually, our romance—which had never been especially deep—just petered out. We met one night after the show in a bright coffee shop on Second Avenue, with shiny red banquettes, stained plastic tablecloths, and one of those revolving cake-display cases. We drank coffee under the harsh overhead lights, and he fiddled with the sugar packets, looking down at the table. I could tell he was worried I'd be hurt, so I spoke first and assured him that I understood and felt the same way. He didn't want to two-time her anymore, and I had begun to feel badly about my role in it, too. It was over; we said good-bye.

Lincoln had been fun, a sexy Band-Aid that made me feel wanted after my celibate summer in Colorado. With all the men I felt drawn to—Michael, Oedi, Lincoln, and even Stanley the Mormon—something was always missing; they were unkind or unavailable in some way. But if I was honest with myself, I wanted a real boyfriend, someone to call my own.

The next day, I splurged and took a taxi to my screen test. I arrived at the studio, was shown to a dressing room—where I put the pretty celadon-colored silk blouse and skirt that Didi had loaned me—and went over my lines one more time before the AD took me up to hair and makeup. The actor I was reading with was on the set when I got there. He was one of the handsome young leads on the show—very Ken doll meets Bobby Sherman. I told him I was nervous.

"Don't worry—you'll do great. Just relax and look at me," he whispered, placing his hand on my shoulder.

"Thanks, I'm just afraid I'll forget my lines." I noticed his hair was perfect.

"Hey, if you do, just make stuff up—they're only looking at how you look on camera anyway."

The second I saw my face on the TV monitor, I knew it was over. My round Irish face blew up all over the screen like an oversized dinner plate. I got through the scene, miraculously remembering my lines and blocking. When it was over, I thanked everybody and took the subway home. When Didi called to tell me I didn't get it, I wasn't surprised. My head was far too big for television.

So when *Spring Awakening* closed, this young starlet had no job and wasn't going to be famous anytime soon.

I went back to being the chief cook and swabbie at the apartment on Ninety-seventh Street. I perfected my navarin of lamb, a French stew with vegetables and potatoes, and my chicken curry, playing house with Pete and Jenny.

My doldrums were lifted a short time later when my pop-star pal, Lee Thompson of the band Madness, arrived in New York. We'd met almost two years before at WBCN when I was hanging out at the listener line with my girl-friend Amy and his band had come to the station for an on-air interview. Madness was just blasting through town on their way to dates in other cities, so Lee and I didn't have much time to explore our relationship—which was a curious combination of crush at first sight with a kind of brother-sister, I-knew-you-in-a-past-life thing tossed in. Plamantic? Romontic? This meet-up was only the third time we'd ever laid eyes on each other—the last time had been in Boston after a gig at a club called the Paradise, where he was drunk out of his mind when I finally found him. I had been angry at him and he probably didn't even remember. So I decided now to live in the moment and not overthink it. It wasn't as if I was his girlfriend. He was here for twenty-four hours, and we had larks together.

I popped down to the Wellington Hotel on Seventh Avenue in Midtown, dressed in a little black dress, a blood-red toreador jacket I'd picked up somewhere, and long, dan-gly gold earrings I'd borrowed from Jenny. Walking through the seedy lobby, I felt I was being watched. Having been in many hotel lobbies in my day, I recognized the gaze and uni-form of the house detective. He sidled up next to me.

"Excuse me, miss, are you a guest here at the hotel?"

I turned and looked at his olive, wide-lapelled polyester jacket, the Brylcreem comb-over, the bulge of his .38. Bingo.

"I'm visiting a friend, actually." I smiled effervescently, putting on my best Hayley Mills accent.

"May I ask whom? And on what floor?" He pulled at the

knot of his wide tie, giving me the steely gaze he'd probably learned in security-guard school.

"Mr. Lee Thompson, room 1702."

He evidently decided I wasn't a lady of the evening and nodded wearily, waving his hand to dismiss me. I headed for the elevator, remembering the only other time I was mistaken for a prostitute—in the lobby of the London Hilton, where I had been propositioned by a Japanese businessman. I was fifteen, so he must have been into young girls. When I told Lee that the house dick had thought I was a hooker, he laughed. I pulled one shoulder of my jacket down and puckered up my lips, doing my best floozy face.

"It's those earrings, girl! Take 'em off. Not nearly classy enough. Here, I've got something for you."

He rummaged around in the top drawer of a dresser, then handed me a little red-and-gold silk pouch. Inside was a pair of simple pearl studs.

"Really? Lee, thank you! They're beautiful."

"We were just in Japan, and I picked them up."

"I love them." I did. Even though I wasn't sure they had been intended for me specifically, they made me happy. I stashed Jenny's harlot earrings in my purse, put on my new pearls, and we went out on the town. Since Lee had just been in Japan, we took a taxi downtown to have sushi before the show.

Madness was playing that night at the Ritz, a club in the East Village. Instead of staying down on the floor, I watched from the first row of the balcony. The place was packed, and when the band came out, the audience went absolutely, well, mad. From the first blast of Lee's saxophone, the opening chords of the band's eponymous monster hit "Madness," the audience went berserk—the balcony was shaking from all the people dancing, threatening to come crashing down at any moment. Madness's energy onstage, combined with the pounding sound of dancers jumping all over the floor and singing along to every song, created a prolonged explosion of giddy joy and rock-'n'-roll mayhem. They blew the roof off the joint, and by the end, after the third encore, everyone was glistening and rapturouslike with a great after-sex glow.

I waited at the bar for Lee, not wanting to go backstage with all the groupies; there were far more of them now than at the show I'd seen the previous year. I was different from those fangirls—above it all. *Hell*, I thought, *I'm practically with the band.* Lee came out, shaking hands with people and posing for Polaroids, eventually making his way over to me. His hair was soaked and sticking up; I thought he had the sweetest face and loved the little crinkles around his eyes.

"So, you up for checking out a club? It's in Times Square—we're going over to meet the owner and have some drinks. Might play a gig there."

"Let's go."

Bond's International Casino on Broadway at Forty-fourth Street had been a swanky supper club in the 1930s, then a department store in the seventies, before it was transformed into a nightclub with an enormous dance floor that claimed to be the biggest in town, bigger than Studio 54's.

You entered the lobby and climbed a musical staircase that sounded notes and lit up with colored red and purple lights as you walked up to the second floor. It was like being in a Busby Berkeley musical, except darker; you had to hang on to the silver railing, as it was hard to see. Crazy water fountains—leftovers from a Liberace TV show—were on the dance floor, and velvet banquettes lined the walls. Silver balloons shaped like people hung from the ceiling along with huge, spiky star sculptures. The bare-chested bartenders wore gold bathing trunks. When we arrived, the Clash song "Magnificent Seven" was blasting through towering piles of speakers the size of refrigerators.

Lee and the rest of the boys were huddled together, talking—I couldn't hear anything except Joe Strummer and Mick Jones singing, "You lot! What? Don't stop! Give it all you got!" I danced my way over to the ladies' room, which was filled with women riffling through suitcases, swiftly changing their outfits to get back out on the dance floor, and piling on more makeup in the murky blue light. Three punky types did coke in one of the stalls. I used the other one.

After about an hour, the band determined that the club was too big for them—it would look empty until there were seven or eight hundred people in it.

Lee came home with me, citing his need for sleep and a bit of quiet, as the rest of the band would keep going into the wee hours. He placed his black Keds high-tops on the ledge outside my window, which I assumed was a weird British custom, and we squeezed into my tiny single bed and fell asleep immediately. The next day, he met Jenny and Pete, had a cup of coffee, and I walked him downstairs to put him in taxi. I didn't know when, or if, I would see him again.

"Write to me, okay?" I asked, sad to say good-bye.

"Will do. Jesus, I'm tired. Still, it's the life I chose, I suppose."

I smiled. "Yeah."

"Take care, my girl." He folded himself into the taxi, gave me a thumbs-up, and was gone—my ship that passed in the night.

It was another relationship with a man who wasn't free—an English pop star with a girlfriend back home—but I kept it locked in a treasure chest, just like the cards and letters he wrote me that I tied in black ribbon. Our affection for each other would never come to anything, but it was fun being on his arm, if only for an evening, and he made me feel unique. Out of all the girls, he had chosen me.

Nina's Broadway show, *The Curse of an Aching Heart*, starring the ultra-famous Faye Dunaway, was now in previews, about to open. Nina left a message on my service about coming to the play. I didn't have anything else to do and she was a pal, so I trotted off to get the subway to Forty-second Street. We met before the show at Charley O's, a local restaurant popular with the pretheater crowd. After we drank Chablis and shared a chicken breast, her boyfriend, Paul, met us and we walked across Forty-fourth Street to the Little Theatre.

The play was a bit flimsy and saccharine, I thought, though the supporting cast gave some good performances. Miss Dunaway, sometimes calling for her lines, struggled valiantly to embody a woman much younger than herself, as she traveled through the story of her character, Frances Duffy, and her life of heartbreak and disappointment in a lower-class Irish Catholic family. *Mommie Dearest* had just come out in movie theaters six months before, so perhaps she was trying to erase "worst Hollywood mom ever" from all our memories by portraying this sweet, sad, and unlucky woman onstage. Apparently, Dunaway was difficult to work with, had quit once, and had driven everyone crazy with her tantrums and demands.

The stress had been too much for Nina's boss, Gerry Gutierrez, a dumpling-shaped gay guy with a big, bushy mustache, so part of Nina's job description began to include acquiring marijuana and cocaine for him—to calm him down or to keep him going. She'd be dispatched in a cab to an address, pick up the drugs, and bring them either to his place or to the theater. I went on one of the runs with her, waiting in the taxi while she ran up the steps next to a crepe restaurant to make the score. It had added an air of paranoia to her lately. She was always closing curtains and making sure doors were locked, as if she expected the narcs to burst into the room any minute.

One night, I hung out at Nina's mom's apartment after the show. In the Eighties between Park and Lexington, it was not far from one of my childhood homes on Park Avenue and Ninety-fourth Street. Her mom was out of town; Nina shuttled back and forth between this place and Paul's. The apartment was very seventies with floor-to-ceiling mirrored walls and white shag carpeting in the living room. A leather sofa and a brown-tinted glass coffee table sat in the center of the room, where you could almost imagine Jack and Anjelica lounging before they headed out to the bar at the Pierre. French doors led to a small galley kitchen on one end of the flat, and the bedrooms and bathrooms were on the other. A few actors from the cast joined in, and then Paul arrived with a woman I didn't recognize, a willowy, generically pretty blonde.

"Hey, everybody," Paul addressed the room, "this is Sandy. I met her at the gym."

"Hello, Sandy," the crowd said in unison. Then, everyone went back to their drinks and conversations except for Nina, who walked swiftly to the windows and pulled the curtains shut. Then she turned off a few of the lights so that it was even darker.

"Hey, guys, Gerry gave me some of his coke—like a work bonus." Nina giggled. She went over to the Danish teak credenza, slid open one side panel, and pulled out something wrapped in silk scarf. She unraveled it while walking to the coffee table, revealing a small plastic bag filled with white stuff, rolled up in a tube. Paul opened the bag and, in perfect *American Gigolo* mode, began cutting the coke into thin lines on the surface of the coffee table. *Oh my God*, I thought, *everyone's about to do drugs!*

My exposure to narcotics had been limited, to say the least. I had smoked pot once with two girlfriends from high school when I was eighteen. I remembered laughing quite a bit and then eating an entire carton of chocolate ice cream. It was fun, but I hadn't done it since.

With a flourish, Paul produced a bill from his jacket pocket and rolled it up. People began circling the table and taking turns snorting up a line or two. Someone put on music, Fleetwood Mac's *Tusk*, and I heard a wine-bottle cork pop free.

"Wendy, want some?" Nina ran her index finger under her nose, sniffing in deeply.

"Sure, I mean, I've never tried it."

Nina looked at me, clearly shocked. I think because I'd lived abroad, had traveled, and dressed kind of downtown, people assumed I was more sophisticated than I was. Despite, or because of, having been raised by a woman who overindulged in all things—sex, alcohol, money, and drugs—I was kind of an avowed dork. "Very cool, I wish I was you," a guy said to me as he nodded in approval.

I got down on my knees, closed one nostril, as instructed by Paul, and snorted it up. Then, I switched sides. It burned, and I tasted something bitter and slightly metallic on the back of my tongue.

"Amazing, huh?" the nodding guy said.

I didn't feel anything; maybe it took a while to kick in. "Um, yeah." I poured myself a glass of red wine and walked over to an armchair in the corner near the window.

The evening went on—people got their coats and left. The stragglers, of which I was one, sat on the floor or plopped on the couch, smoking cigarettes and drinking more wine. The records kept changing. Nina was telling crazy-train stories about weird Faye Dunaway, such as how she had showed up at rehearsal with a newborn baby she claimed to have just given birth to.

"Like she expected us all of a sudden to believe that she'd been pregnant with this baby during rehearsals—which is impossible—and then just had it on her day off and brought it to work. It was so bizarre!"

"Instant baby." Paul nodded.

Things seemed to be winding down; I looked at my watch and it read 2:15 a.m. Deciding to head out, I got my coat and walked over to Nina to say good night and thanks. She grabbed my hand and dragged me to the bathroom, pulling me inside and closing the door. A moment later, Paul came in. We stood there lit up in the bright lights that ringed the wall mirror.

"What is it?" They were both looking at me intently. I wondered if they wanted to borrow money from me or something.

"Well"—Nina looked at Paul, and he sort of smirked— "we have a question for you."

I looked back and forth between them. Nina told me that she and Paul wanted to sleep with me—and include the girl from the gym, Beth. I wasn't sure if Nina thought I was bi or gay or just a decadent European; maybe the suits and ties made me look that way? I wasn't shocked by the *ménage à quatre* idea—and didn't want to seem prudish and disapproving. Nina had been generous to me, but I wasn't willing to go that far to repay her.

"Um, no, thanks," I said to Nina. "Just not my thing, but you guys go ahead. I'm going home. Great party." I opened the door and turned to say good-bye over my shoulder before heading out the front door, smiling to show them it was no big deal.

The next day my phone rang. When I answered, I was surprised to hear Nina's brother Lincoln. He asked me if I'd meet him for drink and said he had something to tell me, something about Nina. He sounded weirdly terse, but I agreed.

We met at the Grassroots Tavern on St. Mark's Place. It was a seedy dive in the bottom of a tenement house, with a low tin ceiling and, for some reason, a grimy glass case full of dusty trophies, sports memorabilia, and tchotchkes. When I arrived, Lincoln was sitting in a booth at the back, and I slid onto the bench across from him. An open pack of Winstons lay on the table, and he was drinking a Bud out of a bottle.

As I sat down, he lit a cigarette. "So, Wendy, I wanted to tell you this in person, not on the phone. Nina went to the ER last night."

"What? What happened?"

"Well, I was hoping you could tell me." He raised his eyebrows.

"I have no idea what you are talking about, I swear." The

waitress came by and I ordered a bourbon. "We were at a party together last night, there were a bunch of people there, I left around two thirty or so."

"Yeah, well, she told me you left with some guy and she was worried about you—and followed you downstairs and that's when it happened. She was tapping on the glass to get your attention."

Stunned into silence, I gaped at him.

It turned out that right after I left, Nina had had some kind of freak-out, run downstairs to the lobby, and put her arm through the glass panel in the front door, shattering it, and slicing a twelve-inch gash along the underside of her arm. She was rushed to the hospital by Paul, where she received over sixty stitches and a blood transfusion.

I sipped my bourbon, trying to process this. I guessed that Nina had got upset about the whole foursome thing and maybe became afraid that I'd tell someone. Drugged-up and paranoid, she'd freaked out. I never would have said anything; I certainly wouldn't tell her brother.

He squashed his cigarette in the ashtray and lit another.

"Can I bum one?" I took a Winston out of the pack and lit it with his book of matches. The smoke felt strong and harsh, and I had an immediate head rush from the nicotine. I was purely a social smoker—occasionally at a bar or a party. Or in this case, to stall for time when I didn't know what to say to my former lover and the brother of the woman who'd propositioned me for a foursome the previous night. "I guess I didn't hear her, I didn't hear any sounds after I left the building." I shrugged, hoping I would look more clueless than I was.

"You should go to see her. I mean, in a way, it's kind of your fault, don't you think?"

"Um . . ."

"I sort of blame you," he said. "I mean, she was just looking out for you."

"I'll go see her."

"And don't go home with strange guys. This city is full of fucking maniacs." He shook his head in distaste, smoke pluming from his nostrils.

"Right. Good advice." I tossed a few dollar bills on the table, got up, and left. The temptation to say anything more was too great to stay any longer.

When I took Nina flowers at her mom's place one morning later that week, the housekeeper let me in and ushered me into the bedroom where Nina was tucked into a single bed and propped up on pillows. The shades were drawn, shutting out the sunlight, which gave the room a sort of hushed Blanche DuBois, Chinese-lantern feel. I sat by her bedside on a little brocade chair. Her arm was along her side on top of the coverlet in a sling, bandaged from her wrist up to her shoulder, and she was on pain meds.

"The show's closing," she told me somewhat woozily.

"That's too bad."

"Yeah, Gerry's bummed because it was his first Broadway show."

I nodded sympathetically; she was out of a job, too. But I knew it wouldn't be for long. She was mercurial and always went after what she wanted and usually got it—the fancy education, the handsome boyfriend, the impressive job that would lead to something bigger. A part of me had always wanted to crawl up her butt and be her, to be Nina Franco, to feel so certain about it all—what she wanted, where she was going, and what her next project would be. But I was the sort of girl who didn't ask the person in the aisle seat on the airplane to stand up when I had to go to the bathroom. I was way behind Nina in lots of ways; I didn't know if I'd ever catch up. But if lying in a dark bedroom with sixty stitches and a drug hangover was the price of catching up, I wasn't positive I wanted to get there anymore. My mother had always shot first and asked questions later—going after the brass ring, or at least the guy who was holding it, and the endings had never been happy. After my time with the high-flying crowd of New York theater, I saw that maybe it was okay that I was making my own way, even if it was in baby steps.

chapter seven

GET OUT OF TOWN, GIRL

I decided to escape from New York after another round of auditions, during which I was criticized by, well, everyone I tried out for. My boobs were too small—I should consider having implants. I wasn't pretty enough—I should have a nose job. I should dye my hair blond. I could afford to lose ten pounds. I was too funny. I wasn't sexy. And what the hell was I wearing a suit and tie for? Just a month before, I'd read for a part in a John Sayles movie and had been told by the doyenne of New York casting, Bonnie Timmermann—who got Mickey Rourke and Scarlett Johansson their first acting gigs—that I was going to be a star. The role went to Rosanna Arquette, and it seemed now that I was the dog girl that no one wanted to hire.

Everyone, except for me, seemed to have something going on that enhanced his or her life in a major way. Pete and Jenny had each other. Nina had applied and gotten into

the graduate program at NYU. My old BU roommate Julie
had bought a loft in an industrial building in Dumbo, underneath the Brooklyn Bridge, and begun fixing it up with
her boyfriend. I was an out-of-work actress who answered
the phone in a deli. Having inherited a strong cut-and-run
gene from my mother, the urge to skip town was fierce. I felt
like Toby Tyler—the little orphan boy in the Disney movie
who runs away to join the circus—except I always seemed to
be one town away from where the circus was playing, trying
to find where there might be a place for me.

Antsy and trying to come up with a plan to find my own
circus, I decided to go to Minneapolis for a while. I had only
spent a few days with my father since our reunion. Maybe
if I lived nearby, I could have quality time and get to know
him better. And perhaps I would have more luck finding
acting work there, since nothing had panned out in the city.
I was also anxious to escape a furtive love affair I was having
with a handsome, cerebral Italian American actor, who had
the most gorgeous black hair that sprang in lush curls from
his head. His name was Mark, and as in my last relationship, he had a girlfriend. I was worried that this was becoming a pattern—or maybe New York was just filled with guys
who were taken and wanted to cheat on their women. I had
met him at a party, and we ended up standing fully clothed
in the bathtub, singing "The Girl from Ipanema" and drinking bourbon on the rocks out of highball glasses. Oddly,
it turned out he had worked with my dad at the Denver
Center in Colorado.

"I can't believe you are Jimmy's daughter," he'd told me that night. "What a great guy! I spent many an evening after the show in the bar with him."

Mark drove me to his apartment in Inwood in his snazzy vintage Lincoln Continental—it was black and had suicide doors, which I had never seen before. The sex was fraught with angst: he seemed to be enjoying himself but in the most tortured way. Maybe it was some kind of Catholic thing. I just hung in there and waited for it to be over. Men who seemed to need a road map of the female form still amazed me.

Afterward, he kindly drove me home. I had seen him one more time, and we had the same Kafkaesque sex, but now he wanted me to meet his girlfriend. He seemed to think we could all go to a movie together or something—which I thought was just plain weird. After I'd decided to bolt, I left a message on his service, saying good-bye and that I was moving to Minneapolis to hang with my dad. Neither of us would be brokenhearted.

A few days before, I'd gone down to Didi's office to let her know I was splitting.

"Minneapolis in February? Are you fucking insane?"

"I'm gonna live with my dad—get to know him better."

"Okay, keep in touch, though. Don't disappear—write, call, whatever."

I promised that I would. She wrapped her arms around me and squeezed me tightly.

So I packed up my possessions, leaving some books and

the futon behind. I kissed Jenny and Pete good-bye and promised to write and call them, too.

Minneapolis in late February was gray and freezing cold, but I didn't care because I'd made my escape. It felt like a new adventure—and I'd be with my father.

Dad drove me to his house from the airport on wet roads banked with dirty snow and ice. It occurred to me that, aside from Christmas, I had never been here in the depth of winter; Robbie and I had spent only summers with our dad. They were days of carefree fun, playing outside, swimming in the lake, or riding our bikes along the sidewalk. Dad drove us past Seven Pools, where our babysitter had sometimes taken us on a hot day. Now it was frozen over and buried in white.

"I have a job prospect for you, sweetheart," Daddy said as he confidently maneuvered his Buick LeSabre on the slushy streets. "I didn't want to say anything until I was sure you were coming."

"What is it?"

"A wonderful man, a good friend of mine, Lou Salerni, runs a small theater downtown, and he's found a play he thinks we could do together."

"Wow! That would be great." *Work as an actor again and with my father?* My imagination raced.

"Now, you'd have to read for the part—but I saw you in action, so I know you can do it."

"Thanks, Dad." I beamed.

"I'm very glad you're here." His blue eyes got a little moisty.

"Me, too." I reached over and squeezed his hand where it rested on the gearshift.

I was staying in the guest room, on the second floor across the landing from my father and Sarah's bedroom. A big, comfy bed was covered with a puffy white duvet, and a built-in window seat with floral-patterned cushions looked out over the side garden. The wallpaper was a navy-blue-and-white geometric pattern, and a bookcase filled with novels, plays, mysteries, and assorted knickknacks, along with a large white wicker chair in one corner, and a dresser with a mirror on top, rounded out the furnishings.

I unpacked my things, hung up my James Dean calendar, and placed a framed picture of my sister and my little red paisley makeup bag on the dresser. A little at sea in my unfamiliar surroundings, I was also giddy to be here. I had slept in this room once before, but now I felt more that I belonged. Determined to leave all those sad feelings behind, I was going to spend quality time with my new family. If I could make a home with Jenny and Pete, perhaps I could find one here with my dad and stepmother. I practically skipped to the bathroom to put my toothbrush in the little silver rack above the sink.

The next morning, I awoke to find everyone had gone off to work—Sarah to her job as business manager of the Children's Theatre, and Daddy to do some voice-over work at a sound studio downtown. I wandered around the house in my pajamas like Goldilocks, sitting in all the chairs, running my hand across the leather sofa in the den, looking at old photos and books, leafing through records, mostly classical and jazz, near the stereo. I opened the cupboards in the kitchen, studying the silver-rimmed, snowflake-patterned dishes and blue-bottomed glassware. I riffled through the packets of pasta and rice and cans of tomato soup and deviled ham. In the medicine cabinets, I found boxes of Alka-Seltzer, cans of L'Oréal hair spray, Dexatrim diet pills, and rolls of Tums. I opened my dad's bottle of Dunhill cologne and sniffed its woodsy leather scent, remembering the way I had smelled it on his neck whenever I'd kissed him on the cheek as a little girl.

In the closets hung my father's dark suits and ties, shirts and sweaters, his wing-tip shoes lying along the floor. My stepmother's clothes smelled of her Cinnabar perfume, and her assortment of chunky necklaces, made from silver, pottery, and beads, hung on a rack on the wall. I tried on a pair of her shoes, which were huge on me. Next, I went down into the basement, where my dad kept an office. It had dusty blue carpeting on the floor and rectangular windows along the tops of the walls that let some light in from the garden. I imagined he sometimes took a nap on the small beige sofa. A massive wooden table with thick, ornately carved legs served as a desk; I browsed the items on top: a paperweight with a swirly-colored-glass center, a heavy brass letter opener with his name on it, gas bills, rolls of stamps, and restaurant receipts. Guthrie Theater posters and costume sketches of characters he'd played there—some from productions I'd seen when I was little, the dandy Lelio in *The Venetian Twins* and Trinculo the jester in *The Tempest*—lined the walls.

I was like a spy, trying to cram every object and smell into my mind, to familiarize myself with this place, so that I wouldn't feel like a guest in my father's house. I would learn it and know it—and it would become my own.

Later that week, Daddy and I went downtown to the Cricket Theatre to meet his friend Lou Salerni, the artistic director, and talk about the play—a 1940s comedic chestnut by Norman Krasna called *Dear Ruth*. My dad read a scene from the play with me; Lou laughed out loud and eased my anxiety, and then we went to lunch. The part was clearly mine, and Lou was excited about the actual-father-and-daughter casting angle. Lou was convinced that, combined with Dad's local celebrity, would bring tons of people in. A director was coming in from New York, but all the actors would be from the Twin Cities. Rehearsals would start at the end of the month. I listened attentively to Lou's plans, unable to get enough.

In *Dear Ruth*, Dad played the long-suffering Judge Wilkins, who lives with his wife and two daughters in Kew Gardens on Long Island during World War II. I was playing the younger daughter, Miriam, who has been writing letters to a soldier overseas but signing her pretty, older sister Ruth's name. When the handsome young soldier shows up one day with a bouquet of flowers to meet Ruth in person—

hilarity ensues. After doing *Spring Awakening*, I found it fun to do a play that was just fluff; it wasn't anything but a kooky story. As the precocious sixteen-year-old Miriam, I got to play a deranged teenager of a different kind—I had a delicious drunk scene, getting shnockered while I clutched a giant stuffed panda bear, and got to wear forties clothes such as rompers and dirndl dresses and saddle shoes. I had permed my chin-length hair and wore a hairpiece that I thought made me look like a young Lucille Ball, whom I was trying to channel in my performance. The director was a charming, elfin man named Bob Moss, who had founded Playwrights Horizons in New York and who genuinely adored the material. Our stage manager, Brian, roly-poly in his tight, wrinkled clothes, reminded me of a wacky character from a Gilbert and Sullivan opera with his booming voice and ribald sense of humor. The cast got along like a dream, and I bonded with the other actresses, Louise, who played my sister, and Mary Sue, who had a small part as a young newlywed.

For press to promote the play, Daddy and I were interviewed by the *Minneapolis Tribune*, and the story ran with a photograph of us sitting together backstage, smiling. Daddy told of the time when I was three or four and Dr. Guthrie scooped me up in the greenroom of the Guthrie Theater and said, "My goodness, aren't you a tiny little thing! I should like to take you home and put you on my mantel." I felt like a debutante being introduced all over town.

During rehearsals, I'd go to lunch with Louise and Mary

Sue. We didn't have that much in common, besides being actresses. Mary Sue was married and had two little boys at home. She was a pretty brunette with a caustic wit that went against her sweetheart looks. Louise was a round-faced, cheerful blonde engaged to a guy I didn't think was good enough for her. But what did I know about relationships? Since breaking up with angry, negative Michael, I'd only given a Mormon an erection and had a few uncommitted love affairs with men who were technically taken. I kept my mouth shut.

Dad and I came home from rehearsal one evening to find my stepmother looking peeved. "Your mother called here— I just got off the phone with her."

"Oh no." I wondered how she'd found me.

"I didn't know it was her at first." Sarah lit a cigarette while my dad poured them both bourbons. "She was pretending to be a school friend of yours from London." It had a theatrical flair to it that I recognized as Mother's, and accosting people by telephone was a favorite hobby of hers. "She had this ridiculous English accent, and then I figured out who it was—and I'm afraid I told her off."

"Perfectly understandable, sweetheart." My dad handed her a tinkling rocks glass.

Over dinner, Sarah told the story of the only time she'd ever seen my father lose his temper. When they were first dating, after a particularly harsh call from Mother, he'd slammed the phone down, ripped the cord out of its socket, and punched his fist through the wall.

"I'd never seen him act like that—before or since."

My father smiled, cutting into his steak, and said quietly, "God, I hate that woman."

"Well, of course you do, Jimmy," Sarah said.

Then she told me how devastated Daddy was when my mother first took me and my sister and disappeared. He just sat in a chair and stared out the window for two weeks.

"Well, she may know where you are, Wendy," Sarah said, "but she can't get to you. You're safe here, and if she shows up, well, I'm sure as hell not going to let her in."

"Christ, no." Dad shook his head.

I was moved by their protectiveness toward me; they weren't going to allow her to swoop in with her banshee-like cruelties and melodramatic high jinks. I was safe here, tucked away in the shelter of their home.

But I lay in bed that night in the dark trying to imagine my father in a fury, shoving his fist through a wall—and I couldn't picture it. Rationally, I knew Mother would never show her face here, although the fear of her sudden appearance was often in the back of my mind, like a bad dream you can't forget. I took some solace in knowing that she was being driven crazy knowing that I was safely ensconced with my father and stepmother. She couldn't control that, and I knew it made her batshit crazy.

Every day was a party, working on this silly, sweet play—we were having a blast. Rehearsing with Dad was marvelous—

he was so generous as an actor, funny, and was always coming up with surprising bits of business that made the play better. I felt that by playing father and daughter we were bonding in a new way, becoming closer through our work. Growing up, I had always been a daddy's girl and was excited for everyone to see us onstage as father and daughter playacting the relationship I'd always dreamed of.

We opened to boffo reviews—the run was extended, and then we were offered a chance to perform it at a summer theater in Denver called the Elitch Gardens. It was in an amusement park, had been operating since 1890, and everyone from George Arliss to Tyrone Power to Robert Redford had played there. The entire cast signed on—it all seemed so glamorous, akin to going on tour.

Right before we departed for our run at the Elitch, a casting person at the Guthrie Theater contacted me. He'd seen me in *Dear Ruth*, and they were looking for a replacement for the part of the boy Cherubino in Beaumarchais's play *The Marriage of Figaro*. It's a trouser role, meaning that it is performed by an actress in male clothing. The woman playing the part now, Caitlin Clarke, could only do the first two weeks of the run, then had a TV commitment in L.A.

The Marriage of Figaro was directed by the renowned Romanian director Andrei Serban, known for his unusual postmodern and avant-garde interpretations of Shakespeare and Chekhov. Serban had become an overnight sensation at nineteen when he directed a Kabuki-style *Julius Caesar* as a student in Bucharest, causing an uproar. Not able to get a job in his native country as an enfant terrible, he came to America, where he was regarded as the hot theater genius of the moment and directed to great acclaim all over the country. With my heart in my throat, I croaked that of course I'd love to audition.

I hadn't been able to see the production as it was running on the same schedule as *Dear Ruth*. I studied the sides, agonized about what to wear—finally deciding on straw-colored linen overalls and a white, sleeveless blouse that were easy to move in and slightly tomboyish.

I arrived at the Guthrie feeling horribly nervous, hands shaking and my knees quivering as if they'd give out at any moment. I milled around in the lounge outside the greenroom with a few other women clearly there for the audition. Although I noticed that I was the least girlie actress there, with more crossover boyish appeal, I still had to pee every thirty seconds from fear, and my face was flushed. I tried to calm down by remembering the times I'd been here as a kid, waiting for my dad to get out of rehearsal, or killing time while he was performing in a matinee. I had dreamed of working at this theater, where Daddy had launched his career.

A pale guy in a black turtleneck with a bowl haircut entered the lounge and called my name.

"Hello, Wendy, I saw you in the show—are you ready?" *Well, no,* I thought even though I was grateful for his kind words, *but here goes.* I smiled and nodded, shaking his hand.

We went backstage through a door I remembered using

many times when I was eight or nine, and I smelled that marvelous backstage cocktail of sawdust, paint, and old, burned coffee. The turtlenecked man led me through the darkness as we carefully made our way around coils of electrical cord, large, standing lighting instruments, ladders, and, for some reason, a grocery cart.

"Andrei is sitting in the audience, waiting for you." He made an "over there" gesture with his arm, like a headwaiter. I took a deep breath and walked out onto the set, which was blindingly bright because the floor was coated with Mylar and the back walls were mirrored.

The great man was blond and quite handsome, as I had heard. He was slumped in his seat, his hair long and stringy past his shoulders. He was wearing a heavy, white wool sweater, looking a bit like a vacationing Irish fisherman. The sweater seemed odd, as it had to be at least ninety-five degrees outside that day, but I took it as a sign that he might be a little out of touch with his surroundings.

"Yes?" He looked at me as if to say, *Who are you?* A doughy, young woman in a short, tight plaid skirt with flaming-red hennaed hair handed him my résumé. She backed away from him as if she were a servant and he were the king of Siam.

"Hello, Mr. Serban. My name is Wendy Lawless."

He gave my résumé, which was pretty flimsy, a once-over. Then he looked up at me. "Begin."

I read with the red-haired girl—a scene between Cherubino and the Countess, with whom he is in love. My scene partner read in a flat voice, which is always difficult for an actor—you have to work harder when you aren't getting anything back, you almost have to play both parts, in your head anyway. We finished the scene. He looked back down at my résumé. There was a silence, then he spoke.

"Do you know how to roller-skate?"

Not the question I was expecting. "Um, no, Mr. Serban. I can ice-skate . . . a bit." I wasn't going to tell him that I hadn't ice-skated since I was a ten-year-old taking lessons at Rockefeller Center.

"No problem—we can get you a teacher." He signaled the redhead, and she dashed off up the stairs and out of the theater.

So I was hired, but only after negotiating for myself with the most terrifying man, the managing director, Don Schoenbaum. Dad had told me stories about actors coming in to discuss their contracts, and some lowly assistant would be feeding him grapes as he lay on a chaise. Dad told me to be tough and hold out for more money.

"And I always ask for my own parking place," he said proudly.

That seemed a little cocky, but I'd see what I could get. Because they were putting me into the show the day after I got back from the *Dear Ruth* tour, and I had to learn to roller-skate for the part—Dad thought I was worth a hundred bucks over the offer they'd make.

When Mr. Schoenbaum called me into his office, he was sitting behind a massive dark-wood desk. I slipped into a small chair across from him that I noticed was quite low to the ground. I had to strain to see him on the other side of the desk, like a little old lady peering over her car dashboard.

"Hello, Miss Lawless—here is the contract we are offering you." Using his index finger, he slid the contract across the desk. I saw that I was being offered $350 a week, which sounded fantastic. But I felt I had to try to ask for more because Dad had told me to.

"I was hoping for four hundred, Mr. Schoenbaum. I do have to learn to roller-skate, after all, and will have very little time to rehearse before opening." I attempted to flash a winning smile.

He fixed a withering gaze upon me. "We feel, Miss Lawless, that this is an adequate sum for an actress of *your* talents."

I signed the contract immediately.

Negotiations complete, I was sent to my costume fitting. The costume shop had been another haunt of mine as a kid. My sister and I would often while away time here, playing with ribbons, buttons, or the little Clytemnestra and Electra dolls that had been made for the design presentation for Dr. Guthrie's landmark production of *The House of Atreus*, and that we got to keep—our very own Greek-tragedy Barbies.

When I walked into the large, well-lit room with padded tables for cutting fabrics, ironing boards, sewing machines, and racks of clothes, it smelled like hot glue and freshly starched and pressed shirts.

"Ah! There you are!" A deep, bellowing voice welcomed

me—it was Jack Edwards, the Guthrie's costume shop director. An enormous man, he was like a huge bear standing on its hind legs. He had a Friar Tuck hairdo and a long white beard and mustache. He was wearing a muslin smock that hung from his huge frame over soft brown leggings and wild, oversized metal jewelry all over his body, looking like a New Age monk. His hands, decorated with many rings, curled up in the air when he saw me. He ushered me into a little changing room, where we were joined by Annette Garceau, a darkly ravishing French costumer with brown ringlets about her creamy-skinned face, her beauty mark fluttering on her cheek as she smiled at me.

"Yoo probablee don't remembeh mee," she said in her fabulously accented English. "I haven't zeen you seence you were leettle. But yoo look dee zame! Just like your fahzer."

She kissed me on both cheeks.

"Of course I remember you. I'm so happy to be here."

Annette had been the resident siren of the original 1963 company—all of the men, and some of the women, had lusted after her.

"First, Miss Lawless, we must try this on." Jack held up a hanger with a funny little flesh-colored vest with a zipper up the middle dangling from it.

I had to wear a chest suppressor under my costumes.

When I joked that I was flat-chested and there was no need, he looked at me solemnly. "There can be no movement beneath the clothes."

Luckily, popping it on, I found I was exactly the same

size as the actress I was replacing, so no adjustments needed to be made.

"Wonderful!" Jack was pleased.

"How eez your mohzer?" Annette inquired as I tried on a champagne-colored satin footman's coat that was decked out in lace and fake jewels. Standing behind me, she placed a matching tricorne on my head and looked in the mirror in front of us.

"We're not really in touch at the moment." That familiar queasy feeling when my mother was mentioned rose up in my gut.

"Ah . . . *tragique.* I always wondehred what would become of her."

Annette was referring to the scandal that broke at the theater when my mother and Pop announced at a lavish cocktail party in front of everyone at the Guthrie and half of Minneapolis society that they were in love. This public declaration of their affair was followed by two quickie divorces and our hurried departure from town. It was more than fifteen years ago now but apparently was still local gossip. I briefly imagined Mother in her condo in Connecticut, ears burning, knowing she was being talked about.

So, I did *Dear Ruth* at night, and during the day I was locked in a dungeon-like room beneath the Guthrie with a short, sixteen-year-old boy clad in black spandex, with feathered dirty-blond hair, named Mike, whom they'd found at the local roller rink. The first thing he taught me was how to fall down. He pushed me so many times onto my butt, I started to look like an abused child. He was a good teacher but somewhat angry and impatient—maybe because he was super short for his age.

"Get up!" he hollered like an angry disco munchkin as I lay splayed on the floor.

Soon he had me doing all the tricks I needed to learn for the show—I could jump, walk on my tiptoes, skate backward, and shoot the duck—crouching all the way down and extending one leg in front of you while you roll forward. Mike was very pleased with himself and pronounced his job complete.

I needed to learn to roller-skate because the entire production was on wheels. Skateboards, wheeled ladders, a bicycle, a large rolling laundry hamper, and a grocery cart had all been incorporated into the show. When I asked the stage manager why, he told me that Andrei had seen a shopping cart in the lobby of an apartment building and was suddenly struck with this concept of a *Figaro* on wheels. I was to learn my lines and work with a director—not Serban, as he was leaving town—on my blocking and characterization. I would leave for two weeks to do *Dear Ruth* on tour—hopefully retaining everything I'd learned. Then I'd have only one technical rehearsal with the entire cast the day before going on.

When I wasn't rehearsing or acquiring more black-and-blue marks, I'd go over to Mary Sue's for tea or dinner, and sometimes play with her little boys, Larkin and Andrew. They were quite rambunctious and loud; just watching them run around Mary Sue's ankles and jump off the furniture made me tired. But I couldn't take my eyes off them; they were like little fires. I wondered if I would ever get married and have kids. I couldn't picture it in my future, somehow. I was still sorting out my own childhood, or lack thereof, trying to make sense of what had happened.

I sometimes went to the Uptown movie theater with our *Dear Ruth* stage manager, Brian. I had developed a little crush on him, attracted to his eccentric manner and hilarious banter. We seemed completely in tune, finishing each other's sentences, and I was the only one in the cast who got his Monty Python references. Even though he needed to lose fifty pounds or so, was a terrible dresser, and wore his bob-length hair thick across his forehead like a girl—he was quite handsome. After seeing *Harold and Maude* together at the Uptown, we felt inspired by Maude's loony and larcenous activities—stealing cars and abducting a forlorn city tree to replant it in the forest—to run out and steal some blinking sawhorse construction signs and stash them in his cramped bachelor flat. Another time, we saw *Lawrence of Arabia* and dressed up in bedsheets at his place, striding around in our best bedouin fashion and calling each other Orance, the name Peter O'Toole's character is given by the Arabs in the film. Brian was desperately in need of a makeover—and I was desperately in need of a boyfriend—but I could just never get that close to him. He used his humor, and perhaps his girth, as a shield, and I strongly suspected that he was gay or simply asexual. After a few romantic stabs in the dark, mostly made up of playful hints that I was a bit sweet on him, I gave up my boyfriendly aspirations and just enjoyed his friendship.

Dear Ruth closed at the Cricket, but none of us felt sad, as we were off to Denver to do it all over again. We rehearsed in the Elitch for a few days before opening, adjusting to the enormity of the space. A classic proscenium theater with seats that went straight back for what seemed like a mile, the Elitch was made entirely of wood, so the acoustics were wild; it almost had an echo. The actors had to work harder to project their voices, beef up their eye makeup so people could see them from the last row, and wait for their laughs to surf all the way to the back wall before continuing with their next lines. Definitely an adjustment after the intimate, little Cricket.

We had a funny little man backstage named Freddy, who had a limp and dressed like the skipper on *Gilligan's Island*. Freddy was in charge of the costumes, assigned our dressing rooms, and delivered our mail, telegrams, and flowers. He showed us a brick wall backstage where all the actors who had ever worked there had signed their names. Huge framed headshots of Grace Kelly, Julie Harris, Burgess Meredith, and many others hung high above us. It was surreal to imagine these legends walking the same boards as I was—as exhilarating as it was humbling. The bar was high, and I imagined them all watching us from their picture gallery up above.

The Elitch was run by a charming older couple in their

sixties who both had been actors in the theater, television, and movies before becoming producers. Haila Stoddard and Whit Connor had old Hollywood charm, simply oozing grace and glamour. Whit was tall and handsome with a Clark Gable, toothy smile and a head of silvery hair. Haila was a petite, bubbly blonde who told fabulous stories about palling around with Noël Coward and understudying big stars such as Rosalind Russell in *Mame* and Uta Hagen in *Who's Afraid of Virginia Woolf?* I was starstruck and developed an instant mom-crush on her—she was part gentle June Allyson combined with a wisecracking-dame sense of humor à la Eve Arden. Haila was an actress, a mother, and a writer who had forged her own career in the arts, someone I could look up to and try to emulate. She was kind to me, perhaps sensing that I was motherless and a bit lost in life. I was sure that we would have been best friends if only I'd been born sooner.

We packed the Elitch every night of the two-week run—the screams from the roller coaster accompanying the laughs in the theater. The reviews were glowing, and the audience went wild every night, often jumping to their feet at curtain call.

"I got a standing ovation," Daddy would say, coming offstage after the show. "How'd you do?"

Haila and Whit threw a party at a Mexican restaurant after our last show, complete with a mariachi band. Everyone got wasted on margaritas, and while we were conga-lining across the dance floor, Mary Sue shrieked into my ear as she was goosed by the guitar player when we bopped by. The next morning we all staggered down to breakfast, hungover, and said our good-byes. Knowing we wouldn't be meeting up in the evening and twice on matinee days to play together was bittersweet, but I didn't have time to dwell.

My only full rehearsal for *The Marriage of Figaro* at the Guthrie with the cast and crew was the following afternoon—in true showbiz, flying-by-the-seat-of-your-pants tradition, I'd be going on that evening. It was a bit of a struggle remembering the blocking I had been given, and I warmed up my roller-skating skills in the halls beneath the stage to get ready. I had never met any of the other actors in person—when I skated to sit down next to the man play-ing the Count, he turned, looked at me, and purred, "I think you're wearing the same cologne that I do," which I was—still Givenchy Gentleman. This was David Warrilow, a founding member of the avant-garde theater company Mabou Mines and renowned interpreter (and friend) of Samuel Beckett. Dandily dressed in a cream-colored suit and tie, his hooded eyes were reptilian, and he was as slim as a cigarette, of which he must have smoked a lot, as his voice was gargling and low, tangy with nicotine.

In the first act, I had to sing a song to the Countess, while her maid, Susanna, accompanied me on the guitar. The sim-ple tune was not difficult to perform, but Jana Schneider, who was playing Susanna, decided it would be funny to play off-key so that I sounded awful, and she would mug to the audience and stick out her tongue. She got a big laugh. Being a replacement means fitting in to the way the originator of the part played the role, not giving your own interpretation. So I incorporated everything my predecessor had done, including bits of business like that with the other actors.

Opening night, I somehow remembered everything I'd practiced—even though I had a few *I Love Lucy* moments, where someone had to whisper to me from behind a piece of scenery or their fan, "Go over there!" or "Exit stage right!"

When I got back to my dressing room, I answered a knock on the door to find Mary Sue with a chilled martini and a small tin box that had a scantily clad man in a leopard-print thong and pasties dancing on a stage on the front. Opening it, I found a condom inside—a great example of her raunchy sense of humor. Daddy and Sarah came in to congratulate me on my Guthrie debut, hugs and kisses all round, and we went upstairs to the bar to continue the celebration.

I enjoyed doing the show for the rigors of the skating and for the spectacle—but it was completely different from any other experience I'd had. It seemed superficial, as if we were puppets, with our stylized movements and white face makeup. I felt I was working from the outside in, instead of the other way around. It wasn't realistic, nor was it psychological. I finally decided I was part of a pretty picture and left it at that.

Even though I loved living with my dad and Sarah, after a few months I moved into a studio apartment in an older building on Oak Grove Street, near the Guthrie, just off

Loring Park. Many of the other actors in *Figaro* had places on the same street and had told me the neighborhood was just fine as long as you avoided the park at night, which was a notorious gay-cruising destination. I didn't have much in the way of furniture—my friend Louise loaned me a bed and a table. My stepmother gave me some spare dishes, silverware, and kitchen equipment from her cupboards, as well as a set of sheets and some towels. The rest I cobbled together, but it was quite spartan.

Despite my newfound privacy, my love life was fairly nonexistent. I had a few dates—an usher at the theater who was only eighteen years old, a grain salesman, a mannered and lugubrious actor someone set me up with. None of them panned out or even made it to a second date. I got a lot of reading done, caught up on old movies on TV, and wrote long—perhaps too long—letters to Jenny and Pete and my sister. Sometimes I'd go out to see a Prince concert at First Avenue by myself or go to a double feature at the Uptown. I would take a sandwich and sit in the dark watching *Les Enfants du Paradis*, *Hiroshima Mon Amour*, or *Seven Samurai*. I tried to be Zen about my lack of friends, but I was lonesome.

The show closed the first week of October, and it grew cold and dark outside. By Halloween, it was freezing and snow was on the ground. Just as after *Spring Awakening*, I had hoped my successes would translate into more work, but the phone didn't ring with any offers. I auditioned for the Guthrie's annual production of *A Christmas Carol* but wasn't cast. I ended up getting a holiday sales job at Dayton's department store, in the toy department, right outside the Santa World display. Mary Sue went home to her boys; Louise moved to Florida with her soon-to-be husband. Brian took a job at an arts center in Staten Island. I would come home at night hoping to see the light on my answering machine blinking—but it rarely was. On Sundays, I went to Daddy and Sarah's house for dinner, which I looked forward to, even though it made me feel a bit low as I had no other invitations and yearned to be with people my own age.

Then one night I was out to dinner with Dad, Sarah, my stepsister Jules, and her boss, Chris Kirkland, from the Playwrights' Center, a local arts organization that supported new playwrights and their work. We were at the Black Forest Inn in Minneapolis, a German restaurant with blue-checked tablecloths and antlers on the walls above large paintings of German castles and farmhouses. In a small-world co-incidence, Chris was Haila Stoddard's son from her first marriage. A few people were at dinner from the Children's Theatre, where Sarah worked, including a young playwright who had tagged along, probably hoping for a free meal. Chris's half brother (Haila's son by her second husband) was in town visiting from Denver and was sitting at the op-posite end of the table from me. Chowing down on spaetzle, bratwurst, and Wiener schnitzel—I also appreciated a free meal—I noticed Chris's brother. A big guy, Tarquin was red haired with a kind of Henry VIII exuberance, a larger-than-life quality. He was a misfit mongrel like me, a stepchild from the theater who'd grown up in a multiply divorced home with half brothers and sisters who were ballet dancers, journalists, and playwrights. Our eyes met across the table and we ended up together in a corner.

He wasn't in the arts, though his father had been a producer and a director. Living in Denver, he was a lawyer working on behalf of men wanting sex-change surgery in the prison system in Colorado. His job seemed exotic and dangerous to me—I imagined hormone-charged convicts growing out their hair and painting their nails, brandishing their tease combs in the cafeteria; it had miniseries potential.

He sent me an eight-page, poetry-laden letter the next day, with a mysteriously beautiful silver pin of a face. I hardly knew him, but he invited me to go to Nassau with him to an annual charity ball that raised money for disadvantaged Bahamian children with heart defects. The Sir Victor Sassoon Heart Foundation Ball was being thrown on the island over Valentine's Day weekend. Lady Evelyn Sassoon, an American who had been married to the late Lord Sassoon and founded the charity after her husband's death, would preside over the affair, and Tarquin and I had been invited to stay at her house. I just needed to buy my own ticket and meet him in the Bahamas. How could I resist? It all felt heady and tragically alluring, like a scene from *Brideshead Revisited*, which I was currently reading after watching the PBS television adaptation starring Anthony Andrews and Jeremy Irons.

Tarquin and I hadn't even exchanged a kiss yet, which

made it all seem courtly. It was certainly more attention I'd had from a man in ages. And it meant a break from the bleak Minnesota winter.

When I arrived at Lady Evelyn's estate after my flight and taxi ride, a sixtyish, diminutive bleach-blonde greeted me wearing an aqua-blue, floral one-piece bathing suit, silver high heels, and a pearl necklace. I introduced myself, wondering if I was supposed to curtsy, then decided not to, as she was in a swimsuit.

"Aren't you a pretty young thing!" she exclaimed warmly, then, without even looking, lifted a goblet off a waiter's tray next to her and presented me with crushed peaches in champagne. My first Bellini.

"I'm Lady Evelyn, but you can call me Barnsie. I'd like you to sit next to me at dinner, my dear."

"Thank you, um, Lady Evelyn. I mean, Barnsie."

As she went off to greet her other guests and dispense glamorous cocktails, I drifted over to a grand piano in the corner, where a morose man with a retreating hairline and slightly bulging eyes in a plum-colored velvet jacket and monogrammed evening slippers was tinkling on the keys.

"My name is Wendy."

He looked up at me glumly. "And I'm Peter Pan."

I found out later that his name was Stephen Barry, and he'd been sacked by Princess Diana, who felt that Prince Charles shouldn't have a gay valet. It seemed the fairy-tale wedding that Robin and I had watched all googly-eyed on the small television in the Rocky Mountains hadn't worked out so well for Barry in particular. I wanted to ask him for some juicy insider details, but he probably hated the princess's guts and didn't seem keen to gossip.

Tarquin appeared, looking wrinkled and sweaty in a seersucker suit, mopping his forehead with a cocktail napkin from his flight. We were shown to our room by a maid wearing a pink uniform. I was relieved to see it had twin beds, like in a *Thin Man* movie, because the moment I saw Tarquin again, I knew nothing physical would happen between us— he was sweet, but with his ginger hair and beard and large, pale, doughy body, I wasn't attracted to him. Luckily, I had paid my own way, so I owed him nothing except to be his occasional arm candy.

That evening at dinner, I wore the little black dress I used to go clubbing in with the pearl earrings Lee had given me. A wire-haired, bespectacled composer I had never heard of was there, with his frowsy wife, and some snooty society-type Brits in from London, a leathery-tanned lady antiques dealer who had a shop in town, and a photographer who was covering the event for the local paper. The composer stood to raise his glass and toast all the white people on the island; I reflexively pulled a face and looked around to see if anyone else thought this guy was as much of an asshole as I did. Stephen, who was there with his eighteen-year-old boy toy, fell asleep in his dinner. He began to snore loudly, but everyone politely ignored him and simply raised their voices over the noise.

The next day, I was sitting on a deck chair under an umbrella on the terrace reading *Brideshead* with great relish.

I'd even dressed that day like the main character, Sebastian Flyte, in white trousers and shirt with one of my striped ties threaded through my belt loops and knotted at my waist. Suddenly, Stephen was standing next to me, in a tiny Speedo, his white skin seemingly untouched by sunlight during all those years in Buckingham Palace. He held two bottles of beer, one of which he offered to me. I stood up, and we walked to the wall that looked out over the ocean that churned below us, filled with brown seaweed. It looked as if a huge teapot had been emptied. I sipped at the icy beer, which I didn't normally care for but it seemed perfectly suited for the scorching sun and a decadent daytime libation.

"Oh, Wendy!" Stephen exclaimed dramatically, raising his pale, skinny arms up in the air as if addressing not me but the heavens. "Whatever shall I do?"

"Do?" I wasn't exactly sure I knew what he was talking about, but I had an idea.

"About work. You've probably heard I was sacked by that viper, Diana." He spat out her name as if it were a hot coal.

"No, I hadn't," I fibbed to draw him out. "That's too bad."

"The problem is that I don't really know how to do anything else." He pouted.

"I'm sure . . . something will come along," I said encouragingly, although just how vast the market for unemployed valets was, I wasn't sure.

Who was I to advise the former manservant of Prince Charles on job strategies anyway? With my acting career on pause, I was just a salesgirl in a department store. He had my sympathy, though; I could hear him and his boyfriend fighting in their room at night.

"I suppose." He sighed, and squinted, looking out over the sea.

That evening we all piled into cars and went to dinner at a restaurant that served grouper and conch myriad ways. Shellacked blowfish hung from the ceiling, and—for some strange reason—German oompah-pah music churned through the air. From there we went on to the Playboy Casino, where I won $25 at a slot machine. Finishing the evening at a nightclub called Peanuts Taylor's, where all and sundry downed copious rum cocktails, we danced the limbo to loud steel-drum music till 1:00 a.m., and the British antiques lady put her hand up my dress. When I emitted a loud whoop, she winked at me and told me I was dishy.

A hedonistic crowd, they seemed to be always one step away from an orgy. At Sunday lunch at James Bond movie producer Cubby Broccoli's house, his handsome blond son, Tony, who wasn't that much older than me, preened around and introduced himself to me as "the son and heir." I walked around the enormous backyard, where the palm trees were equipped with speakers so that piped-in music could be heard wherever you were. The Police sang "Don't Stand So Close to Me" in stereo.

It reminded me of the sort of weekend my mother would have raced to when I lived in London as a teenager. She was constantly dashing off in a backless dress with a crowd of pagan types to a fancy, raucous party or some country inn to go hot-air ballooning. I couldn't help but think what a great time she'd have barreling around Nassau with this bunch of reprobates. It was like her wet dream. I was half tempted to send her a postcard.

I caught a little cold from going in and out of the air-conditioning, and a woman in the kitchen made me a cough syrup from limes and ginger that I remembered my nanny Catherine making me when I was a child. My mother had fired her when I was ten, and I knew I would never see her again. I didn't even know her last name. The elixir the woman brought me had the same sharp, peppery taste, meant to blast out whatever gunk you had in you. I lay in my little single bed drinking my syrup, thinking fondly of my old friend, the times she held me against her ample bosom, shushing and rocking me when I'd had a nightmare, or the times my sister and I sat on her lap watching cartoons on Saturday mornings in her little room at the back of our apartment. In contrast to my mother's frosty, rigid inconsistency, I had felt utterly loved and protected in Catherine's presence, and I carried her devotion with me long after she'd been banished from our lives. So I raised my glass of cough syrup and drank a little toast to Catherine, wherever she was.

Before going home to the dirty ice cube of Minneapolis, I placed giant hibiscus flowers in baggies to carry them back with me for their warmth and sunshine. And a bottle of Mount Gay, of course.

Between icy beers, dinner-plate pillows, and rent boys, Stephen Barry figured out something to do. He wrote two tell-all books about the royal family, for which he was paid

$1 million in advance. Because he had signed an official paper before his employment forever barring him from talking or writing about the royals, the books were only released in America. A year after the second was published, he died of AIDS at thirty-seven.

Plunged back from my Bahamian fantasy island vacation into the gloomy, sunless land of the Swedes, I hunted around for another paying gig. My stint at Dayton's had just been for the holidays, and I needed an influx of cash.

I had been living in the Twin Cities for a year; my experiment of being in the same place as my dad had been a success, from my standpoint. We had spent time together and had bonded by doing the play. It was like a honeymoon period for me—basking in the love of my father and the admiration so many other people had for him. But I wasn't a little kid anymore, waiting for him to come home from work to ask me about my day. Our relationship cut short, we had sort of picked up where we didn't leave off and there was a lot he didn't know. Having always been a daddy's girl, and someone who never rocked the boat, I didn't see the point of sitting him down and giving him the blow by blow of Robbie's and my hellish childhood with our mother. I didn't want to ruin things or make him feel guiltier than he may already have. I already knew he felt regret over not coming to our rescue; he had told me as much. I wanted to protect him from those painful feelings, but at the same time, I wondered if we would even be spending time together now had I not picked up the phone myself.

I had made a few friends since moving to Minneapolis but still yearned for my life back East and missed Pete and Jenny and my sister, who was waiting tables in Boston and going to school part-time. Robin had opted not to come to Minneapolis for the last Christmas holiday—it was just too upsetting for her, she told me. I understood; my sister had more of a "don't look back" take, which was quite different from mine. She didn't seem to feel the bond with my father and his family, and she was moving on. I preferred to hang in, inserting myself in that sometimes uncomfortable limbo, trying to find a connection, real or imagined. I would will it into being if need be.

By April, there was still snow on the frozen, gray ground. I got a call from Mark Cuddy, who had directed *The Importance of Being Earnest*, the show I'd done in Steamboat Springs. He offered me a summer job acting at a Shakespeare festival in Boise, Idaho. I wasn't sure I was interested in traveling to another wild frontier; Idaho sounded like a place filled with lumberjacks and man-eating animals. I was unsure of what to do when, on a visit to Mary Sue, I saw a four-inch object on the low stone steps that ran up from the sidewalk to her house. At first I thought it was a Christmas ornament, but when I got closer, I discovered that it was a wooden piece from a jigsaw-puzzle map of the United States. It was Idaho. Perhaps it was a random way to make the decision to go, but maybe it was a sign? It seemed to make more sense than, say, flipping a coin. I picked up the piece and put it in my pocket.

Before leaving for Idaho, though, I received a phone call from Peter Hackett, the artistic director at the Denver Center, the theater in Colorado where my dad had been working. He wanted me to come and audition for the next season there, which would start in the fall. Amazingly, I wasn't being asked to do just a general audition, but to read for actual roles—a first for me. One of the roles was Juliet in *Romeo and Juliet*, which I'd dreamed of playing. Another was Cecily in *The Importance of Being Earnest*. Mark Cuddy had recommended me to Peter. I figured I could swing through Denver on my way up to Boise. I said good-bye to my father and stepmom, packed up my car, and hit the road again.

I stayed with my pal from my summer of flowing Moët and theater in a tent, Barbie in Boulder. She was engaged to be married to a new guy, not the one from the naked photo, and was singing in nightclubs with a vocal quartet that reminded me of the Manhattan Transfer—sort of white, groovy harmonizing stuff. I met her fiancé, Kip, who was laid-back and nice. They seemed so happy and relaxed as a couple. I just marveled at people in relationships—especially since I couldn't get arrested by the love police. I seemed doomed to be the third wheel, hanging out with my girlfriends and their menfolk.

Onstage, it was a different story. It was always a great feeling, despite whatever nerves I was experiencing, to walk out on the stage of a big theater. Hearing the echo of my footsteps as I crossed the stage, looking out on the sea of

seats, was thrilling. Especially delicious was the moment before I launched into my audition; that hush made me feel as
if I were about to invite the audience to join me and hopefully hold them in my hand.

Peter sat in the middle of the house with another man,
perhaps an assistant. Peter smiled and nodded at me, saying
hello. I started with Juliet's balcony speech, then read for a
smaller but juicy role in Tennessee Williams's *The Night of
the Iguana*—a sexpot teenager chasing after the defrocked
priest, Shannon. And then, finally, for Cecily in *Earnest*. I
finished and looked expectantly out from the stage.

"We'll be in touch." Peter smiled and shook my hand.
"Thanks for coming in."

After thanking him, I walked off through the backstage, breathing in that marvelous theater perfume, past the
heavy black drapes hanging in the wings. I reached out and
brushed the velvet with my fingertips, hoping they would
bring me good luck.

The drive to Idaho was wildy scenic—I had to go
through Wyoming, with its buttes and buffalo, and through
Utah, with its mountains and dry towns. Idaho itself was
ever changing. One moment, I'd be going along a flat road
surrounded by shimmering, cerulean lakes; suddenly sand
dunes would appear; and then I'd be climbing up a twisty
mountain road redolent with the smell of pine, snow glinting above the treetops. It was like God's country.

I arrived at the actors' housing and met my roommates.
Ursula was the company vocal coach and also acting in the

summer Shakespeare festival. She was five years older than me, engaged to be married to an actor in New York, and had this sweet, pretty cartoonlike face that was so expressive that she reminded me of Bugs Bunny when he's dressed like a girl. She would drink half a lite beer and have to immediately lie down, even if it meant on the kitchen floor, and I'd bring her a pillow; she was a cute drunk. Our other housemate was Wayne—a towering, slender gay guy from Florida with a goatee. He used to give us a funny look and say, "I'm going to the post office."

"But it's ten o'clock at night, Wayne," I would say.

"Uh-huh," he'd drawl as he grabbed his car keys and headed out into the night. It took me a while to realize that the *post office* was a euphemism for "gay bar." One night, I dressed up like a guy and Wayne took me with him to one of his haunts. Here we were in Boise, Idaho, God's Country, USA, and the bar was stuffed with more trannies, leather boys, and screaming queens than I'd ever seen in the Village. It blew my mind. He also introduced me to an after-hours disco that didn't serve alcohol, but you could dance your ass off till three in the morning on a strobe-lit floor. It was the only place I saw African Americans in town; it was as if they were Idaho's vampires, who only came out at night to party down.

We started rehearsals for *Henry IV, Part 1* on the bottom floor of an old department store that was now defunct but owned by this mellow hippie couple who lived in a loft-like space on the second floor with their baby. The woman's name was Star, and she worked in the costume department.

They threw all the opening-night parties and, to my dismay, didn't have a door on their bathroom.

The theater itself was outside, next to a golf course. We were lucky to have a huge hardware megastore across from the stage on the other side of the golf course, which improved the acoustics, as you were competing with people talking and eating their dinners on the grass, traffic noise, and the occasional airplane, helicopter, or ambulance. One night, a duck waddled up onstage during a battle scene and caused quite an uproar, bringing everything to a screeching halt. An actor in chain mail gently herded the duck offstage with his broadsword.

I enjoyed performing in two of the three plays. I had a tiny part in *Henry IV, Part 1*, as Lady Mortimer. Just one scene, but I had to speak and sing in Welsh and play being madly in love with my husband, who can't understand a thing I'm saying but thinks I'm adorable. This was the only play we performed in period, and wearing a long wig and a wool dress with fur trim under the blazing-hot lights was definitely a challenge. The sweat would start trickling down my back as soon as I got out under those hot lights, forming a little puddle in my underpants, even as we pretended we were in a drafty English castle.

My favorite role of the summer was in *The Merry Wives of Windsor*, in which I played Mistress Ford. It was done in present day, we had a terrific female director, and Ursula—who played the other merry wife—referred to it as *I Love Falstaff*, because of its sitcomlike plot: the local lounge lizard, Falstaff, fancies himself a ladies' man and causes all kinds of trouble. Of course, the wives turn the tables on him, and he gets his comeuppance. It was loads of fun, a comic romp jacked up by screwball antics.

In the last play of the summer, *Love's Labour's Lost*, I played Rosaline—I was awful and I knew it. The director was a swaggering cowboy type who paraded around with his two witchy girlfriends, whom he referred to smarmily as his "bookends." Idiotically, he set the play in the future, so we wore these ridiculous yellow jumpsuits and makeup that made us look like overgrown parrots. It was agony for me to be up there, saying these lines that were way over my head in terms of understanding and delivery—Rosalind was just so much smarter than I was. To make it even worse, the actor who played my love interest, Berowne, took an instant dislike to me. His name, Bill Fears, gave me my catchphrase of the summer: "There is nothing to fear but Fears himself." Since he was here in Idaho, from New York, and slightly older than the rest of the cast, he felt the whole experience was beneath him. He was slumming, and having to do scenes with me was a waste of his valuable time—so much so that he would often cut to the end of our scenes and walk off the stage. In a way I felt he was justified in doing this, as I was so obviously out of my league in terms of the language. The other part of me thought he was a dick.

I felt embarrassed by how horrid I was in the play—it was like Nina at the end of Chekhov's play *The Seagull*, where she talks of being onstage and knowing she's acting badly and doesn't know what to do with her hands. It was painful to come out from behind the curtains after each performance and not have anyone say something nice to me. I'd sneak home, my head low. I was lost in the part, and it showed.

Toward the end of the season, a director and old friend of my dad's, Ed Call, came to see the plays. He was going to be directing John Osborne's kitchen-sink drama *The Entertainer*, with Daddy playing the lead—a washed-up, bitter music-hall performer named Archie Rice—and Ed wanted to see me read for the role of Archie's daughter, Jean. It was a great role, and I'd be working with my dad again—and at the Guthrie.

Unfortunately, Ed saw my horrible performance in *Love's Labour*, but also my wacky take on *Merry Wives*, in which I thought I showed some comic chops. Not that comedy was what was required for the role of Jean—she is a disappointed daughter, trying to make sense of her postwar life, against the sadness and bleakness of England at that time and her father's unhappy marriage to her alcoholic stepmom.

I met Ed in the ground floor of the department store, where we'd rehearsed the plays before moving to the golf-course stage. I was even more nervous because Mark, who ran the Shakespeare festival, was there—the two of them together felt a little like a firing squad. I made it through the scene but felt distant from the material and frozen with fear. I knew in the first thirty seconds of the audition that I wasn't going to get the part.

"You know, Wendy," Ed said after I'd read, "you should really think about getting some training."

I nodded, not knowing what else to say. I stuck my hands under my armpits, tapped my foot, and pursed my lips, in an attempt to show that I was tough and didn't need his fucking job.

Ed saw right through my act. "I mean, you're really good, but *if* acting professionally is what you want to do, you need a program. You need to go to school. You know they're starting one up at the Denver Center."

Oddly, I hadn't heard about the new program until now. "Thanks, Ed."

"Jesus, when are these goddamn Lawlesses going to leave me alone! See ya around, kid, and think about what I said."

Ed ended up casting another actress named Wendy, Wendy Makkena. She had more experience and was gangbusters in the role. I was jealous, but she was better for it than I would ever have been.

At the end of the summer, my phone rang again—it was Peter, the guy at the Denver Center. He offered me an "as cast" contract—basically small roles and understudying leads for the season—which both surprised and disappointed me. Maybe my tryout before I came to Idaho hadn't gone as well as I'd thought. Then I remembered what Ed had said about going to acting school and the program starting up there.

"Peter, thank you so much for the job offer, but what I really want to do is get some training. Would you consider admitting me to the new conservatory there instead, in lieu of offering me a contract?"

He said yes. I was twenty-four years old and going back to school—for the third time.

chapter eight

WILD, WILD WEST

The National Theatre Conservatory (NTC) was a three-year graduate acting program affiliated with the Denver Center for the Performing Arts, a multimillion-dollar arts complex with three theaters. Coincidentally, my stepmother had been asked to be the managing director of the theater company—she'd left the same position at the Children's Theatre in Minneapolis when the artistic director, John Donahue, had been arrested for having sex with underage boys. My father was staying in Minneapolis but would visit often, and it was nice knowing some family was around.

Our school was in the old jail building around the corner from the theater. It was under the stewardship of Allen Fletcher, who, along with William Ball, had founded the American Conservatory Theater (ACT) in San Francisco.

The NTC's first class was composed of students from ACT whom Allen had invited to come with him to the new program. Some went straight into the second-year class, and I was in the first, along with nineteen others. We were going to have scene study and acting class in addition to training in voice, movement, the Alexander technique, phonetics, speech, dance, and singing. Many of the faculty Allen had brought along from ACT; others would be hired from around the country. Guest instructors, such as the well-known Shakespeare teacher David Hammond, would be coming in to teach specific skills.

The plan was to spend two years studying and then, in the third year, be paid a stipend and act in the resident company. We were all awarded scholarships of various amounts—mine allowed me to stretch the last of the money my grandfather had left me and cover the three years.

Acting school was, for me, a way to commit to the profession, to finally fill that lonely place inside me with something that captivated and drove me. I wanted to land, to no longer drift aimlessly from place to place. After a lifetime without guidance or structure, I hoped it would be good for me. As always, I was looking for a home.

I was here to learn who I was, and what kind of an actor I wanted to be. I was terrified. Since many of the people in my class had known each other at ACT, I called upon my new-girl-in-town bravado—Wendy Lawless, breezy world traveler and bon vivant—honed over years of constant moves with my mother and sister. Putting on a plucky, insouciant front, I tried hard to put my insecurities aside and concentrate on trying to learn. I didn't have to be the best—

it wasn't about that. Still, many days I felt like jumping off a tall building. I'd take a running leap off, eyes wide-open, hurtle through space, and land in a net held by my classmates and teachers. After a while, I started to find conquering my initial fears and doubts exhilarating.

The main idea behind our first year of school was to strip us all down, erase everything we thought we knew about acting, and—when we were broken of all our old tricks—to start rebuilding us, hopefully into better performers. More than a way to free myself from any prior notions I had about acting, I also saw this time as a way to break free of the past. That was over and couldn't hurt me now, and no amount of replay would change it. I'd already mucked through my macabre childhood—how much harder could this be?

The first two weeks were a crash course of exercises as the class got to know each other by playing theater games so that we would bond as a group and become a unit. We played charades, red rover, and a game I'd never heard of before called hunter/hunted—one person is blindfolded (the hunter) and placed in the center of the room, and everyone else (the hunted) has to cross the room, one by one, without getting caught. We did trust exercises where we took turns falling backward, expecting that the rest of the group would catch us, or we led each other around outside in pairs, taking turns being blindfolded. We performed our monologues for each other. Dancing, living, singing, breathing, and tearing our guts out in class together was simultaneously invigorating and exhausting. Getting in touch with my raw emotions during the day, I had trouble sleeping at night and dreamed vividly about being chased by monsters or my bike hitting a rock and going over a cliff. People got pinched nerves in their necks, headaches, and torn tendons. There was a fair amount of crying, and many shoulder rubs were dispensed among us. Quickly, the class morphed into a little dysfunctional family of sorts.

I liked many of my classmates right away. M.E.—short for Mary Ellen—had brown hair she washed in laundry detergent because she didn't have any money to buy shampoo. She wore headbands, holey jeans, and white boy's T-shirts, and her eyes popped ever so slightly out. M.E. had a tony lockjaw accent, which I suspected was a put-on. Maybe that's why I felt drawn to her—she was a bit of a phony, and so was I. We'd find odd bars to go to with the class—such as the Buckhorn Exchange, the oldest restaurant in Denver, which served Rocky Mountain oysters and had walls covered in gruesome stuffed animals.

Two of my classmates, John and Jen, were the resident "parents," whom everyone flocked around because they were newly married, the only couple in our class and sort of still on their honeymoon. They were still unpacking their wedding presents, and Jen would bring her homemade bread to school for us to gobble down. I liked just sitting at their kitchen table, watching them be domestic, the way I had with Pete and Jenny at Ninety-seventh Street.

Rounding out the group were JB, Graham, and Anna. JB was a rangy jock from Indiana who'd been a track star in high school and had a sunny, laid-back disposition that made him easy to talk to. Graham was the tall, dark, and handsome guy in the group, with a loping walk and a sly smile, a practical joker who'd put plastic flies in my drink or on his tongue. Anna was statuesque and had fluffy, layered, dark blond hair, a booming voice, and fierce brown eyes.

NTC had some kick-ass teachers. Ethan, our main acting guru, was like our Yoda. He was blunt, brilliant, and kind of a drunk. In his late thirties, he wore John Lennon–tinted spectacles and shuffled into class looking as if he'd slept in the park. His shaggy, long brown hair hung perilously close to the cigarette he always had going, threatening to set fire to his unkempt beard. Even when he conducted class lying down with a wicked hangover, he had this amazing ability, using one or two sentences, to zero in on what was lacking in a scene or an exercise. Our voice teacher, Bonnie, was tiny—barely five feet—and had clearly compensated for her size by developing a huge persona. Bonnie sported a Saint Joan haircut, had big sea-glass-blue eyes, and was passionate about absolutely everything. She threw herself fully into teaching us to use our voices. We spent a lot of time in her class bent over with our mouths hanging open— drooling onto the floor—or massaging our faces, and saying "Aaaahhh" to relax our jaws and tongues. She tolerated no crap, called us on our laziness and our bad habits, and pushed and challenged us in every class. "Tears are a garbage can!" she'd bellow when someone started to fall apart in class. "Especially for women!"

After all the game playing and trust falls, we were broken up into two groups and were told to choose two-person scenes with a partner, which we'd periodically be doing during the year. I chose to do *Our Town* with Jeff, who had a soft, rumpled face and sad eyes; he seemed to have so many original ideas and impulses. We'd meet up to work on the scenes after school and perform them in class at the end of the week, in front of the teachers and our classmates.

At the end of the day, we'd all limp home, wiped out after a day of classes. I was living in a studio in the Capitol Hill area of the city, near a few of my classmates—John and Jen, M.E., and Graham. JB and Anna were living in cheaper digs on the wrong side of the tracks with roommates. If we had the energy, M.E. and I would get a drink or go to a movie after school, or Graham and I would go get a burger at Chesby's, a local watering hole that served killer martinis. Graham's girlfriend was an actress in the company and was working all the time, so he sometimes stopped by for a chat.

One night about a month after school started, a bunch of students—along with Ethan and a few of our other teachers—went out to the Wazee, a bar and restaurant in the industrial part of town that had great burgers and pizza. Ethan's protégé and our assistant acting teacher, Ned, was there, too. We were all sitting at a line of small tables pushed together, listening to Ethan talk about gestalt therapy and watching him chain-smoke.

I was talking with Nancy, our dance teacher, who was sitting next to me. She was petite with a black bob haircut that made her look like Louise Brooks. I adored her class—Contemporary Movement Technique—which she claimed she made up on the spot every time. It was a mélange of ballet, jazz, and modern; it was all very free and fun. We leaped and spun across the floor, forgetting our bodies as they flew through the air.

I could see Ned at the end, working the table, and making his way toward me. I hadn't talked to him yet but had seen him around the building. He was barely taller than me and had short, brown, tightly curled hair. His face was smooth, like a boy's, as if he had never shaved.

When he reached my seat, he knelt down beside me. "Hi, I'm Ned. You're Wendy, right?"

I nodded. He was wearing black jeans and a black leather motorcycle jacket because, as I later found out, he was from New Jersey and worshipped Bruce Springsteen.

"So, where you from? Back East?"

"Yeah, New York, Boston." The short answer.

It turned out he had gone to Tufts, in Medford, Massachusetts. We talked about the Boston music scene for a while. He smiled at me constantly, and I got the feeling he was flirting with me, but I dismissed it, as my radar for such things was rusty and, although he was just a few years older than me, he was also my teacher.

After that night at the Wazee, I often felt Ned's eyes burning into my skin, in class, in the hallway, on the sidewalk in front of school. I tried to ignore that I had developed a little crush on him, convincing myself that it was just temporary, that soon he would do something that totally ruined it for me—pick his nose or fart—and I'd be off him. But that didn't happen. Instead, he continued aggressively flirting with me, and I started to flirt right back, but perhaps not as fervently. After being on my own with no man for so long, I was ashamed of how desperate I felt, how much I looked forward to his somewhat brazen attention. I tried to keep at least the semblance of a boundary between us; he was my teacher, after all. I certainly didn't want anyone, especially Ned, to know how love-starved and pathetic I felt.

One day, we were all lying on the floor in his class doing a visualization exercise, and he came over and sat on my stomach. I was flustered and worried by what my classmates might think. I looked around nervously, but no one was paying attention and everyone else's eyes were closed.

"I heard about your astronaut exercise. Ethan told me that at the end, the two of you looked like a painting. That's awesome."

The day before, in Ethan's class, after avoiding taking a turn for as long as I could, I'd finally volunteered to go up and do what he called Given Circumstances—an exercise in which he gives you the who, what, and where of a scene, then puts another actor in it with you who has no knowledge of what's going on. Ethan took me out of the room and told me that my husband was about to go to outer space, and that we had one hour to spend together before he was taken to quarantine for the flight. The trip was dangerous, and he might not return. Ethan and I went back into the room, where I set up a space—moving furniture and props. Then Ethan chose Jeff, with whom I was working on an *Our Town* scene, to be my partner. I threw myself into it, and Jeff was amazing, intuitively picking up on some of the details and the seriousness of the situation. At the end, I had a vision of the rocket ship exploding and him being a million miles away; I broke down.

"Please don't go," I pleaded, tears running down my face. "I'll die if you leave."

"I have to go."

I ran to him and threw myself into his arms. "Why?"

"For the world," he replied solemnly.

The exercise had only lasted seven or eight minutes, but I had never felt that sort of electric connection with another actor or the truth of playing a scene moment by moment. I was, in actor talk, completely "in the now." That *coup de foudre* realization made me see everything that was wrong with my acting up until that point. It hit me, suddenly, that this was why I had come here.

"Yeah, it was incredible," I said now, looking up at Ned from my space on the floor.

"Well, everyone's talking about it."

Feeling shy about all the attention he was paying me, I laughed. I couldn't remember this happening to me ever before with a guy, and I was drunk on it.

The next day, I saw Ned in the hall and ducked into the library—hoping that he would follow me in, my heart racing. He did, and we were completely alone. He walked right up to me, hugged me, and kissed my cheek.

"I like you a lot," he said, smiling in his adorable way.

"Aw." I reached up and tugged on the sleeve of his leather jacket, too bashful do anything more forward, in case what I thought was there really wasn't. "I like you, too, Ned."

He looked at me, turning his head to the side, and put his hand on my forehead. "Are you having your period?"

I was, so I felt completely freaked-out that he'd guessed. "Um, yes. How did you know?" I was mortified, discussing menstruation with my acting teacher and my crush. All of a sudden I felt twelve years old.

"My dad is a gynecologist," he replied matter-of-factly.

"Wow. Weird. Well, I have to go to class." I crept over to the door, checking the hall to make sure no one would see me leave, my heart pounding, my face flushed.

And that was it—but I ran it over and over in my head a hundred times, each time feeling the delicious flip my tummy made as I thought of that moment, his eyes, his smile. It was fun to torture myself. I waited, wondering what would happen next.

He invited me out to dinner, which neither of us ate because we were so distracted by each other. We were like a screwball-comedy movie team with a quick back-and-forth banter to all our conversations. After he paid the check, we walked out to his car, and once inside, a marathon make-out session started—we each could scarcely breathe; it was as if we were inhaling each other. He drove me home, and I was surprised when he didn't want to come inside. It was for the best, even though I just wanted to throw him down on the car seat and fuck his brains out. He wanted to take it slow, and I was eager to keep our relationship a secret—for now—which only added to the thrill of it all.

Back at school, we students danced, sang, learned phonetics—which seemed useless to me—practiced our *a*'s and *o*'s, and had Alexander technique with teacher Michael Johnson-Chase, whom we called MJC for short. I learned that F. Matthias Alexander was an Australian actor born in 1869 who started having vocal problems while he recited his speeches. He stood in front of a set of mirrors to try to figure out what was causing him to lose his voice. He observed that he pulled his head back and lowered his chin when he spoke—MJC called this "chicken necking"—which pinched his larynx. He developed a method, which became famous internationally, of correctly balancing his head on top of his torso, which then led Alexander to discover that the entire spine could be lengthened—allowing a postural flow to the body. We all ran around school with our heads floating on the tops of our spines.

Jeff and I performed the George and Emily scene from *Our Town* in which they walk to the soda shop and she tells him how stuck-up she thinks he's become. It went fairly well—and it was Ethan's favorite play.

"There's a reason this play gets performed all the time—it's iconic. *Our Town* is like ground zero, man. It's life, death, and that fucker time. I'm telling ya, if actors connected with this piece, it would heal a lot of shit we encounter along the way." Ethan listed around the room, pulling on his cigarette, holding a Styrofoam cup—the contents of which I couldn't guess. "Wendy, you really have to cry in the scene—confront him, you are so pissed off at him. Let him have it, you know?"

Ethan pulled me into the corner and asked me what I found attractive about Jeff. I said his hands, which were large and soft with thick, long fingers. Then Ethan took Jeff aside and whispered something to him. Jeff nodded.

We did the scene again, and Ethan seemed pleased. "At the end, you know, I was really beginning to see the soda shop." He smiled as he said it. Praise from Ethan—our leader! I was over the moon.

My stepmother and I usually got together once a month—she often treated me to lunch or dinner out, a welcome respite from my student fare. That October we met at the Café Promenade—a charming old-school restaurant in Larimer Square, a trendy shopping district in downtown Denver. The maître d', Fred, always made a fuss over her. He reminded me a bit of Jackie Gleason. Though very overweight, he moved like a dancer, dressed nattily, and was so incredibly charming that you almost didn't notice his size.

"Mrs. Lawless and Miss Lawless! How wonderful to see you, come right this way," Fred boomed, showing us to a corner table, theatrically waving our menus in his gigantic hands as he waddled across the room.

Because Sarah and Daddy were living in different cities, rumors were flying around the regional-theater community that they were separated and even getting divorced. My step-mother found this hilarious.

"It's ridiculous, isn't it?" she said over lunch after Fred left us. "I'm telling you, it's the most perfect way to be married. I think Katharine Hepburn said something once about how couples should live next door to each other and just visit now and then." Sarah laughed and lit a cigarette. I couldn't help but think of my mother's long-term affair with my ex-stepdad, after their divorce. After we had moved to London and he had remarried, they rekindled their romance—as if the distance of an ocean between them had made it easier to be together. Maybe being in a part-time, commuter relationship was the key to happiness—tethered together instead of handcuffed, with enough room to keep longing alive.

Sarah switched topics. "So how is school going, cookie?"

I filled her in on my classes, my favorite teachers—Bonnie, Ethan, and MJC. I didn't mention Ned; I was worried that she'd think I was a floozy, or that I wasn't taking my studies seriously enough.

"Well, I've certainly noticed a change in you since you've been at the conservatory. You're so focused and sparkling. It's wonderful to see." She smiled and gave my hand a little squeeze.

"Really?"

"Yes." She sipped her glass of red wine and looked at me intently. "I've been meaning to tell you for a while that your father and I think of you as the child we would have had together."

"Thanks, Sarah. That makes me very happy." I meant it, but I also felt a tinge of guilt about being favored over my sister.

After she'd paid the check, we walked out of the restaurant into the chilly evening.

"I'll see you soon. Always feel free to come by my office, okay?" She hugged me.

I was working with Graham on a scene from a dated kitchen-sink drama called *A Hatful of Rain*. He played Polo, the supposedly no-good brother of my character's—Celia's—junkie husband. Polo is in love with Celia, and she is pregnant with his brother's child, so the scene is loaded with tension and the unsaid, and both our characters experience a meltdown. We rehearsed in my kitchen late at night.

After we ran it a few times, we were both sort of jazzed by all the conflict in the scene—I'm supposed to throw a glass of water in his face, and he confesses that he loves me.

"I thought that went pretty well—you?" I was trembling slightly.

"Yeah. I have to tell you something."

"What?"

"I'm crazy about you."

"What?" I sputtered.

This seemed preposterous to me. Graham had a gorgeous girlfriend, Liz, who was the star ingenue in the company—he could have any girl he wanted. He was good-looking in a conventional, strapping, telegenic way, with broad shoulders and a head of thick brown hair. I'm sure it upset him that his all-American looks and build caused people to regard him in a sex-slob way. Everyone probably thought he'd just move to Los Angeles after school and become the next Tom Selleck. But he wanted to be a serious actor and worked hard at his craft.

"You're kidding, right?" Completely shocked, I couldn't believe he was serious. "I mean, what about you and Liz?"

"I never wanted it to be serious. She feels differently, so it's a problem. She kind of hates me right now." He glowered and looked at the linoleum.

"I'm really flattered," I blustered on, trying to avoid sounding insensitive by telling him I thought he was nuts. "I think your feelings are coming from working on the scene, you're projecting them onto me. But it's not . . . me, you know?" Falling for your scene partner, at least temporarily, was common. I was sure that this phenomenon, combined with all the information we were being bombarded with at school, had caused his temporary insanity.

"I don't know what else to say. If you think that, okay, but I'm in love with you."

"I'm sorry, Graham. I really like you. I hope we can still be chums."

He put on his long, herringbone-tweed coat, wrapped a tartan scarf around his neck, and stuffed his script into his pocket. He strode purposefully to the door and turned back to me. He looked miserable. "If this is all upsetting to you, well, think about how I feel." He threw open the door and left with a slam.

What the fuck? I thought. I just wasn't the kind of girl who had more than one guy running after her. The last time this had happened to me was at the Town School in Manhattan, when Tommy Rosenberg and Arthur Flatto had both professed undying love for me. I was seven. So it had been a while.

I threw myself into classes: ballet, singing, voice. November arrived, and we were all cast in projects. One group would be doing Lanford Wilson's *Balm in Gilead*, which Ethan would direct, and Ned would be directing Tennessee Williams's *The Glass Menagerie* for the other group. Ned had told me, in secret, that he wanted to cast me as Laura, the fragile sister of the main character, Tom. I was thrilled that he thought I could do it—I wasn't sure I could myself, and it scared me. I was also unsure he could pull it off and worried that it wasn't a good idea, considering our relationship. But the casting lists went up—and I was to play the part. My classmate Leslie was to play Amanda Wingfield, Graham was cast as her son, Tom, and JB as the gentleman caller.

We worked hard learning our lines but also did a fair amount of improvisation in rehearsals. We cooked dinner and ate together as the Wingfield family. We went out on an excursion, and I shoplifted a little bottle of pink nail polish at the drugstore, thinking it would be good to have a secret—one that could be discovered in a way similar to Amanda's discovery that Laura has not been attending her typing lessons. I worked with MJC in Alexander class on Laura's physicality—she had pleurisy as a child and has a pronounced limp, another reason for her fear of people and the outside world. I scribbled in a notebook, answering all the questions Ethan had told us we must answer when working on a character: Who am I? What's around me? What time is it? It was a new approach for me, and I relished the process. For the first time in my life, I was working to build a character from the inside out, instead of simply projecting my own past onto her or just playing pretend as I went along.

On the weekends, Ned and I would often go off on an adventure. Not ready to out our relationship at school, we usually drove into the mountains, where there was little chance of running into anyone we knew. We drove to Central City one weekend, an old mining town that was now a quaint tourist attraction with original storefronts from the 1850s lining the streets. We had Bloody Marys at the Teller House bar, where the famous portrait of a beautiful woman looks up at you from the barroom floor. Next door was the opera house, built in 1878, where Buffalo Bill had once performed and P. T. Barnum had presented his circus. Once we drove to Estes Park and ate corned-beef sandwiches at the Stanley Hotel—a supposedly haunted hotel that had inspired Stephen King to write *The Shining*. We had fun wherever we went, so much so that people stared and pointed at us. I was head over heels in love with him and told him all the time, and he told me he loved me, too. It was as if my blood moved faster when I was with him. He was always buying me thoughtful gifts—a copy of my favorite children's book, *Eloise*, a red bomber jacket that I'd admired in a store one day, and a thin, beaded silver friendship bracelet.

But our sex life was kind of a letdown. With all the intense feelings we had for each other, it didn't seem to translate into amazing sex. We'd spent what seemed like weeks doing what my mother would have called "heavy petting." I had rug burns on my ass from rolling around naked on the floor in front of the fireplace at his apartment, a sort of consolation prize for waiting for things to get to the next level.

He was a fantastic kisser and generous in bed, but when it came to the actual mechanics—he had trouble. The first time we were together, at my apartment, he couldn't get hard. I didn't know how to react, having never encountered this before—unless the guy was fall-down drunk.

"Is it me?"

"No, no, it's not."

He got out of bed and sat on the floor next to me.

"It doesn't matter. I mean, we can do other stuff." I didn't want him to think I thought it was a big deal—like lack of penetration was a deal breaker. I smiled while he looked down at the floor. Maybe this was why he'd wanted to take it slow and not jump into bed right away. I couldn't ask him.

We were entering the holiday season—which I always had mixed emotions about. My stepsisters and my dad would be flying out to spend Christmas in Denver. I started to hear an old sound in my head, the usual dread I experienced as the holidays approached. I knew my sister wasn't coming—she'd told me it was too painful for her and she planned to stay in Boston with her friends—and I understood, but I felt deserted by her, by her choice to spend Christmas with someone other than me. Ned invited me to go with him to visit his parents in New Jersey. No matter how much I wanted to run away, I knew that I never would. It ended up being fine—my stepmother taught me how to knit. I had fun with my stepsisters: we chatted, played cards, smoked, and drank bourbon. I didn't die. I tried hard to be a joiner and not feel outside the group. There were other people, friends of Daddy and Sarah's, and stragglers from the theater who had no place to go, so it felt more like a party than a holiday. But I missed Ned.

After the holiday break, school started back up, rehearsals continued. We had a new teacher for mask class, Craig Turner. Mask eluded me, it seemed so difficult and vast. When an actor puts one on, it's a way of vanishing into this other world—to the time of the Greeks—but every gesture is wildly magnified because the face is covered. Sometimes, in classes that intimidated me, such as mask, I threw something together at the last minute. Arriving only partially prepared, I could shrug off not being good and pretend it didn't matter to me.

My relationship with Ned, on the other hand, seemed effortless. We finally ventured out to the Wazee as a couple—our public debut—for a large gathering of students, actors from the company, and a few of our teachers, including Ethan. People ogled and nudged elbows—a bit too much, I thought, as if we were suddenly back in high school. Ethan, noticing all the unwanted attention we were getting, shrugged his shoulders as if to say, *So what?* I appreciated the gesture. But I still felt self-conscious because Ned was my teacher and I didn't want anyone to think I was receiving preferential treatment. When someone introduced me as Jimmy Lawless's daughter, I balked a little, too, because I wanted to be judged on my talents, not thought of as someone who had an advantage because of her father or her boyfriend.

One morning after I had slept over at Ned's place, he was in the shower. His roommate, Ken, was making coffee in the kitchen—I helped myself and thanked him. Walking around Ned's small bedroom looking for my shoes, I saw his wallet. Without thinking, I picked it up, opened it, and looked at his driver's-license picture. He looked super cute. I set down my coffee mug and looked inside the fold, thinking I'd slide out a couple bucks to make a joke when he got back about hoping he'd had a good time. A few twenties were in the billfold slot, but I saw something else. I pulled out a small photograph of a young woman, beautiful with dark long hair and a beaming smile, wearing a yellow sweater with a locket hung around her neck. Behind the photo was a clipping from a newspaper in San Francisco. The same photo I held in my hand appeared in the article. I read that she was an ACT student who'd been offered a ride home from her movie usher job by a coworker. He had murdered her and dumped her body by the side of the road. My hands tingled as I read about how they'd searched for her for days before finding her body. I looked at the picture. Who was she? Why did Ned have a picture of her and a clipping about her murder in his wallet? Was she his girlfriend? Why hadn't he told me about her?

I didn't hear the shower turn off. I was standing next to his bed looking at this girl's smiling face when Ned walked in wearing a towel. He saw me, and I looked at him. Because it was so strange, I didn't feel embarrassed about being such a snoop.

"Who is this?" I felt a little flipped out.

"She was a very good friend of mine." He started to get dressed, pulling on his usual all-black ensemble.

"Was she your girlfriend?" It seemed so bizarre to me. I thought we were so close, and he suddenly had this huge secret. A secret he carried with him in his pocket every day.

"No. We were close."

I put the picture and the clipping back in his wallet. "Why didn't you tell me about her, about this?" I didn't understand. I was jealous and hurt—how could I compete with a dead girl?

"I'm going to have to go back next week to the inquest."

"Okay." I gulped, trying to comprehend how he and I could be together all the time and he'd decided not to say anything until I looked in his wallet. Would he even have told me if I hadn't found the photo? "It's just . . . I'm surprised, that's all."

He didn't respond.

A week later, I drove him to the airport—he was heading to San Francisco for the inquest. I told him to call me. I waited to hear from him that evening but never did. I was worried and would have called him if I'd known how to reach him.

The next day at school, during voice class, there was a fire drill. We all spilled out onto the street. I saw Ken, Ned's roommate, and ran over to him to ask if he'd heard from Ned. He said Ned'd left a garbled message on the answering machine. Then he glanced around shiftily, lowering his voice to a whisper. "Ned really wants to be alone. He doesn't want anyone to know where he is. And he told me he was afraid he'd hurt your feelings by telling you."

"Um . . . all right." My mind was reeling—Ned's weaselly roomie as the messenger in our relationship? What the hell was going on?

"I'd be happy to keep you posted if I hear anything."

"I don't understand."

"He said he'd talk to you when he gets back."

Ken smiled and looked at me with saccharine, insincere sympathy. I walked away, trying not to burst into tears.

When we got back inside the building, I saw my classmate Adam, who'd been at ACT the year before with Ned and the dead girl, leaning on the soda machine outside the bathrooms. I walked over to him and asked in a quiet voice if he'd known her that well. It turned out that Adam had been close to her—I remembered seeing his name in the clipping in Ned's wallet. Looking pained, Adam told me some things that made me feel uneasy. He said that Ned hadn't been that close to her, that he wanted to be, but she wasn't interested.

"We were both in love with her. It was so fucking horrible when they found her."

I nodded.

"She would have been in our class, you know. But she's not here."

Then Adam looked at me gravely—as if he wanted to say something, but wasn't sure he should.

"What is it?" I reached out and touched his arm.

He ran his slender fingers through his hair and looked off down the hallway. "It's just that . . . well, we were really tight, and . . ."

"Tell me."

"You remind me of her."

"But she had dark hair and—"

"No, I mean, you're like her. The first time I saw you, talked to you, watched your audition pieces—that's what I thought. It's really weird. You have the same sort of, I dunno . . . talent and openness that she had." He shook his head. "Ned always goes after the shiniest thing in the room. This time it's you."

I didn't know what to say to this. Feeling sick to my stomach, I took the elevator downstairs. I walked the streets for a few hours, bewildered, wondering what the fuck was going on. Did he love me? Or did he love the part of me that reminded him of her? Did I love him? Was he even in San Francisco? All of a sudden I felt as if I were in some creepy Brian De Palma movie.

I thought about how strongly Ned had come on to me when we first met, all the compliments, and the wildly inappropriate comment he'd made in the library about my period, which had thrown me at the time, but now seemed like a manipulation—something he'd said to make me feel vulnerable, and in awe of him, as if he could read my mind. In rehearsals for the play, he only said positive things about my work, whereas I worried that I wasn't learning or growing in the role. All the weird sex problems and the murdered girl in his wallet. Suddenly, he seemed false to me, and I didn't feel I could trust him. It was as if it were all a mirage.

When Ned got back, I didn't tell him about my conversation with Adam. He didn't say anything about the inquest, and I didn't ask. Instead, I told him that I thought we should take a break. It was too much, going to school, rehearsing the play. I had to start working harder—there were so many distractions, and I wasn't taking it seriously enough. I told him I was overwhelmed and needed some time to myself.

He listened patiently and nodded. "Okay. If that's the way you feel."

I was surprised he'd taken it so well. I expected more of a fight.

But that night, when I got back to my apartment, I saw Ned's car driving slowly down my block as I made my way inside, and my answering machine was full of hang-up calls.

Meanwhile, Graham and I had been spending a lot of time together, rehearsing and running lines for *The Glass Menagerie*. In the wake of this weirdness with Ned, I kept thinking back to the time Graham had told me he had a thing for me. He'd stop by my place for a cup of coffee or we'd pop out for drinks. We had a lot of laughs, and though I didn't know if he still cared for me that way, I found myself wondering more and more if he did.

One night, after a rehearsal in my kitchen, Leslie left and Graham lingered. I told him that I thought about him a lot. He said he still felt the same way he had back when we were scene partners. We discussed it all in a logical, grown-up way—and decided we shouldn't get involved, just remain friends. He'd had a bad breakup recently, and I had just dumped Ned. It seemed best not to plunge into a relationship when the rose garden was littered with our victims.

Rehearsals complete, we performed *The Glass Menagerie* and received a fair amount of criticism. Ethan felt that I was too resilient as Laura. I had been too afraid to go too far with the character's disability. I didn't want her to be a victim. Allen said that it was a "tragic mistake" to have made in my performance. But he praised other things and he cried through a couple of scenes, so I thought he'd been moved a little.

"This is the place where Wendy should be allowed to branch out and play roles of depth and power! Not wallflower parts," our voice teacher, Bonnie, said somewhat angrily, zeroing in on what would become one of my biggest challenges at school, and my bête noire: I was in jeopardy of being typecast as ingenues because of my height and sweet appearance. My whole life, people had called me "flower" or "butterfly" or patted me on the head as if I were a kitten.

I often felt that I shared something with Bonnie: we were both little people who were big inside and pissed off about the way other people saw us and treated us because of our size. When I had performed a monologue from *Romeo and Juliet* for David Hammond, an expert teacher of interpreting Shakespeare, he told me that it was "cute." That was all—dismissing me in one little, and little-sounding, word. I was furious and embarrassed, trying to pretend I didn't care what he'd said even as my face turned red and my ears prickled with anger.

After the feedback on *The Glass Menagerie*, I was determined to change the faculty's perception of me by working in scene class on ballsy women—Marlene in Caryl Churchill's *Top Girls*, a cutthroat executive who's given her child to her housewife sister to raise; Irene in *Idiot's Delight*, a pathological liar and con artist; even Shakespeare's Cleopatra, who was larger-than-life and a drama queen. I also started working with Bonnie, when we both had time, on a *Richard III* speech that was filled with fury and darkness.

"This is some of the best work I've seen you do, Wendy." She beamed at me. "I see all the rage inside the character, and your voice dropped to a lower octave as well! Excellent."

I kept working away at showing my range as an actress, praying it would make a difference onstage.

During a sunny January after projects were over, our Alexander teacher, MJC, had a big bash at his house, to celebrate surviving projects. It was loud and boozy—everyone was letting off steam. We'd all been under so much pressure. I was standing in the hall outside the bathroom, talking with MJC and nursing a Jack Daniel's when Graham walked by. MJC reached out to take Graham's arm and dragged us both into the bathroom with him. I was confused, until MJC spoke.

"You two are such special people. You should really be together."

Without another word, he walked out, closing the door behind him. Graham and I looked at each other for a long moment. Then we fell into each other's arms, tumbling onto the cold tile floor.

I worried that, like my mother, I was going through men at tramplike speed—but I was searching for something real. A true love. I'm sure many people looked at me and thought, *Slut*. But I was filled with hope each time. For me, it wasn't about sex—it was about finding the love and acceptance I'd never had. Not knowing what to look for in a guy, I gravitated toward the ones who seemed to want me. I figured that was half the battle—getting some man to hanker for me—so if he did already, why not give it a go?

Graham and I were happy, at the start. He had a great sense of humor and would play silly practical jokes on me. We'd make pancakes and eat them in bed. He was kind of pent up sexually, and I felt that I could help him be more relaxed and have more fun. He'd grown up in Sonoma, with WASPy, stern parents who didn't support his decision to be an actor. I felt comfortable with him, maybe because we'd been friends first. I wished sometimes he could be more affectionate, more giving—but I thought that would come in time. I blamed his starchy upbringing for his inability to express his emotions. I also blamed myself for his reticence in showing his feelings for me; maybe it was my fault that he didn't want to French-kiss or go down on me. It was as if he thought sex was dirty, but maybe he just needed more time to be intimate in that way.

One evening a few weeks into our romance, we were at the Oxford Hotel, a fancy hotel in downtown Denver, having a drink, when he told me I was the only woman he felt he didn't have to charm the pants off. Was it that he could relax around me and be himself, or was I so easy he didn't have to work so hard? With his good looks, I couldn't see how hard it would be to get any woman to fall into bed with him. His smile, the husky magnetism of his delivery, made me feel special—it was a compliment, right? But after a beat and a slug of my bourbon, I wondered what it meant.

Suddenly at school they dropped a bomb on us. The artistic director, Donovan Marley, called a big meeting with the entire class, Allen Fletcher, all the teachers and the administration and told us that our class would be cut in half at the end of the year, after our final projects—from twenty-four to twelve. Our only previous interaction with Donovan had been when he threatened the kids who were late with their tuition payments. When Anna, who was working nights as a waitress to put herself through the program asked what would happen if they couldn't come up with the money, he snarled through clenched teeth, "I'm not the kind of person to be handed ultimatums. I'll close this goddamn school down!"

He was a real charmer.

Donovan claimed that reducing the class was a way to save money; the theater didn't want to waste time and talent on those who weren't cut out to be career actors. We were stunned, having been told that we'd be together for the three years. Allen looked as if he were going to throw up, and Ethan stood up and said, "This is fucking bullshit!"—and stormed out of the room, slamming the door behind him. People were crying, shaking, and hanging on to one another. Though I didn't show as much outwardly, I was devastated by this threat to the new home and family I'd found.

After that day—dubbed Black Thursday by all of us, who felt as if our front teeth had been punched out—we all walked around in a daze, feeling doomed and breathing what felt like poisoned air inside the building. Initially, we had bonded and functioned as a group, but now it seemed we were expected to pit ourselves against each other, to compete to be "the best." I couldn't help but wonder who was going to get the ax, who I thought deserved it, and who didn't. Would I be cut? And what would the ratio be? Five women and seven men? Six of each? It changed everything in an instant; I felt the tenuousness of my position in the class and was more determined than ever to shine as best I could. I prayed that I would get a plum role in final projects, where I could strut my stuff and impress the faculty.

The roller-coaster week at the conservatory was punctuated—of course—by a telephone call from my mother to the school. I was pulled out of class and informed that Cindy, a young Mormon woman who answered the school office phone, had spoken to Mother. Poor Cindy was distraught not only by my mother's tone but from her profuse and creative use of the F-word during their brief conversation. I rushed to the office and practically had to peel Karen, who ran the NTC's office, off the ceiling.

"Oh my God, your mother screamed at me! And cussed me out when I refused to bring you to the phone." Karen was quite shaken, as many people were when they were confronted with Mother's tsunami of venom. It could be overwhelming, especially if it was the first time it had hit you.

"I'm really sorry, Karen. My mother is, um, well, she's nuts."

"Jeez, she scared me to death! What a way to behave. Poor woman belongs in a hospital."

Karen shook her head and hugged herself for comfort. I had no idea how Mother had found me. I had often wondered if someone, perhaps an old friend from Kansas City when my parents were first married, had stayed in touch with both of them after the divorce. Perhaps Mother had put in a phone call to her old friend Sylvia Browne, now a famous psychic. But I would never find out how she did it. Mother herself had always claimed to be telepathic; maybe she was. The poison phone call was just Mother's way of saying, "I know where you are. You can't hide from me."

The final projects were cast later that week, with all of us preoccupied with how our performances would be the deciding factor in who would be asked back. Ned would be directing *Chekhov in Yalta*, a play about actors from the Moscow Art Theatre visiting Chekhov when he is sick with consumption; Allen had chosen to do Somerset Maugham's *Our Betters*—a 1923 satirical comedy of manners set in London about American expats marrying impoverished British nobility to increase their own social stature.

After trying so hard to change my good-girl image at school, I was hoping I'd get a meaty role, preferably not in Ned's show. So I was disappointed and devastated to be cast as the ingenue, Bessie, in *Our Betters*. Apparently, I was still considered a lightweight, and the character had a cow's name. Why had I bloody bothered to try to show my versatility? I thought briefly of going to Allen to beg him to recast me but knew it was too late for that.

One of my first pieces of direction from Allen was to

enter the room and bury my face in a bouquet of roses. My character was a total simp; I had to say lines like "I've just begun to live!" I looked up *ingenue* in the dictionary to prepare; it read, "An unsophisticated young woman." My ambition to be taken seriously was screwed.

Graham was cast as Tony, the cad, a gigolo who chased women and drove fast cars. Plunging into one of his dark moods, he told me he was convinced that all those in *Our Betters*, or *Bed Wetters*, as we came to call it, were the people who were most likely to be cut from the class. Feeling despondent over my casting, I went back and forth about giving a shit if I was cut. I'd skipped class, turned in a lackluster performance as Laura, and was now saddled with this boring wallflower part. I figured if they cut me, screw them; I'd just move back to New York and live with Jenny and Pete. Then I would flip-flop back to wanting to be one of the twelve who got to stay, be with Graham, and continue my training.

Graham and I started arguing—maybe the stress of the impending class cut hanging over us made us feel tentative about our relationship. Only a few months of school were left—would we even still be living in the same city six months from now?

His black mood was worsened because he rarely had any extra money, was still dependent on his folks, and his roommate moved out suddenly, leaving him hanging. I tried to help him, but he seemed to resent the meals I cooked him— knowing that it might be the only meal he'd eat that day— as well as the cash I offered to lend him. Instead of being appreciative, he was distant, and I thought just plain mean sometimes. He thought I overreacted to what I perceived as his withholding tendencies and his general thoughtlessness. He would stop himself from saying nice things to me—he rarely told me he loved me or even complimented me. Maybe it was my problem that I liked to be told I looked pretty or to have my boyfriend save me a chair in class. His behavior brought out the needy, insecure side of me. The more he pulled away, the more I wanted him. This feeling of being off my game, uncertain of what would happen from one day to the next, was a mirror of my relationship with my mother. That painful feeling of floating along waiting for the next slight, the next fight, was familiar. I knew how to do it; I was even good at it.

Soon after rehearsals started, I entered the dance studio to find Graham with Val, a Malibu Barbie type whom I didn't know that well, as she'd been in the other group. Luckily for her, she had been cast in the lead of *Our Betters* as a rapacious, man-eating socialite named Lady Pearl, who was carrying on behind her husband's back with Graham's character. Graham and Val were lying on mats next to each other with their faces turned toward each other. She was wearing a short skirt. He hardly noticed when I walked in; they appeared to be sharing some private joke. They were both laughing, she breathily, as I stood there, watching them "running lines." I turned and walked out.

Later, I made the mistake of telling him I was miffed.

"What the hell are you talking about?" he fumed.

"You were lying on the ground together!" I didn't point out that nowhere in the script does anyone lie on the floor.

"We were rehearsing, for Christ sakes."

"Do you enjoy all that giggling and gushing she does? Jesus, it's embarrassing."

"We were doing the scene!" He stomped off.

Afterward, I was sorry I'd said anything. We sort of patched it up later; he said he thought I'd overreacted and I said I was entitled to my feelings. I told him he could be cruel at times and he agreed. "I know I gave you a hard time. I'm sorry."

Part of me couldn't help but blame his attitude on his good looks—it was as if his whole life he'd been getting away with murder because he was handsome and charismatic, like a modern-day Hubbell Gardiner from *The Way We Were*. He was fucking Robert Redford, which made me the ugly duckling trying to hang on to him—like Barbra Streisand's character in the movie. I wasn't sure I was willing to stick it out as she had.

One evening a few days later, Graham borrowed my car, as his was in the shop. After he'd been gone for two and a half hours, I had this weird, sick feeling and walked straight to the Scotch N' Sirloin, a local bar where the actors in the company hung out. Maybe I'd inherited some of the clair-voyance my mother claimed, because parked right in front of the bar was my car with Graham and Val inside, in some sort of a clutch. He had his hands on her shoulders, and her face looked all dewy and drunk. I turned and started to walk away, feeling as if I were going to puke, but also gratified that the crazy radar in my head had been right. Graham must have turned to see me. I heard him getting out of the car and heard Val screech as he threw her out of my car onto the sidewalk. He chased after me.

"Wendy, I love you!" he shouted at my back.

Funny time to tell me, I thought. I kept walking

"Wendy, stop! It's you that I love!"

He caught up with me and grabbed my shoulders to turn me around to face him.

"Is that why you're in my car with another woman?" I yelled.

He clutched me to his chest. I could hardly breathe.

"I'm in love with *you!*" his voice boomed through his chest into my ears. I tried to pull away from him, but he was so much stronger than me. I used my fists to punch his back, hitting him as hard as I could.

"I don't understand," I screamed. I continued flailing at him and exhausted myself breaking away from him. I ran home through the alley.

Then, as if by magic, Val suddenly vanished. A rumor started circulating that Ethan had been having an affair with her. He slunk conveniently out of town and back to his wife and kids; she just disappeared. I sort of felt sorry for Val; it was hard to imagine what would happen to her now. With her beauty-contestant looks and her slatternly ways, she seemed headed for a career as a game-show hostess or a trophy wife. We never saw her again. As everyone huddled by the soda machine in the hallway and discussed Val's fate, I was annoyed that Graham seemed to be concerned for her. I returned all his belongings from my apartment by dumping them on his front porch, which felt really good. *What an asshole*, I thought.

The next day, Allen announced that I would be taking over the role of Lady Pearl. I was terrified—but I also knew I could do it and that it was my chance to show the faculty what I was capable of. Or so I hoped. My classmate Reenie was moved into my old ingenue role, and we started all over again. Lady Pearl was a delicious part; she was a complete reprobate, a conniving snob, and a gold digger. She reminded me of my mother, so it was easy to channel her. I wore vintage dresses to rehearsal and carried an elegant carved silver cigarette holder. The role came naturally, and for the first time since being at NTC, I felt I was filling my space. I was grounded and sure-footed.

Two days later, I walked into the building, pressed the elevator button to go up, and felt something was amiss. In an eerie quiet I walked down the hallway and into the rehearsal room. Ned was there, looking somber. I took a seat and waited in silence for everyone else to arrive. When we'd all sat down, Ned told us that Allen was in the hospital. He had always looked frail, but this was sudden. He had a rare blood disorder, had contracted pneumonia, and had some sort of wound on his ankle that wouldn't heal. I knew he wouldn't be coming back. Ned would be taking over the last ten days of rehearsal, in addition to his own project with the other half of the class.

We did the play. In my critique, a teacher (whom I loathed and whose voice class I skipped often because he told us to breathe through our assholes) said my performance was "professional" and he marveled why I had slacked off the year. I had high marks from everyone—many of them surprised I had the role in me. Still, I wasn't sure that pulling off a strong performance at the last minute would be enough to save my ass. Other people had worked a lot harder than I had.

The next few weeks were ruled by an electric anxiety you could practically taste as we all waited for the big showdown. Who would be chucked out, and who would make up the second-year class? When the day came, we were informed in alphabetical order. Everyone paced in the hall, waiting his or her turn to the guillotine. I went in to Karen's office to see Bonnie and Michael. They told me I wasn't being cut, but that I had just squeezed by. I started crying and got up to leave.

"I think that actors are the bravest people in the world," I sobbed, before joining the group downstairs in the lobby.

The hardest lot was reserved for the people toward the end of the alphabet—when Jen, whose last name began with a *W*, heard M.E. crying, she knew M.E. had been cut and she was getting the last remaining woman's slot.

I had made it. It was ugly, and maybe I'd been saved at the last minute by wowing everyone with my portrayal of the reprehensible Lady Pearl, but it felt good. I may not have been sure of who I was yet or where exactly I belonged, but I felt for once I'd played my hand well. I'd wanted a spot and I got it. For once I felt that I had set my own rules. Maybe home wasn't somewhere you found or were born into but something you made. And I had made this one—at least for now.

chapter nine

SLAVE TO LOVE

That summer, I packed up my apartment and moved into John and Jen's to house-sit. They would be gone for a large portion of the summer visiting family and taking a trip to Ireland. Oddly, Graham would be traveling with them to Europe in August. He seemed a rather unlikely traveling companion, and I didn't know how he could afford it, since he was always saying he was broke, but what did I know?

It had taken me about a month to wise up, but I broke up formally with Graham a month after school ended. After catching him with someone else, in my car, it seemed prudent to end it. I didn't feel that I could trust him. Despite his claim of having not really cheated on me that night, that it was me who he loved, Graham's attitude had hardened into an aloof and unkind dead calm. I wasn't his "physical type," and that's why it was so difficult for him to be warm toward me. In other words, I wasn't attractive enough to warrant his romantic attentions. Apparently, it was all my fault. Still, it was painful and made me miserable. After I ended it, he made a big deal about how we should be friends and that he didn't want me to think badly of him. It was as if all he cared about was that I didn't tell people the truth about what a dick he was.

Things were made a million times worse when none of the summer acting jobs I'd tried out for came through, and I was stuck with a gig at the theater selling season subscriptions over the phone, two cubicles away from the big dick. So I had to see him almost every day before he took off to meet up with John and Jen in Europe. I was cordial in the elevator, but I felt that he was always watching me from his cubicle. If Kafka had written a relationship guide, this would have been the breakup chapter.

Summer dragged on, and everybody left town except for me. I holed up at John and Jen's, listening to Bryan Ferry's new LP on cassette, *Boys and Girls*, playing "Slave to Love" over and over. And singing along to the lyrics: "Now spring is turning your face to mine, I can hear your laughter, I can see your smile."

Feeling wretched and alone, I chain-smoked, killed John and Jen's fish, and drank all of their booze. I invented the scotch-and-M&M's diet and lost so much weight my hip bones stuck out and my arms looked like string beans. I found a copy of *Inside Daisy Clover* and read it over and over, identifying with the main character, a trailer-trash urchin with a crazy mom who becomes a movie star, but all she

really wants is love. She makes the mistake of falling in l[ove]
with a devilishly handsome matinee idol, but it turns out [he's]
gay. I could relate to a lot in the story.

I took tryptophan to try to sleep at night, but usua[lly]
couldn't and ended up watching old movies on TV or VC[R]
tapes of screwball comedies starring Carole Lombard, Jam[es]
Stewart, Myrna Loy, and William Powell that I found i[n the]
bookcase. *Why can't life be like the movies?* I wondered, s[it]
ting in my borrowed, darkened living room.

At the end of the summer, driven crazy with boredo[m]
and forlorn at my solitary, too-thin state, I flew to New Yo[rk]
to see Jenny and Pete. They were busy with plans to mo[ve]
to Buffalo so Pete could go to medical school, but my o[ld]
room was waiting for me. I hung out there for a few week[s]
and helped them pack up their stuff, playing house aga[in.]
On one of my last days in the city, I was standing in line [at]
the stinky Red Apple grocery store, buying pasta for dinn[er]
and tampons for Jenny, when I grabbed a *People* magazin[e]
and started leafing through the lives of the rich and fabulou[s,]
many of whom—I felt sure—had never had to stoop to [a]
job in phone sales. On the last page, where they usually ha[ve]
little tidbits of juicy news, or the next go-to celebrity haird[o,]
was an article about a movie that Frank Sinatra was set t[o]
star in, which was being produced by his daughter Tina. [It]
was called *Somebody Turn Off the Wind Machine,* based on [a]
novel by Georgann Rea. I was thunderstruck. My mother['s]
book was a thinly fictionalized account of a trip Robin an[d]
I had made with her to Kansas City in 1974 to see our can[cer]

tankerous and frosty grandfather before he succumbed to cancer. So Frank Sinatra was playing my grandfather, and JoBeth Williams was attached to star as Samantha, the gorgeous, bilingual, brilliant mother of two, the character my mother had based on herself. I was perturbed at the casting choice of Sinatra—my grandfather was more like the grouchy guy Henry Fonda played in On Golden Pond—but JoBeth would totally work. After my initial shock at seeing my mother's name in print, and a kind of strange, almost jealous dip in my stomach, I laughed. She'd spent years writing that damn book on her typewriter while torturing my sister and me, and now she was in a national magazine? It was like a sick joke, but still a joke. She worshipped Old Blue Eyes and craved money and attention. It was so exquisitely my mother; she always landed on her feet. I left the People at the checkout.

Right before I was to go back to Denver to start my second year at NTC, Graham called me. I was surprised when he asked me to meet him. His voice sounded so different; lighter somehow and happy to talk to me.

"Wendy, I need a favor." He was in a pay phone about ten blocks away.

"How did you get my number?" Why was he calling?

"From John and Jen. So can you come?"

I knew I should say no. But I didn't. I couldn't help myself, like a little kid picking a scab. "Sure, I guess. What's up?"

"Well, I need to go shopping . . . for clothes." He laughed. "So I was hoping you'd help me pick stuff out."

He said he wanted me to meet him on Broadway and Eighty-sixth Street because he was staying at an aunt's house on the Upper East Side.

I met him about an hour later. He was standing on the street, wearing what he always wore—khaki pants, a striped button-down shirt, and worn gym shoes. His sleeves were rolled up, showing his tan arms. He was probably the only person who could go to Ireland and get a tan. He had a ragg wool sweater tied around his waist. I noticed that his clothes looked odd; they were ripped and stretched out, and his sweater had huge holes in it, as though he'd caught it on something sharp. His shirt was torn at both elbows.

I gave him a modest hug, then looked him up and down. "What's with the scarecrow routine?"

He told me that while he was in Ireland, he had saved a ten-year-old girl from drowning in the ocean. She was on a school trip when she fell through a blowhole in a cliff and down into the water below. Everyone stood there, watching her float out into the rough sea. Graham looked around, expecting someone from her group—an adult or a teacher—to jump in, but no one moved. He explained that many people in Ireland don't know how to swim. Watching the girl wailing with fear and being swept farther out from shore, John and Graham quickly discussed who was the stronger swimmer. Clearly it was Graham, who had grown up in California and was endowed with an almost supernatural outdoorsy zeal. So while John and Jen, the girl's teacher, and her classmates stood on the shore watching her flail about in the ice-cold water screaming for help, Graham took off his shoes and dived in to save her. When he reached her, she was as cold as a stone and had already given up, having gone down a few times. Graham grabbed her in a lifeguard hold. The waves crashed on the beach, threatening to toss them into the rocks if they got caught in the tide. Graham towed her to a small rock outcrop close to shore, and everyone started tying their clothing together, making a sort of wet, woolen towline to bring her back to shore. Graham became a local hero, made all the Irish newspapers, and would be receiving a citation and a medal from the mayor of the small town in Ireland from which the girl hailed.

Stunned and impressed, I walked him to Banana Republic—telling all the people in the store why he needed new clothes; that his had been ruined rescuing a girl lost in the sea in Ireland.

"He saved her life!" I exclaimed to the smiling saleswoman. I basically picked out his usual uniform—he was like the guy in *The Fly* in this regard—a few pairs of chinos, some oxfords, and a couple of sweaters. He put on some of his new duds; the rest were wrapped in tissue and put in shopping bags by the adoring cashier.

"What an amazing thing you did! You are a brave man." She beamed at him.

We walked out of the store, and he placed his old clothes in the garbage can on the corner of Broadway.

"Hey, you want to come over to my aunt's place? It has a killer view of the park."

"Okay."

We took a taxi across town to his aunt's; she was away someplace. The chichi building on Fifth Avenue had a uniformed doorman and shiny brass railings holding up a forest-green awning. I followed him through the apartment's vast foyer into the dining room, where a long, gleaming wooden table was surrounded by stately upholstered chairs. The rambling prewar flat had way too many rooms, all decked out in WASPy, Scalamandré fabrics, chinoiserie, crystal, and antiques. Where Nina's mom's apartment had been an au courant, brick-and-glass, 1970s, new-money pad, this was old money, ever so tastefully displayed above the elegant front yard that was Central Park. I was beginning to understand how a "broke" Graham could get to Europe for the summer.

He poured us each a large vodka, plopping ice cubes in from the bucket he had brought to the bar. The grown-up flat made me feel as if I were back in another time; the antiques, Persian rugs, and beautiful oil paintings reminded me of my childhood home at the Dakota. But I wasn't a child anymore. What the hell was going on? I had broken up with this man four months ago, suffered his cubicle surveillance; he was an asshole, and now I was in someone else's apartment, alone with him, with a giant tumbler of vodka in my hand in the afternoon.

I was guessing that all of this was some kind of passive bid to get me back. But you never knew—especially with him. It might just be a friendly shopping trip followed by a drink at his aunt's sumptuous pad. We talked about his trip, my horrible long summer. Then neither of us spoke for a moment. I walked over to the window to look out over the dusky light on Fifth Avenue and the trees beyond the low stone wall that encloses the park.

"You know, when you marched in like a Trojan and proceeded to break up with me, I didn't know if I should kill you or kiss you."

"I didn't know what else to do. You were so indifferent to me." I shrugged.

He wordlessly took my glass from my hand and put it down on a side table and led me back to his bedroom. We didn't talk. He pulled me down on top of him on the luxurious bedspread as it grew dark outside. We kissed, and I decided this probably didn't mean anything. It was just easy, familiar.

Seeing him again had made me miss him. But as we rolled around on the bed, rubbing against each other, I realized that despite what I thought or hoped—that saving the little girl had miraculously changed him into a different person—it hadn't. I was the one who was open and offering myself to him, getting never quite enough in return because that's all he had to give. It was the same old story played over again.

"I think we should stop." I got up and walked back into the dining room. He followed me, and we went back to our vodkas, looking out across the street at the trees trembling under the streetlights.

"I missed you," he said. "I thought about you a lot."

Really? I wasn't sure that he meant it, or if I could believe it. I had never felt beautiful with him—not once. He couldn't accept my love or return it; something in him was broken.

"Graham, I just don't think we can ever be happy together," I said to him in the dark room. "I can't help but think that we'd both be better off with other people."

As my words faded from the air, I heard the slight whistle of his glass hurtling toward my head and then shattering on the window behind me. Glass, ice cubes, and vodka sluiced on the floor at my feet. I calmly put down my drink and walked out of the apartment.

In the cab on the way home it hit me—the raggedy clothes he had worn to meet me. He wore the fucking torn, sea-stretched clothes from his gallant rescue over a week ago and thousands of miles away! As if he'd been wearing them all this time. As if they were the only clothes he owned and he needed help getting new ones. And I'd fallen for it. *How dumb am I?* I thought. Then I realized: not that dumb—the saleswomen at Banana Republic had been fawning all over him as well. The story of the rescue was true, but everything else was bullshit. Except for one undeniable fact: he had totally played me.

At the end of the summer, as we were all heading back to start our second year of conservatory, Allen, who'd been in the hospital for five months and hadn't been improving, passed away. Many people, including his wife, blamed the theater and its staff for his demise. He'd been working too hard, it was too much of a strain—not only had he been teaching acting, he was also directing main-stage productions, including a nearly four-hour production of *Hamlet*. They had worked him to death. Crazy rumors about the theater's having been built on a Native American burial ground started circulating among the students. All of the teachers whom Allen had brought with him refused to return, citing his harsh treatment at the hands of the administration. Ned would not be returning, either. Only Bonnie stayed—everyone else would be new.

With no one to lead the school and time running out, the administration pulled in a married couple from the American Conservatory Theater in San Francisco—combat teacher J. Steven White, who would be running the school for a year while a search was conducted for a new head, and the leading ingenue of ACT—Annette Bening, who'd now be in the company in Denver.

J. Steven was a swaggering macho guy who liked to quote Machiavelli and had a tendency toward malapropisms. He was short; perhaps this, combined with being married to the star actress in the company, made him overcompensate by being even more he-man in his behavior. On the first day, he made it clear that he thought we were all a bunch of babies, and—much worse—soft, out of shape. He was going to transform us into lean, mean acting machines by having us start aerobics. This was to make us strong, seriously buff, and would hopefully increase our lung capacity. And he was going to teach us all how to fight onstage. Toughen us up. Pussies can't do Shakespeare, right?

It was a one-eighty from our first year, where we lay on the floor a lot, softening our tongues and jaws, vocalizing, doing ballet, and delving into emotions and the senses in scene study and acting class. Soon we were all jumping up and down to bad synthesizer music, following the frenetic motions of a headbanded, Lycra-bound, relentlessly cheerful brunette whom J. Steven had brought all the way from California to teach us aerobics. She looked and behaved like a demented chipmunk, and just watching her ponytail whipping around her head made me dizzy. In our motley array of leg warmers, sweatpants, and ripped-up T's, we looked as if we'd escaped from an audition for *Flashdance*.

In combat class, we rolled around on mats, learning how to run into walls and pretend-punch and smack each other, then we moved on to fencing. I was horrible at all of this. I was terrified of hurting someone or, worse, losing a finger and therefore couldn't commit to it enough to be convincing. The strongest fighter and fencer in our class was Anna. Anna fought as if she were going to kill you; it was thrilling to watch. She kicked some serious ass in that class, and how cool was it that our best combat student was a woman?

We'd be doing three plays in class that year—a Shakespeare, a Chekhov, and a musical. Starting off with the Bard—J. Steven cobbled together parts of four plays in which the character of Queen Margaret appears—all three parts of *Henry VI* and bits of *Richard III*. He then divided Margaret's lines among the women and cast the men in the other roles. Because Anna was the best fighter, she got to play the twisted Richard—I was so jealous, but she was fierce in her black leather jacket and gloves, looking like a demonic punk tearing up the stage. I, of course, played the young, innocent version of the princess, before she becomes queen; the sweet English rose.

J. Steven came from the louder, faster, funnier school of directing. He would often tap on his watch while we were rehearsing, and say, "Get off, get off, get off, get off." By the time he'd finished speaking, you had best exited the stage. Stanislavski and Alexander were tossed out the window, to be replaced by Jack LaLanne and Speedy Gonzales. We ended up performing the play in the Denver Center's movie theater, running up and down the aisles, dodging pretend cannonballs. This all built up to what he called the "Hello, Dolly!" of sword fights. I did not lose my eyeballs, but there were a few close calls.

Next up was Anton Chekhov's *Three Sisters*, directed by our new acting teacher, Archie. Archie, who looked worn-out because he was directing us in the play in addition to re-hearsing at the theater, immersed us in the world of Chekhov. Why did people sit around talking in his plays? There was nothing else to do! No radio, television, and limited access to newspapers and mail. Talking was how everyone learned about what was happening in the village, politics, or the theater, and—in Chekhov—it's how they fall in love.

For J. Steven, the most important part of being in a Russian play was learning how to hold your vodka. Not only was he going to turn us into acting dynamos, he was going to teach us how to binge drink. The trick, he told us, was to have a little bite of something—fish, salted cucumber, or bread—in between each little glass. It was beginning to be a trend—getting blasted with our acting teachers.

So we had a "research" Russian party, and J. Steven supplied the vodka. Someone passed out with their head in a closet, I remembered dancing on the dining-room table (but not much else), and JB, who hosted the party along with Anna, fell off a wall while getting some air outside and landed in a snowbank, the vodka glass still in his hand.

Whether it was a talent for Chekov, or my ability to hold my liquor, I was enormously pleased when the casting went up for *Three Sisters*. I had been afraid of being, and expected to be, cast again in the younger-sister role, Irina, but instead I was cast as Natasha, a young woman who marries the sisters' beloved brother and turns into a shrew. I was excited to play the meaty part, someone mean, provincial, and a bit stupid. Once rehearsals started, though, I found that playing such a bitch made my stomach hurt. For years afterward if I played an unsympathetic character, knowing that the audience— or some of them anyway—disliked me, I always felt slightly queasy. Although the hisses and boos proved I was doing my job well, it also made me feel like my mother, with her keen taste for cruelty and her self-serving machinations at other people's expense.

J. Steven's wife, Annette, was often held up to us as a shining example of the consummate actor. She had what was coined at ACT "the thrilling voice," and her technique was flawless. Watching her, you could see everything coming together to give an ace performance, but despite her skill I found her rather cold—I preferred to see someone willing to take risks, someone warmer and more emotional who put himself or herself out there. We all thought she was about as sexy as a stick of gum, so imagine our surprise when she showed up a few years later, buck naked, playing a depraved con woman in a movie called *The Grifters*. I overheard one of the company actors say in a bar one night, "Well, J. Steven will be a good first husband for Annette." I guessed that was true; she went on to become Mrs. Warren Beatty.

Graham and I kept a civil distance from each other at school that year, and I went out with a lot of guys. Most of them were actors—I had yet to learn my lesson, and they were the only men I met. A tall, dark, and handsome leading man in the theater company courted me with chicken-fried-steak dinners, walks in the snow, gifts of books, and little trinkets such as feathers and seashells that he left in my mailbox. He was nine years older than me, and having sex with him was sort of like sleeping with an excited German shepherd. He would leap enthusiastically on top of me, his weight crushing my chest, and whip his head around while he climaxed, then emit this loud, self-satisfied sigh, as if he'd just won an Oscar for all his hard work. He was not wildly imaginative in the sack, but at least he was consistent. I felt like hot shit dating him and imagined our relationship increased my cachet in some way.

We had fun—he took me to the Ringling Brothers circus, and we partied on the train afterward with some clown friends of his. It was all lovely until a few weeks after he'd gotten me into bed. The German shepherd became elusive, making excuses not to see me. I spotted him one night in a restaurant with a woman from my school who was a year behind me, a young, dewy thing who looked sixteen. She wore his sweater to class the next day. Feeling frantic and cast aside, I went a little crazy, driving past his house repeatedly at night. I wasn't in love with him, I was just obsessed with the idea of his no longer wanting me. One evening, I threw a rock at his window to try to rouse him—the story was all over school the next day that I had hurled a brick through his window in a fit of rage. My mother had been a stalker; she had once even staked out her married lover's house, sleeping in her car in the driveway until the housekeeper came out to tell her he was out of town. Was this where I was heading? The deranged, jilted woman from *Play Misty for Me*? Luckily, the German shepherd left on a yearlong tour shortly after the rock incident and saved me from having to confront this question more squarely.

After he left, I began dating a guy in the class behind me whom I called Sweeney because every morning I woke up at his house, he'd put on the cast album of *Sweeney Todd*. Full blast. It didn't last long, though I did knit him a sweater and gave it to him before I broke up with him as a consolation prize.

Next came the flannel-clad, dour actor from the Pacific Northwest with acne-scarred skin and a chip on his shoulder about being short and having grown up poor. He had a rough-hewn charm, with his spartan flat, where everything was on the floor—the bed, the TV, his ashtray. He seemed to own nothing—he was like a monk whose religion was smoking cigarettes. At first, he bought me gifts—a copy of *The Joy of Cooking* and a beautiful vintage pin. Then, after telling me I was "oversexed" (because I liked to do it more than once a month and not only in the missionary position), he dumped me, claiming I was too needy.

I hadn't set out to be the school siren, but by the end of my second year at NTC I'd slept with over twice as many men as in all my previous years of dating combined. I didn't know if I had changed—become bolder as a person and an actor—or if I simply had more opportunity. I'd had my heart stomped on or twisted and torn, but most often I'd cut and run before that could happen. I didn't know what I'd learned or garnered in these entanglements. I was just as devastated by Mr. Flannel's cruel assessment of me as I had been by Oedipus's casual dismissal of my pregnancy. Blindsided by Ned and wising up just in time with Graham, I didn't feel any closer to knowing what I wanted or needed in a relationship or what love meant. Perhaps, I reasoned, my mother's crazy love life wasn't all the ravings of a psychotic seductress—maybe some of it was just the desperation that comes with wanting love but not finding it. Whatever the answer was, it seemed that Boston's J. Geils Band had one thing right—love stinks.

chapter ten

CRIMES OF THE HEART

I was determined not to spend another lonely, deathly dull summer in cow town. Luckily, I was offered a summer gig at a small theater in Westerly, Rhode Island, doing the Beth Henley play *Crimes of the Heart*. My married NTC class-mates John and Jen would be in the cast also, along with two other actresses being brought in from New York. The pay was small, but I jumped at the chance. I could be close to Manhattan, my sister in Boston, and friends—and I'd get to spend some time in a pretty New England coastal town. I gave up my apartment in Denver, put my junk in storage, and flew to New York to hang out at Ninety-seventh Street before rehearsals started.

Jenny and Pete were living in Buffalo these days, where Pete was doing his residency. But Jenny's brother Dave took up residence in the apartment on Ninety-seventh Street with his girlfriend, a flame-haired, zaftig, brainy beauty named Della, as well as a friend of Jenny's from Barnard, Martha, leaving my old room available. I thought of Jenny as another sister and Dave, whom I'd known since he was fifteen, as a brother. So even though I'd only lived at Ninety-seventh Street for maybe twelve months if you added all the stays together, I felt that I was home for the summer like any other kid from school.

Dave had graduated from the French Culinary Institute and was working for a hot young chef named David Bouley at the new restaurant-of-the-moment, Montrachet. There, Dave was the *poissonnier*, or fish chef, but was taking the summer off, with Bouley's blessing, to hone his skills apprenticing at Roger Vergé's famous restaurant on the Côte d'Azur, Moulin de Mougins. So Della was throwing Dave a going-away party, a big one—the kind of party you have in your twenties where you tell everyone to tell everyone and before you know it, your nine-hundred-square-foot apartment has three thousand square feet of people in it, most of whom you've never met.

The front doorbell of the building rang so often, we just left the door propped open. The fridge was packed with Budweiser, and industrial quantities of gin and tonics fizzed in pitchers and vases in the kitchen. Everyone was hot and sweaty, and Django Reinhardt, Charlie Christian, and Fats Waller records on the stereo helped with the sway.

It was a marvelous party, every room packed to the rafters. The only thing missing to make it perfect were Jenny and Pete. Then, at midnight, a strange couple arrived with a noisy fanfare, the woman sort of braying and tossing her hair, and the man executing bizarre kung-fu moves. In their early twenties they were decked out in tight, cheap clothes. Her purple hair fell sloppily around her pasty face, her eyes were done raccoon-style with a ton of kohl, and her red lipstick was smeared across her cheek as if they'd just had furious sex in the elevator on the way up. He was wearing black spandex pants, which left little to the imagination, no shirt, and a limp, gold vest like a reject from the slutty Ice Capades with ratty white Nikes instead of skates. He was shorter than she was and had jaw-length, feathered, dirty-blond hair that hung stringily from his head. They both smelled as if they hadn't bathed in a month, opting instead to walk through the mistings of department-store perfume sprayers or to rub under their arms with those little tree-shaped air fresheners that hang from cabbies' rearview mirrors. Almost immediately, the odd couple ran in to Dave and Della's bedroom and began jumping on the bed. We crowded in after them to watch. The girl wasn't wearing anything beneath her tight pleather skirt, which flew up, revealing her dimply white thighs and that the furry patch between her legs had been dyed to match her hair. The guy started licking her face—it was like a bad Coney Island act or a scene from a John Waters movie. Who were they? What were they doing here?

"Thank God, the drugs have arrived!" someone shouted over my shoulder.

Cheers erupted throughout, and suddenly a crush of

people pressed into the room behind us. I found myself wedged in between or—given their height—under an old friend of Pete's, Jay, a sort of dark hippie with a demonic surfeit of facial hair, and a black guy named Dwon in leopard-print pants and no shirt who worked either at the John Jay College of Criminal Justice or a hair salon, I was never sure.

Our pushers started dispensing little white pills. Apparently, a friend of Martha's, an aspiring lawyer, had arranged for sixty hits of ecstasy for Dave's bon voyage. I stood in a mass of people all holding out their hands like beggars or congregants at a bizarre communion rail. The first sixty of us got a hit, and the stragglers were out of luck.

Their work done, the spandex twins cavorted out the door with a couple of beers to go, never to be seen again.

I had never taken ecstasy—not yet illegal, it was being used at that time mostly by therapists trying to unlock their patients' inhibitions, so it was considered a "truth" drug. I was a little afraid, turning the small tablet over in my hand. I hadn't experimented with that many drugs but, *Oh, fuck it*, I thought, and swallowed it down. A bunch of us sat on the dining-room floor, waiting for it to take effect.

Slowly at first, then suddenly, the ecstasy hit us each like a wave. People got up and ran around the room, then we were holding on to each other, then laughing our asses off. Someone came running in from the bathroom with a fistful of toothbrushes.

"Try brushing your teeth! It's incredible!"

Even doing something as mundane as teeth cleaning became a wild sensory experience. You could feel the bristles massaging the inside of your mouth, like those huge soapy brushes in the car wash—but it was in your mouth and tasted better. Other things tasted weird: beer, orange juice, gin. Suddenly water was the most wonderful beverage in the world. The more mundane, the more ordinary the experience or substance, the better it felt under the drug's influence. Kissing was better than having sex. Strangers started petting each other, stroking each other's faces as the party spilled out of the apartment and up the stairs to the roof. People stood transfixed by the dark, undulating surface of the Hudson River and the glancing slivers of silver light from cars driving on the West Side Highway and across the river in New Jersey. Guys were driving golf balls off the roof into Riverside Park, and the rest of us hugged and declared our love for one another, recounting first meetings rapturously. To the sober or merely drunk person, I can only imagine that it looked like a party of overgrown preschoolers experiencing the world and each other for the first time. For us, it was a lovefest.

At one point, Dave came over to me and said, "See that guy over there?" He pointed to a skinny young man on the far side of the party with blond hair combed back against his head, making his nose look even bigger than it was, as if he were flaunting it or something. He was dressed in a white shirt, white trousers, and black espadrilles, leaning against a wall, smoking a Marlboro Red. His name was David, and he was a friend of Della's, a boyfriend of one of her roommates from Smith, who was in town visiting from Philly.

"Yeah." I nodded. I'd always had a thing for guys with big noses—Gabriel Byrne, Pete Townshend, the actor who played him in the *Quadrophenia* movie, Phil Daniels.

"Why don't you go over there and be nice to him. His girlfriend just dumped him."

"Sure. Okay."

I navigated the crowded room and asked him for a cigarette. And that was it.

We spent the rest of the night and into the morning talking as the ecstasy surged through our brains: on the couch, on the stairs, on a blanket on the roof watching the stars; at one point, every other room being packed with people, we sat on the edge of the bathtub for a good thirty minutes just talking. He was from Philadelphia, but his parents now lived in Ohio. He'd gone to Penn and was helping to run a catering company a friend had started as a student; he'd lived in London. I can't remember what I told him about myself. Somehow, it wasn't what we said that was important, it was just . . . the connection we seemed to have, something spoken through our eyes maybe, or the supersensitive touch of our fingers. Maybe it was the drugs.

Dawn found us in each other's arms dancing slowly across the chipped parquet floor of the dining room while Django Reinhardt played Kurt Weill's "September Song." Half-naked partygoers stumbled out of bedrooms or down from the roof. A bearded imp of a man wearing only a sheet sat on the couch playing a guitar with only one string he'd found in one of the closets. Dwon, the criminal-justice scholar or hairdresser, walked out of the kitchen with a white dress shirt on but his trousers gone—replaced by a pair of leopard bikini underwear. David and I walked to the bodega down the street for cigarettes and on our way back found Dave and four other guys sitting on the front stoop in 1960s prom dresses, also from one of the apartment's magical closets, drinking beers and smoking while Della photographed them. We kissed everyone good morning, went upstairs to my tiny room, and fell asleep for a few hours, clutched together in my single bed.

That afternoon, we had our first date. David said he had enough money for some mediocre food or two exceptional cocktails, so we walked from Ninety-seventh Street all the way down to One Fifth Avenue and its eponymous bar, One Fifth, just up from Washington Square Park in the Village. I hadn't been back to this part of town since I'd been a miserable film student at NYU. That Wendy felt like another person from another planet. David and I pushed open the doors and entered a hallway with gleaming-white tile walls, teak paneling, brass portholes, and other nautical trim salvaged from an ocean liner. The first room on the left held a white-marble bar backed by mirrors facing the large windows that looked out onto the street. Pressed against the far wall, between an assortment of potted palms, a jazz trio—piano, bass, and electric guitar—played to a smattering of early customers. We got a table. Having talked all night and as we'd walked halfway down the island of Manhattan, now we just sat and listened to the music and smoked. It was easy. Right. Just as we took the first sip of two very nice martinis, the band started playing "The Girl from Ipanema"—one of the iconic songs of my childhood I'd fallen asleep to while my mother entertained in the living room of our Park Avenue apartment. I associated the song with the clinking of ice in crystal, and the laughter of grown-ups, the glamour of my mother's youth and a New York that was long gone.

David took my hand. "Would you like to dance?"

I looked around. No one was dancing. There was no dance floor or even space for it.

"Come on. You obviously love the song."

We got up and glided through the other tables to the grand piano, and then we danced in its hollow. It seemed, just as it had the night before, that when we were together, there were only the two of us. I had never before felt such a pull toward another human being—an almost gravitational force that told me we belonged together. We finished our dance and our martinis and walked ninety blocks back home singing every song from Roxy Music's album *Avalon*. When we got back to the apartment, we went straight to my room and ripped each other's clothes off, laughing as we got naked and rolled onto the bed. We made love with our eyes open, mouths devouring each other's body—sweet and tender one moment, fiery wrestling the next. Afterward we lay in each other's arms, listening to our hearts beating.

The following weekend I took the train down to Philly to visit him. He didn't have a car, so he picked me up at 30th Street Station in a big white van that belonged to his boss at the catering company. Our first stop was DiLullo Centro, a spectacular bar and restaurant in Center City, to meet his friend Merritt, who worked for Bonwit Teller, and her mom, Alison, who ran Saks in Philadelphia. We drank Prosecco and ordered fried calamari, which—I didn't want to say for fear of appearing like a rube—I had never had. I vaguely remembered having octopus sometime during my childhood, at a restaurant in Harlem where my mother, during her Radical Chic phase in her sheath dress and circle pin, had met with the Young Lords, a Puerto Rican street gang turned militant civil rights group who were squatting in a church nearby. Mother's meeting with the gang didn't produce anything more than a good cocktail-party story, and the octopus came right back up in the taxi on the way home.

Unaware that calamari and octopus are in the same family, I daintily selected a piece and ate it up. Back in the borrowed van about ten minutes after we'd left the bar, I turned to David. "I know we don't know each other that well, but I'm about to be violently ill."

I frantically crank-rolled the window down and barfed my brains out. Vomit flew across the expressway as people stared at the girl in the nice black dress, hanging out of the van window throwing up like mad. Tears stung my eyes, and puke streaked the side of the van below my gushing mouth.

"Oh my God, are you okay? Should we go to the hospital?" He kept glancing over at me while dodging fifty-mile-an-hour traffic.

My stomach finally empty, I pulled my head back inside the van and nodded and shook my head awkwardly at him, adding that I'd be fine. Wary of the drive he'd planned out to a trendy riverside neighborhood called Manayunk, he decided to take me to a place he knew in Chinatown called Joe's Peking Duck for some wonton soup and Coca-Colas. "It's medicinal," he said.

On our way home to his place in West Philadelphia after our therapeutic Chinese food, we drove up South Street, a strip of cheap clothing stores, bars, and cheesesteak places—Philly's own little Greenwich Village. This muggy summer a garbage strike was on, but the van didn't have air-conditioning, so we rode with the windows down. Stopped in South Street traffic, we heard a saxophone. I looked over and saw the door to a dive bar called Bob and Barbara's Bonfire was open, and way in the back, an African American man in a white suit wailed away on an alto sax—sending its fluttering rasp out into the hot night. We exchanged a quick look, and David drove the van up onto a heaping pile of trash, covered the boom box—the radio was broken—with some newspapers, and we headed over to Bob and Barbara's.

It was dark and crowded inside. A cigarette machine selling Pall Malls, Kools, Salems, and Philip Morris Commanders was just inside the door, next to a long, dark-wood bar with a white Formica top that ran along the left side of the room until it bent back on itself at the opposite end forming a *J*. Small tables lined the opposite wall, creating a narrow path into the long room. The tables held black, molded ashtrays and candles in teardrop-shaped holders encased in plastic netting. A muted kung-fu movie played on a TV mounted on the wall over the bar. The band that had lured us in played at the end of the room against a fake-wood-paneled wall, where the light from a potato-chip machine cast an eerie glow on the drummer. In addition to the drummer and the saxophonist, an older African American woman played the organ with a tall glass beside her music stand. She was wearing a lilac-colored pantsuit and reading glasses on a gold chain around her neck.

We were halfway down the bar when David and I realized that we were the only white people in the place. David was wearing a seersucker jacket and white bucks, making him seem even whiter than he was already. As we moved along the bar, the bartender moved in the opposite direction. We stopped and tried to order a drink. The bartender ignored us, turning away. I started to feel a bit nervous, and after a full five minutes of waiting for the bartender to turn around and acknowledge us, I suggested that we leave and find another place.

David shook his head. "Listen to that sax, Wendy!"

He lit a Marlboro, placed it in one of the slots in the dirty ashtray on the bar, and planted himself on a stool. I sat down next to him. Another five minutes went by, and although the sax was amazing, I still felt uneasy at our lack of a welcome.

"C'mon, David, I don't think he's gonna serve us." I tugged on his sleeve to go.

"Sure he will." David smoked and watched the organist riff on a passage of "Green Dolphin Street."

Just as the song and the set ended, a tall black man wearing a powder-blue suit and a cowboy hat came in through the back of the bar. He talked to a few people as he made his way along the bend in the bar opposite us—clearly he was a regular. Just as he was about to sit, he noticed David and me and stopped talking. I was certain something bad was about to happen.

"Bill!" he shouted across the bar. "It's my man Bill!" he said to the people around him, gesturing at David as if he were an old friend. "Hey, how ya doin'?"

David nodded. "Good, good!" For a moment, even I thought maybe they knew each other. Then David shot me a wide-eyed look of wonder, and I knew that the guy was doing us a favor.

"How was church? I missed it myself," the man said, adding to the people next to him, "He's from the church."

David played along, saying that church was good, and then the man flagged down the bartender. "Reggie, get my man a drink! This is my man Bill. And who's your lovely lady?"

David introduced me and then the bartender came down, took our order—"Two bourbons on the rocks, thanks"—and guided us to seats at the bar around the bend near our savior. With that one vote of confidence, it was as if we were regulars—fellow patrons began talking to us, and we were even invited to the funeral of a local jazz musician that Thursday. The guy sitting on the other side of us was the sax player's brother and a trumpeter himself. My apprehension faded into relief and happiness; I looked at David and it seemed as if we were under a magic spell.

"Let's hear it for Miss Goldie Hill on the Hammond organ!" Everyone clapped as Miss Goldie walked daintily up to the bar for a refill of her giant drink.

"Chivas, no ice," she cooed to Reggie.

A man wearing a backpack came wandering in. The sax player's brother let out a small whistle under his breath. The man with the backpack was a well-known jazz singer and, according to our friend, was here to steal his brother's thunder: "And my stupid brother's just gonna let him." The trumpeter got up and shook hands with the singer when he came around, and then the trumpeter stepped up to do a number with the group.

The singer sat down next to us at the bar and started talking animatedly about Miles Davis and jazz phrasing and the importance of integrity. After a few minutes, just as the trumpeter had predicted, the sax player made a big show of introducing the jazz singer and calling him up to perform. Neutral in the wars of the local jazz scene, we were able to just sit back and enjoy it.

The singer paused after his second song and announced,

"This is for that young couple at the bar, the two who look so very much in love." He sang "My Funny Valentine" to us, transposing the words to fit the moment. "Don't change your hair for him, not if you care for him . . ."

We had to get up and dance on the stained red carpet next to the band, since they were playing a song for and, it seemed, about us. Trying to avoid a crater underneath the rug near the potato-chip machine, we stared into each other's eyes and again were alone in a crowd. It was like a dream or a fairy tale; each day was Valentine's Day. I knew suddenly something I'd suspected since we first met: David was the one.

After a magical weekend in Philadelphia, I headed to Rhode Island to start rehearsals for *Crimes of the Heart*. David and I promised to figure out ways to see each other, and we wrote letters and talked on the phone, cords stretched across our respective kitchens, to stay in touch.

Robin took the train down from Boston for opening night. We went to this funky hotel on the beach for drinks after the show and sat on the wraparound porch looking at the ocean. She'd dropped out of school again, but had made a short film about the fans of Elvis Presley, called *Elvis: I Love You Because*, which she'd shot at Graceland the year before. Now her film was making the circuit—it had been shown at various festivals and had even won an award. I was happy to see her doing something she felt passionate about and was proud of her achievement.

"What about you?" she asked as she sipped her Rolling Rock.

"Well, I met someone."

"Where did you meet him? Does he have a name?"

"I met him at an ecstasy party in New York. We stayed up all night and then walked like a hundred blocks down to the Village. It was magical, he's so romantic, like a character out of a novel. His name is David, and we are crazy in love."

She eyed me skeptically.

"I honestly think this is it, you know? I feel like we're going to get married," I gushed.

"O . . . kay. That's a little weird. I mean you just met this guy, and let's not forget you were on drugs at the time."

I laughed. "It's not like that. I wish you could meet him."

She smiled and looked at me as if I were crazy. "All right, whatever. Maybe I will someday."

The show only ran Thursday through Sunday, so I had a few days off and drove up to see David and meet his whole family at a cabin on a lake in the Adirondacks. We were in separate rooms with thin walls and creaky beds, so intimacy was sort of impossible. His mother and father were kind, and, well . . . parental. They were certainly quite unlike my family—my rageful mother or even my dad and stepmom, who were more like a fun couple you'd meet at a cocktail party than parents. David's mother cooked and quilted, and his dad sat on the screened-in porch read-ing and smoking a pipe. His sister and brother were both younger, fresh faced, and uncomplicated—secure in their parents' love and support. No dark shadows collected in these corners. It made me love David more, seeing this

I limped back to Denver for my final year of school. My last year at the NTC would be an apprenticeship in the company with a small stipend to live on. Some people in our class were lucky enough to get decent-sized parts; the others were in crowd scenes, the chorus, or assigned as understudies.

In my first role of the season, I was a dancing and singing Nurse #3 in *South Pacific*, the Rodgers and Hammerstein musical based on James Michener's book *Tales of the South Pacific*. Learning dance routines had never been my forte, which became clear during rehearsals with the celebrated African American choreographer Donald McKayle, who had worked with greats such as Alvin Ailey and Martha Graham among others, and whose work had appeared in films, on television, and on Broadway. The dance studio had oxygen tanks, in case someone overdid it and passed out from the altitude, which was easy to do. I hoofed around and sang, pushing hospital equipment with the other nurses, washing that man right out of our hair, struggling to hit my marks and keep in time with the other actresses in the scene. I'm sure it showed that I was playing keep up; Donald took me aside the first day and said that I shouldn't worry.

"Wendy, when I'm done with you, I'll have you dancing like a flea on a griddle!" he cackled.

He was kind and patient, and eventually—I got it. When we got into technical rehearsals, however, the director of the show, Donovan Marley—who had made the dire announcement about our class being cleaved in twain two years previously—put glasses on me and stuck me in the back row. I didn't care.

It was an over-the-top production—Dino De Laurentiis meets World War II, with onstage explosions and towering stacks of oil barrels careening around the stage during set changes. Actors falling off or being hit by scenery or large wooden crates being tossed around resulted in many trips to the ER. The theater began to gain a reputation for not putting safety first.

In the second production, I played one of four muck-covered, barefoot Irish village girls in *Playboy of the Western World*. I only had four lines, but the play was a gas nevertheless because my dad played the Playboy's father. When I cut the bottom of my foot open on a nail dancing onstage one night and was whisked away to the hospital, the stage manager made it clear he expected me to return to the show the next day and presumably do the Irish jig with stitches in my foot. My father came to my defense, and I was given a few days off to recover. I knew my understudy, Paula—one of my classmates who'd gotten shafted in her casting for the season—was dying to go on for me.

Daddy's and my last time onstage together in *Dear Ruth* had been a peak experience for me and a lovefest for both of us. I adored my dad, but in the last few years I had started to feel angry and disappointed in him. Having grown up without my father, I had created an idealized version of him, a myth as wonderful and inaccessible as any. After reuniting and spending some time with him off the pedestal, I began to see that my dad was ordinary, with foibles and faults. This kind of revelation hits most people as teens trying to rebel and push away from their parents. But I had spent my teenage years dreaming of being closer to my father, so it felt as if all of the natural father/daughter dynamics were compressed into a much shorter time. He was vague and forgetful; he drank too much and sent me flowers on my birthday, but only at the last minute, after I'd become convinced he'd forgotten. It seemed to me that he only paid attention when I was standing right in front of him.

My friend, Patricia, who was my stepmother's administrative assistant at the theater, recommended a shrink named Marcus Pass. Patricia had become a fast friend to me; a blond Mia Farrow look-alike, nine years my senior, she'd become a single mom at nineteen, raising her son in a tiny town in the mountains. She also worked as a freelance photographer, and I sometimes worked for her, lugging her equipment to shoots or labeling slides. Once when I had confided to her that I was afraid I might be pregnant (a false alarm), I told her that maybe I had an unconscious desire to have a baby.

"Wend"—she'd looked at me wryly, tapping her cigarette on the brim of her ashtray—"you don't have an unconscious desire to have a baby. You have an unconscious desire to *be* a baby."

She gave me Marcus Pass's number and said, "You have to stop putting your ego on the line every time, babe. Men are like streetcars—there'll be another one along in a minute."

A large man in his early fifties stuffed into a rumpled,

blue pin-striped suit that barely contained his girth, Marcus Pass had a head of unwieldy, moppy brown hair that he often brushed out of his eyes with a plump, stubby-fingered hand. He had a wacky, confrontational therapy style. We met in his office, but also in cafés, hotel lobbies, on park benches, and sometimes even in his car while he drove around doing errands. When I first told him about my mother, he picked up the phone on the low side table next to the sofa we were sitting on and suggested we call her.

"What's her number?" He looked over at me questioningly.

"No!" I screeched.

"Until you can do that, pick up the phone and talk to her, you're not free. You must resolve this."

He put the phone down and fiddled with his soup-stained tie, smoothing it over his enormous belly. "We all have our demons," he sighed. "This is mine." He patted his sizable tummy.

During my dad's time in Denver, I decided to ask him to go to see Marcus with me. To my surprise, he said yes right away. During our session, I talked about the dichotomy of my emotions toward my father: my deep love for him, the ways in which we seemed similar and shared a special kinship, but also about the darker side, my anger over what I perceived as being abandoned by him and his lack of engagement that left me feeling as if I was doing all the heavy lifting. Daddy listened patiently, nodding and basically agreeing with everything I said.

"You have every reason to be pissed off, sweetheart." He sort of winced and smiled simultaneously. "But I love you very much, and I always will."

At my next session with Marcus, held over lunch in a Mexican restaurant, he asked me how I thought it had gone with my dad. I told Marcus it had felt good to air some of my feelings, but it didn't look as if anything was going to change.

"It won't. But you can. Your father is a kind and gentle man who loves you. But it's not about him, it's about you. You need to accept what happened, realize that he is a limited person, and get what you need from him."

"How do I do that?"

"By understanding that he did what he could. You know, the pain you went through in the past will always be there. But, over time, it will become smaller and more manageable."

"Promise?"

"Yup. How about dessert? Churro?"

My best role in Denver that year was saved for the last slot in March. I had done a staged reading of Molly Newman's play *Shooting Stars* the year before. Set in the South in the 1950s, the play was about a women's trick basketball team on tour with their coach, a nasty, manipulative guy who ends up croaking onstage. The team then gets a chance to play "real" ball, and the ending shows them all bounding offstage to presumably pound the men's team into the ground. I had gotten a terrific response performing the role of Tammy, the team's none-too-bright mascot. She loved fruitcake and her little brother, Bubba, and would tear up at the mention of her dear dead dachshund. I was fairly sure they would use me in the premiere production of the play—it was the main reason I'd chosen to return for my last year. Without that plum role, I would most likely have stayed in Manhattan and started looking for work. Two of my other classmates, Leslie and Anna, were in the cast, playing other girls on the team, and my acting teacher, Archie, played our coach, the evil Cassius—whom I got to discover onstage dead on the toilet dressed in a Santa suit. The play got strong notices in the local press that singled out my classmates and me for our performances. I even got a terrific mention in *Variety*.

Didi, my lost-then-found stepsister, flew out from New York to see the show, as she had promised she would the summer before. She took me to breakfast the next morning at the Brown Palace, one of the fanciest and oldest hotels in the city, a sandstone-and-red-granite behemoth built in 1892 with an atrium in the center. It reeked of old-frontier charm with its afternoon teas and debutante balls.

"So, have you thought about what you're going to do now?" Didi sipped her mimosa and pushed her Denver omelet around on her plate. I was busy devouring my Monte Cristo sandwich—a sort of fried *croque-monsieur* served with jelly.

I took a pause before answering. "I thought about going and checking out Seattle. They have a big theater scene there."

Didi eyed me somewhat dubiously. "Do you actually know anyone there?"

"Um, no."

"Have you had any offers from agents? That *Variety* review was fantastic."

I told her I'd heard from two agents in New York, neither of whom had seen the show but had called the theater offering to represent me.

"Well, you are an exceptional actress, Wendy, and if you want to move back to Manhattan . . . I'll help you get started."

"Wow, that's amazing. Thanks, Didi."

"Of course, it also helps that you have training and look about fifteen. Both big commodities in New York right now. Do you have any money?"

"Not really, a bit left to me by my grandfather. Maybe a couple thousand dollars."

"That's too bad; every actress should have a trust fund." She laughed throatily. "We'll get you some work. Don't worry."

She picked up the check. I wondered if she was just being nice; maybe she felt sorry for me being my mother's daughter—a woman she'd always despised. I drove her to the airport and said I'd be heading back to the city toward the end of the summer.

"Call me when you're settled, Gwendolyn." She had taken to calling me this recently. I nodded and hugged her good-bye at the gate. I knew she would look out for me— for whatever reason. She was tough, loyal, and brash—good qualities in an agent. And in a friend.

chapter eleven

THE UNSINKABLE
WENDY LAWLESS

Jenny and Pete were getting married.

Their wedding was to be in Cornwall, Connecticut, a beautiful, largely unspoiled, and empty corner of Litchfield County. A low-key location at the time, in ten years it would be overrun by celebrities and famous newsmen. Jenny had lived there on and off throughout her childhood, and her grandparents Bill and Buela had a house there where we all stayed when we visited. An old, low-ceilinged house built into a hillside in the 1700s, it was crammed with large antiques and dusty brocade sofas. I usually slept on the top one of the three floors. If I wasn't lucky enough to snag a room, a bed on the landing was usually empty, wedged Hobbit-like under the stairs to the attic. The house was surrounded by Buela's gorgeous rambling garden. She was especially proud of her lilac bushes, which she liked to say were so tall and beautiful because she made Bill piss on them from an up-stairs window after parties.

The service would be at the white clapboard church in town, with the reception—a large dinner dance—held afterward in a nearby barn belonging to old family friends. Even though Jenny was a staunch feminist atheist, a church wedding went with the long white lace dress and picture hat she had chosen to wear. She'd spent months with Martha Stewart's newly published *Weddings* book under her arm—obsessing over flower arrangements and silverware patterns, fussing over every detail, determined to have a perfect day. It was as if, quite suddenly, she'd become a grown-up, taking on all the concerns that grown-ups in the movies had. I'd thought that none of these conventions were supposed to matter anymore, but suddenly, it seemed they did. And even though I was thrilled for her, I felt I was losing a race I hadn't even known I was running.

The guests—over two hundred of them—started pouring in. Pete arrived with his family, a swarm of Homers: his mom, brothers, sisters, respective girl and boy friends, uncles, aunts, and cousins. Jenny was to be walked down the aisle by both her parents, John and Phyllis, who were divorced but appeared to have an amicable relationship, which seemed modern and civilized to me, as well as completely unlike my mother's slash-and-burn style of breakup and divorce. The only place I could see my parents coming together was at a crime scene in which one of them, probably my dad, would be dead.

I was to be a bridesmaid, as Jenny had promised her best friend in fourth grade that they would be each other's maid of honor. Having lived my younger life moving around, leaving many chums behind, this kind of pledge and long-lived friendship seemed inconceivable—even alien—to me. Friends, to me, were the people who were there for you in the moment, so I was a bit hurt by this interloper from Jenny's past. I decided to approach *bridesmaid* as a role; I wasn't the lead, or the "best friend," but at least I was in the chorus.

The morning of the wedding, the bridesmaids all dressed in an upstairs bedroom at Buela's house. I had bought a pair of grayish-cream-colored pumps to wear, as instructed by Jenny, and had worried that they weren't the right shade, but luckily I passed inspection. I pulled on my tea-length, long-sleeved, minty-green-and-pink floral Laura Ashley number. Checking myself out in the mirror on the door, I thought I looked a bit like a chintz-covered armchair and wondered whether—if I stuck around after the wedding was over—I could live there at Buela's, pretending to be an ottoman.

We arrived at the church all together; it was a hellishly hot day, and as I was almost completely covered in fabric, I began to broil. Standing outside the church before the walk down the aisle and feeling faint from the heat, I had to sit down on the church steps with my head between my legs. Somebody brought me a lukewarm Sprite to sip on, and I started to feel good and sorry for myself. I wasn't getting married, I didn't have a boyfriend, and I had unceremoniously been dumped by the man I'd believed to be "the one."

Jenny's wedding was all about me, the single bridesmaid, right?

This was only the second wedding I'd ever been to, the first being my mother's marriage to Pop in the Dakota when I was seven. I had coughed all through that ceremony, which ended up being a bad omen, since the marriage only lasted eighteen months. I didn't cough this time, but I did tear up listening to Jenny and Pete take their vows. Amazing, I thought, that these two people, whom I loved so much, had found each other and wanted to be together forever. How could they be so sure? Would I ever meet a guy I didn't have doubts over? I was twenty-seven—where was my Pete?

The rings on, Jenny and Pete kissed, and they turned to greet us for the first time as a married couple. We all clapped and cheered as organ music swelled, and we followed them up the aisle and out of the church. Looking at the backs of their heads, as they squeezed hands, smiled, and whispered to each other, I felt a curious mixture of both joyous euphoria and a pain like having an arm cut off at the elbow. My best friend was moving on, and I was happy for her and happy to see them so happy, but I also felt I was losing them and was lost myself.

I decided to handle my mixed feelings as maturely as possible and drink heavily at the reception. Luckily, two different men obliged by chatting me up—one of them I knew from visits to Cornwall. His parents owned the barn and the old farmhouse across from it in addition to a palatial penthouse apartment on the Upper West Side I'd visited a few times. It was the kind of flat where the elevator opened into the foyer, and the buttery-wood floors led to a terrace that ran along the entire side of the apartment. The other potential suitor was the older brother of a girl I'd gone to Town School with in New York in the late sixties; I'd gone to his sister's eighth birthday party in their cavernous apartment on York Avenue, where they screened a sixteen-millimeter print of *A Dog of Flanders* and we played musical chairs and pin the tail on the donkey.

Both nice-looking, smart, and from privileged families, they were your basic preppy-prince types. I decided to send them both to the bar to get me a drink. The first one back got me. I would have denied it had anyone pointed it out, but I was behaving exactly like my mother, who always played multiple boyfriends against each other. Of course Mother was an expert, exacting trips, jewelry, and cars from her champions. At Jenny's reception, I was just a drunk amateur feeling sorry for myself. The brother of my childhood classmate never returned from the bar. I told myself that he was clearly frightened of my raw vagina power, but at the time he probably guessed at my little contest offering myself as the door prize. So the other one, Zander, the inheritor of all this prime real estate, won by forfeit.

We danced our asses off to the deejay until ten thirty, when it started to pour rain. We were bopping around to Springsteen's "Dancing in the Dark" when suddenly the electricity cut out, and we were all plunged into darkness. After some squeals of laughter, people lit candles, and someone started singing "Amazing Grace." Zander took my hand, and we ran into the dark garden on a slope below the barn. While we pushed our tongues into each other's mouth, I used the hand not around his neck to remove my panties and toss them into the bushes like a dueling glove. Laughing, we dashed to his house across the way, climbing the stairs up to an empty room in the attic with wall-to-wall carpeting and no furniture. We were both soaking wet and pretty hammered, but that just emboldened me to take charge and shag his brains out. Feeling Superwoman powerful from all the booze, I ripped his clothes off and threw him onto the floor. I was pretty sure by his reaction that no one had ever done that before. He'd never been with a bad girl like me. I got off on what a good time I was showing him; I was on top of Zander when a man walked in on us—a drunken, lost wedding guest—but I didn't care. I heard the soft mumbling of apology, and the door shut. I continued on my mission to burn this guy to a cinder with sex, to smote him.

"Oh my God," he moaned. "You're amazing."

Good, I thought. *And, yes, I am.*

Afterward, he loaned me an L.L. Bean long-sleeved striped T-shirt and a pair of his sister's jeans, and we went to check out a party where Pete's family was crashing in another big, borrowed house down the road. There were wall-to-wall Homers, drinking Barrilito rum that someone had brought back from a Puerto Rican vacation, and the air was sweet with the smell of weed. We had a pop or two, then drove to a lake in an old, beat-up Volvo station wagon and found another party going on in and around the boathouse. Plenty of people were skinny-dipping, but it was too cold and dark for me. I sat on the dock, hugging my legs, listening to the cicadas strumming along to the screams and shouts of delight coming from the water.

In the morning, at Zander's house, I changed back into my Laura Ashley dress, neatly folding the jeans and placing them on a chair in the corner. I thought about stealing the shirt—it was one of those French sailor tops that had been washed a hundred times until it was impossibly soft and perfectly worn. It was the kind of shirt your boyfriend lets you wear, like a love badge, I thought, as I moved my fingers along the ever-so-gently-frayed neckline. But Zander wasn't my boyfriend, and I left the shirt on top of the jeans.

I sneaked downstairs, hoping that anyone who saw me would think that I had just crashed in a bed someplace. A breakfast spread was laid out on the kitchen table—coffee, bagels, lox from Zabar's. Feeling as if rocks were exploding inside my head, I chugged a glass of orange juice and poured myself some coffee. Zander came into the room, looking nervous, and pulled me into a corner. Through the window over the sink, I could see his mom and dad with sundry guests on the porch.

"Hi," I said, and took a sip of my coffee—any liquid crucial at that moment.

"Hi, listen, Wendy, I don't want you to get the wrong idea about last night." He checked outside to make sure his folks were out of earshot.

and the flotsam of ex-step-, step-, and half siblings strewn across the city and the country.

Didi got me an interview for a day job waitressing in an executive dining room at Teachers Insurance Company on Third Avenue in Midtown. The boss was her soon-to-be-second ex-husband's girlfriend—a descriptive phrase that few people outside of Didi's and my families could appreciate. The girlfriend hired me pretty much on sight and gave me a uniform to wear—a shiny, polyester black dress with a white Peter Pan collar and an attached white apron, like a chambermaid in a French farce.

The dining room was a perfect gig for an actress because it was over by two in the afternoon, so I was free to go to auditions after work. I was the youngest person there by far. The other waitresses were all lifers, all in their late sixties—the kind of world-weary broads played by Thelma Ritter or Selma Diamond who seem to be gone from the city now. The second-youngest person was Mo, who was around forty and had been an actor in 1970s, downtown–New York experimental theater. He'd worked at La MaMa, knew Janis Joplin, and once threw Allen Ginsberg out of the house for hitting on his friends at a party.

"Jesus, I tossed that fucking bum out on his ass! I didn't give a shit who he was—he was bothering my guests!" Mo crinkled his nose and made a bad-smell face. His voice was deep, with the raspy gravel of a lifetime smoker and the jaded inflection of a hepcat.

Mo was originally from San Diego and had grown up

in a succession of bars that his crazy, drunk mom ran. His dad had taken off when he was a kid; his mother, like mine, had a string of boyfriends, whom Mo called his "uncles." He was rakishly handsome, tall and slender, with light brown curly hair and a mustache. Off work, he'd don a sheepskin coat and black cowboy boots and tie a red bandanna around his neck, lighting a cigarette on his way out of the building, looking as if he'd just walked out of *Midnight Cowboy*. He liked to swear, smoke, and drink. We got along great and soon became partners in crime at work. He was incredibly sweet to the crusty, old-broad waitresses, often going to their houses or churches on the weekend to help them with some chore that their husbands could no longer do—stringing up Christmas lights or moving the china cabinet. Their husbands were geezers who seemed to be permanently attached to Barcaloungers, watching old reruns on TV. Among his many other good deeds, he also protected me from Jean, the Bahamian cook who was always putting curses on me. I was terrified of her.

"You little white devil," Jean'd hiss if I so much as looked in her direction, waving her huge spatula in the air, her big, crazy eyes zeroing in on me and making goose bumps pop up on the tops of my arms.

"C'mon, Jean, cut the crap! She's just a kid, for Christ sakes, stop with the voodoo bullshit," he'd holler over the din of clacking dishes and silverware. Then he'd wink at me.

Mo lived in a one-room, rent-controlled apartment across from the Barrymore Theatre on Forty-seventh Street.

The room was filled with puppets and a folded-up, brightly painted wooden theater he'd taken to South America when he'd saved up enough for a ticket, to do shows for little kids there. It was like entering a magical kingdom, although there was barely room to sit down because every available space was dedicated to pieces of scenery and marionettes. We'd sit in his apartment, and he'd tell me incredible stories, such as how he once sneaked a bottle of vodka into the hospital for his friend Nicholas Ray, the famous film director—"He was dying, the poor bastard, so I took him a drink!"—or about running away from home at sixteen and hitchhiking to Northern California with his girlfriend to try to find Jack Kerouac. "We never found him." Mo exhaled a funnel of cigarette smoke and sipped his glass of Chablis.

I adored Mo because he was like someone from another time: a modern-day beatnik. He'd moved to New York, like me, with a couple of dollars in his pocket to pursue his dreams. It seemed to me that he had truly lived the life of an artist and still was. He was an inspiration to me, and a kindred spirit. We worked our day jobs, paid cheap rent, and weren't trapped in the economy of the city. This made it possible for us to do our thing.

One of my first auditions after landing back in New York was for Miranda in *The Tempest* at a theater in Tucson, Arizona. I put on one of the dresses Didi had helped me pick out, and I loaded up the voluminous faux-leather tote bag I'd bought on the street that I carted all my actor shit around in—a bottle of water, a book to read on the subway, my

Walkman, any play or sides I was auditioning for. Taking my cue from the young women in suits I saw dashing around the city, soon to be immortalized by Melanie Griffith's character in the movie *Working Girl*, I wore sneakers to walk around, then I'd change into my dress shoes when I got there. The sidewalks of New York could trash your best pair of heels in a day. The audition was in one of those ratty rehearsal-hall buildings in the Fifties near Eleventh Avenue. I strode purposefully down the trash-strewn street, politely avoiding eye contact with the chicks-with-dicks prostitutes working the early shift in their fake-fur jackets and hot pants.

I read the opening scene with Prospero, when Miranda witnesses the shipwreck, and then a later scene when she meets and falls in love at first sight with the young prince Ferdinand—the only man she's ever seen besides her father. Tapping into my own experience, I connected with Miranda's childlike honesty, her intense love for her father, and her open heart. I felt I had been that girl many times, running with my arms wide-open toward love.

The audition seemed to go well, and they called Didi later to offer me the job without even having to do a callback. I was thrilled—I'd booked my first gig out of acting school, and it was Shakespeare. Three years before, *Love's Labour's Lost* had tripped me up and cost me a job. Now I was back with the Bard and feeling in my element, soon to be a working actress.

It was about four months away, so I kept working at the dining room during the day. Then, about a month before I was due to leave, I got a job playing an incompetent secretary on the soap opera *All My Children*. I didn't have many lines, but worked for a few weeks—on TV, no less—and made some money.

One evening, after a taping of the show that had run late, I saw an actor, Charles Keating, in the lounge on my way out of the building. This dashing Englishman actor had been at the Guthrie Theater with my dad. When I was nine, I'd seen him play Mark Antony in a production of *Julius Caesar* in which he wore a macramé bikini bottom and leaped off a giant head of Caesar at the top of the show. He was simply spectacular and had taken my little-girl breath away. Looking at him maraud around the stage, feverishly spouting his lines, my nine-year-old self felt a warmth in her underwear that she'd only previously experienced when climbing the rope in gym class. I decided to go over to my first crush and say hello.

"Excuse me, Mr. Keating, I'm sure you don't remember me, but you were at the Guthrie with my father, James Lawless. I saw you in *Julius Caesar*."

He was twenty years older but still gorgeous, with thick, long white hair tied back in a ponytail, a distinguished mustache, and the darkest, deepest eyes.

"My dear, how wonderful to see you again! I remember your father very fondly. May I ask your name?"

"Wendy Lawless. I'm working on *All My Children* for a while before going off to do *The Tempest*." I wanted him to know that I was a serious actress, hoping to follow in my father's footsteps.

"Ah, Miranda." He enveloped my hand in his, kissed it, and looked down into my eyes. "What a perfect part for you. She is so young, so innocent."

"Um, yes," I managed to peep. "Do you have any advice for me? It's my first real job since getting out of acting school."

Still holding my hand, he smiled radiantly. "You must remember that when Miranda sees Ferdinand for the first time, it's as if she's grown breasts."

"Oh, I'll remember that. Thank you." I was feeling faint, along with the familiar damp-underpants sensation from when I was nine.

"Have a marvelous time, I must dash!" Charles squeezed my hand and was gone, out the door to Columbus Avenue. I just stood there for a moment, unable to move. All the way home on the subway, I felt a buzzy delight from being the recipient of his charms. It made me feel as if I was beginning to reach that world in which my father lived—as if I was making connections in that long lineage of roles and actors and stages. If a dark theater, any dark theater, made me feel at home, then working with and meeting other actors, especially of this grand, older generation, was like being part of "the family."

Taking a taxi from the airport to my actor's housing in Tucson, I was struck by the eerie beauty of the terrain. The mountains were blue and purple and topped in snow; the soil was pink and dotted with sage-green towering saguaros standing at attention across the desert. Palm trees swayed to and fro against the azure sky. The light was different, too—it was golden and lit up everything as if you were seeing it for the first time. Hummingbirds zipped through the air between flowers as big as your hand amid lush green grass. Everything seemed magnified and more alive. I didn't expect the desert to be so vibrant, so full of life.

The actors in *The Tempest* were being put up in a condominium complex near the theater, so I could walk to work. The man who was playing my father, a Korean American actor named Randall Duk Kim, was so mindful and sweet that it was easy to work with him; he was so generous and giving in our scenes together. I had been nervous, as he was well-known in regional theater, but he instantly put me at ease, and I felt close to him almost at once. A lifelong and profoundly dedicated actor, he had founded his own Shakespeare company in Spring Green, Wisconsin—American Players—but was taking a break from his responsibilities there, telling me he just wanted to act and not be burdened with the day-to-day running of the place. He told me that eventually he wanted to return to Hawaii, where he'd been born, and open an orchid farm.

We did the play in Tucson for three weeks, then performed it in Phoenix for three more. Doing the play in Phoenix was very different—it was an older audience, and I could hear them riffling for their car keys toward the end of the show and see them starting to make for the exit doors during the curtain call to make it home to see *The Tonight*

Show or the eleven o'clock news. Still, the company had fun going to a Japanese shabu place Randall had found, and we also had a private tour of Taliesin West because he knew the widow of Frank Lloyd Wright, who was a patron of his theater in Spring Green. My pal Patricia came to visit, and Daddy popped down to see the show, too.

My first acting experience out of school had been mostly positive, and I had avoided any romantic entanglements, for a change. Perhaps I was turning a corner, taking my first steps toward being a grown-up.

I got on the plane and returned to New York. Didi picked me up at the airport and eyed me up and down. She didn't have to say anything; all that fabulous Mexican food had fattened me up a bit—I was going to have to lose a few pounds.

My old friend Nina Franco, who had directed me in *Spring Awakening*, was back in town, having gotten her graduate degree from NYU. She called me, and we went to dinner to catch up. She filled me in on her three years at NYU; I told her I was just back in town after doing *The Tempest* in Arizona and was now on the dole looking for more acting work. Surprisingly, there was no weirdness between us—even though the last time I'd seen her she was wearing bandages over sixty stitches from the notorious arm-through-the-glass-door incident. Perhaps because we'd known each other on and off for ten years at various stages of our lives, our friendship just plugged itself back in when we saw each other.

"Come back to my place, I'll make popcorn."

I didn't have anywhere to be, so I shrugged. "Okay."

We walked over to her flat on Ninety-eighth Street just off Broadway. The large, dark place had been broken up into bedrooms that her roommate, who owned the apartment, rented out. Nina clanged around in the kitchen, and I heard the popping corn kernels pinging around in a pot on the stove.

I was standing in the small, sparsely furnished living room just outside the kitchen when I heard the front door slam. A handsome man, about my age, with dark hair and a mole on his cheek entered the room. He looked like a young Robert De Niro, the good-looking one from *The Godfather: Part II*.

Nina came in with a bowl of popcorn and introduced me. "Wendy, this is Stewart. This is his apartment."

We nodded at each other. He had a shy smile and tended to look off to the side, as if he were embarrassed about something. It was cute and made him seem sweet and self-effacing.

"Wendy lives a few blocks away on Ninety-seventh." Nina eyed me, clearly seeing an inkling of chemistry between us. My face felt red and warm.

"Oh, my cousin Dave Ott lives over there. At 210 between West End and Riverside." He put his massive messenger bag down on a chair.

"You're kidding me, right?" It was just another crazy example of how small a place such as New York could be. "Jenny's my best friend! We met at BU."

"Wow. Will you say hello to her and Dave? I haven't seen them in a while."

"Sure."

He got my number from Nina and called me the next day, so we met for coffee and exchanged stories. He wanted to be a screenwriter, but his day job was delivering oversized Italian sandwiches from a white van he drove around the city. Like me, he'd had an unhappy childhood—his parents split up when he was young. His mom was eccentric and now lived in a trailer park in Florida. His dad was a charismatic ne'er-do-well who never seemed to have had a real job.

Stewart listened with great interest to the saga of my insane childhood: the batty, narcissistic mother; the ghost father who'd chosen not to come to my rescue; the patched-up relationship with my sister, which at times resembled a broken vase stuck back together with sticky tape. His eyes narrowed with intensity as I cataloged all my strife and my various stabs to sort it all out. He held my hand and said he understood, which made me feel safe and cared for. We were alike in many ways—we'd lacked traditional parenting to say the least, we were both in the arts, and we had experienced the same proximity to money without having any ourselves.

Stewart and I drifted into a relationship, seeing each other a few times a week and on the weekends. In the beginning he seemed to have a gentleness that shone out of his brown eyes; he looked at me as if he loved me. I believed that I had finally found someone who would help me make the leap to the world of grown-ups; that we'd be a real, committed couple and cherish each other. Plus, I'd be joining Jenny's family by being with him.

Then, just as with my relationships with Michael and Graham, it all drastically changed. Suddenly, he turned the tables on me and went from being my sweet boyfriend to my nemesis, full of angry criticisms of me. Why wasn't I confronting my past? Why wasn't I going to Al-Anon meetings because my mother was clearly a drunk? He bullied me into calling my mother—it was the first time I'd spoken to her in six years. Feeling as if I were going to vomit, I listened to the phone ring while he stood there watching me.

"Hello, Mother." There was a pause while I listened to her smoke. "It's Wendy."

"Oh, it's you. You no longer have the right to address me as Mother. You will call me Georgann."

"Okay, Georgann." Just hearing her voice on the phone made me ill. Her palpable hatred and vitriol made me want to curl up in a closet in the dark. "How are you?"

"How am I? I don't hear from you in six years, and you call me up out of the blue to ask me how I am?" Her tone started to become more shrill, becoming slightly louder and even more nasty. I couldn't speak. I was trembling, my hands sweaty from gripping the receiver so hard. "Well, I'll tell you how I am. I have cancer!"

With that, she hung up the phone.

I crawled into my bed and wept. After all this time, she could still reduce me to a quivering mess.

Stewart sat on the edge of the bed, rubbing my back. "See? You did it. You can't let her have all that power over you."

Over the next few weeks, he continued to funnel his frustration over his own childhood disappointments, his stalled writing career, and his resentment toward Jews (didn't I realize they ran Hollywood?) into acting out a drill-sergeant routine on my psyche. I started hearing that old sound in my head, the voices of boyfriends past.

Didi never liked him; she thought he was a loser. "He delivers sandwiches for a living! I mean, come on!" she'd snort.

Reeling from what I perceived as a crushing betrayal and an epic—and repetitive—mistake on my part, I felt that I was back in free fall. Once again I had chosen a man who belittled me the way my mother did. I sank into a monumental depression. Unable to eat, sleep, or stop crying, I frantically called my old Boston shrink, Dr. Keylor, who kindly listened to me, then told me to take care of myself and that unfortunately she didn't know anyone in the city. So I called the only other therapist I could think of—Jenny's mom and Stewart's aunt, Phyllis.

She listened patiently while I blubbered into the phone about, well, everything. Why hadn't I been able to resolve my issues with my mother? Why did I continue to find guys who treated me badly and didn't value my worth? What was wrong with me?

There was a slight pause before she spoke. I blew my nose noisily.

"Well, I think you need to spend some time really mourning the fact that you didn't have a mother. I mean, really feel sad about it."

"Okay." I sniffed.

"Then I think you have to ask yourself a question."

I waited.

"What would happen if you decided to grow up?"

Her words stopped me. I looked into the mirror on my bedroom wall. Tears streaming down my face, I looked so small, so crumpled. Who was that girl?

Phyllis gave me the name of a shrink in Manhattan, Elaine Livingston, whom she'd met at a conference in California. "I only spoke to her for twenty minutes, but she seemed great."

"Thanks, Phyl."

"Hang in there, kiddo. Lots of love. And call Elaine."

Elaine Livingston's office was in London Terrace, an elegant prewar block of apartment buildings in Chelsea on Twenty-third and Twenty-fourth Streets between Ninth and Tenth Avenues. From her first-floor window, she had a lovely view into the courtyard garden. Somehow the hush of this cocoon-like room, with soft, dusky lighting and trembling, leafy trees outside, made it easier for me to pour out my feelings. I felt secure, hidden, safe.

She dug right in. "So, why are you here?"

Elaine was a tiny, fine-boned brunette in her mid-to-late thirties with fiercely intelligent eyes and a warm, caring voice that bordered on the maternal. I liked her right away. She sat back in a comfy chair that almost enveloped her petite frame with a yellow legal pad poised on her knee and listened intensely as I spewed all my problems and concerns out like so many hair balls: my apparently superpower-level ability to find critical guys, the feelings of worthlessness and sadness that threatened to incapacitate me, and my toxic relationship with Georgann. Elaine jotted notes down on the pad, looking up at intervals to smile or give me a look of concern. I sat on a couch across from her, surrounded by piles of balled-up, damp tissues.

She nodded and leaned in toward me. "Let me explain a little about the way I work. I practice something called brief therapy with clients. It focuses on the present and the future. Your past is important, of course, to help me understand where you're coming from, but it's more important to identify the problem and what behaviors are sort of holding up your ability to change or reframe the situation. Does that make sense?"

"Kinda," I croaked. I had been crying so hard and talking so much, my nose was completely stuffed up, and I felt as if I couldn't breathe.

"Next week, I think we should discuss your personal relationships and why you gravitate toward men who don't nurture and accept you."

"Okay." I sobbed, trying not to gag on my own saliva.

"See you next week, Wendy."

"Bye. Thanks." I hobbled out the door and home.

After a few sessions with Elaine, I broke up with Stewart, which I hadn't formally done; I was too afraid of confronting him with my true emotions—that he made me feel weak and preyed upon. She had suggested taking time off from the relationship so I could figure out what I thought I should do, and I agreed.

"The great thing is, you don't have to decide now." She shrugged and gave me a sly smile.

I met Stewart one evening later on the steps of Ninety-seventh Street.

"But why?" He clearly had no idea.

"Because I deserve better." I had thought about this moment for a while; I'd rehearsed it in my mind and now knew it was the truth.

"What do you mean?" He looked at me as if I were speaking Swahili.

"I can *do* better than you, Stewart. Good-bye." I turned on my heel and strode up the steps into the building.

Fuck that, I thought as I walked away from him. A rush of adrenaline pulsed through me from the power of doing the right thing for myself—from choosing what Wendy wanted over what some guy wanted.

I smiled to myself as I punched the button for the elevator.

chapter twelve

GROW UP

My roommate Dave was off in San Francisco for the summer, working at Alice Waters's Chez Panisse in Berkeley, and Molly had followed him out there, so Dave had rented their room and the small one by the kitchen out. Feeling uncomfortable living with strangers and not wanting to run into Stewart, who lived only a few blocks away, I went to visit Pete and Jenny at their new home in Albany—she was four and a half months pregnant, and Pete was doing his medical residency. She and I went trolling the town for baby clothes that weren't ugly, which in 1988 wasn't easy. We cooked and hung out, talked and listened to records—Bonnie Raitt, Dwight Yoakam, Ry Cooder, or the Supremes. Somehow Jenny, a lifelong WASPy New Yorker, had always dreamed of being a Motown backup singer or Dolly Parton. It was great to be together, to reconnect with that part of my found family. But it was not the same. Jenny and Pete had grown up. Albany was a town for grown-ups. I was unemployed and just learning how not to have a bad relationship—clearly just a visitor to the real world.

Back in New York, I camped out at Didi's place during the week, sleeping in the bunk bed above Ali or on the puffy couch in the living room. I kept my stuff in my room at Ninety-seventh Street but stopped in as little as possible to avoid running into Stewart. Sometimes on weekends I tagged along with Didi and Ali to a little guesthouse Didi rented with her mother behind a mansion in East Hampton. We'd roller-skate along the flat, winding roads past the grand houses of the truly wealthy; the constant whirring of lawn mowers accompanied the dragging clack of our skates. I still had my skates from playing Cherubino, and Didi was the only person I knew who fearlessly roller-skated to work in Armani on the sidewalks of Manhattan. And here we were—back in the Hamptons together for the first time since the crazy food-fight summer twenty years ago, when I was a towheaded little girl and she a caustic, cigarette-smoking teenager.

Wall Street money from the go-go eighties was rapidly changing the low-key, old-money tone of East Hampton and creeping out toward Amagansett and Montauk. Even Grey Gardens, the famously dilapidated haunt of Big Edie and Little Edie Bouvier, had been completely renovated—its creepy, broken-down charm just a memory to be visited in the Maysles brothers documentary. We'd walk to the beach at the end of the street and eat fries and greasy burgers to

wasn't taking responsibility for my life or my actions. I wasn't taking care of myself. Maybe this had been what Phyllis had meant about deciding to grow up.

When Mother called back a few days later, shouted her usual tirade, and hung up hysterical, I paused for a second, then called her back.

"Hello . . . ?" she answered in her calm voice, one that I hadn't heard in quite some time. She sounded as if she was sitting on her living-room couch, reading a magazine. At that moment I realized that it was, once again, all an act; and it certainly wasn't worth losing sleep or crying over.

"Georgann, if this is the way you're going to behave—the robo-calling and the nasty messages—I just don't think we can be friends."

Silence.

A declaration of boundaries clearly wasn't the response she had been expecting. She would have preferred if I'd been crying and had snot coming out of my nose.

"Well, Wendy, that's fine. I don't want to be friends; I am too angry at you." She hung up.

A huge rush of relief swept over me. I had drawn the line and she had made her choice, opting out of contact with me. As I turned this small victory over in my mind, I realized that, in a larger sense, all the hurt she'd caused me in the past was over, done with. She could never do that to me again. I simply wouldn't let her.

———

Except for Shakespeare in the Park, summer is traditionally a pretty dead time in the city for work in the theater. I had my unemployment and then got a short-term temp gig answering phones at Juilliard's traveling company, the Acting Company, where Nina was now working with her old boss Gerry Gutierrez. I just took down messages on little pink pads of paper and transferred calls—a skill for which the deli had trained me well. It gave me a place to go in the morning, for which I was grateful. The people were nice, and so was the income.

I took the subway to Times Square, but from the subway station, walking Forty-second Street to Eighth Avenue, the commute could be treacherous, calling for serpentine moves to avoid the bums and drunk guys who harangued me and asked, "Can I see your pussy?"—or if they were slightly more sober, tried to grab my boobs. I carried my cup of coffee like a weapon, in case any of them came too close.

The Acting Company office was a shabby little hole on the second floor, ruled over by a mercurial, fireplug-shaped force of nature named Margot Harley, who yelled a lot in a Bryn Mawr accent and expected everything to be done perfectly, which of course meant her way.

"Get Edward Albee's agent on the phone!" she'd roar at me, even though her desk was less than four feet from mine.

I'd look the number up in the Rolodex and place the call. "Hello? It's Margot Harley calling. You know, Harley, like the motorcycle?"

Margot basically ignored me unless I was placing a call

for her, but I enjoyed trying to get her attention and crack that frosty, upper-class veneer that she was either born with or had picked up from her predecessor, John Houseman.

Nina's boss, Gerry, often called the office and always pretended to be some famous actress—sometimes dead, sometimes a lesbian, always female. I took messages from Rosalind Russell, Agnes Moorehead, Mary Martin, Bea Arthur, and Dame Judith Anderson. When he found out I'd been through a classical-acting program, he asked if I wanted to audition for the company. I had never been sure that he even liked me, so I was touched by his generosity. I did my pieces for him and Nina and was called back and offered the job: small roles and understudying the other actors on the next tour, all of them from Juilliard. Afterward he took Nina and me across the street to a crappy Mexican restaurant to talk more about what we'd be doing. From his point of view, he was giving me the chance of a lifetime—to work with people from the top school in the country. Juilliard actors were the crème de la crème, along with NYU graduates, or kids from Yale.

"And let's face it, darling," he said as he started in on his fourth martini, "it's not like you'll ever be Kevin Kline. I mean, you're good, but you're not *that* good."

I smiled and sipped on my jumbo-sized margarita on the rocks with salt.

"It'll be great to have you along." Nina smiled, reaching over to squeeze my arm.

I was torn. I'd be on tour, living out of a bus with a group of strangers, who most likely had all been classmates. I was afraid of being lonely and far away from my friends—the only family I had, here on this coast—and then I had my appointments with Elaine. Without my newly woven safety net, I suddenly saw myself buying crack in a supermarket parking lot in Nebraska. I stalled for a week, agonizing over whether I should take the job.

When I told Didi about it, she didn't try to hide her disdain. "What the hell are you going to do on a tour bus, playing a lady-in-waiting, booked into every shit-hole town in America?!" She felt I should commit to staying in New York, or at least on the East Coast.

"But I don't have anything else." I moped, imagining the headline: "Classical Actress in Period Costume Jumps off Grain Silo After Bus Stalls in Dubuque."

"Well, I have an audition for you for *Midsummer Night's Dream* at Hartford Stage tomorrow. Mark Lamos is directing. Here are the sides they want you to read. It's for Helena. You're probably not gonna get it because you're not tall enough, but give it a shot. Just go in there like you already have the job."

I knew Helena's big speech in act 1 by heart because I had watched an actress named Lisa Sloan do it every night at the American Repertory Theater in Cambridge, when I was working as a dresser eight years before. So I was able to go in and do it off-book. I had always adored the speech— all about unrequited love and peppered with beautiful images and words. Helena enjoys her suffering and is totally

desperate, throwing herself at this man whom she adores. I identified with her "love is a many-tortured thing" attitude. I had tried to make guys want me and had longed to be truly and deeply loved, searching in all the wrong places for that man who would devote himself to me and our life together. Perhaps that showed because Mark Lamos offered me the job right there in the room.

"I'm sorry. What?" I knew I'd heard wrong.

"I want you to come to Hartford and be my Helena," he repeated with a sort of kindly delight. A slim, puckish fellow, he wore tennis shoes and practically flew around the room like Peter Pan.

I stammered and shook my head, not knowing what to say. I told him I'd been offered a job with the Acting Company.

"Have you signed the contract?"

"Uh . . . no." I almost blurted out my vision of the dive off the grain silo, but stopped myself.

"Well, I think you should come work for me." He smiled. "Unless you're afraid of Margot. Are you afraid of Margot?"

I shook my head. Of course I was a little afraid of Margot—everyone was.

"So, tell her you got another offer—no, tell you got a better offer! And I'll see you in two weeks."

"Thank you, I'm so excited!" I wanted to kiss him, but instead I skipped out of the room and down the stairs out into the street. I found the nearest phone booth right away and called Didi. The theater had already called her with the

offer. I asked her why she had said that I'd never get the part.

She laughed. "I had to psych you out or you'd overthink it. Now you have a job near the city. See?"

When I told Gerry that I was taking the Hartford job, he looked down at me disapprovingly and made it clear that he believed I was making a big, career-killing mistake. It might be, but I knew that for my mental health I was making the right decision. Like ending my relationship with Stewart and standing up to my mother, I had done the right thing for myself—and it was getting easier every time.

Mark only liked to rehearse for four hours a day—he believed that after four hours, your brain just couldn't absorb any more information. Helena was a demanding part—she's brainy and loquacious. Mark told me that I was often behind the metaphorical horse, holding on to its tail, in terms of keeping up with the language. Striving to run faster, keep up, and perhaps eventually jump up on the horse, I felt challenged and lucky to be surrounded by talented people. I worked hard and wanted madly to make the director happy with me.

Hartford was an oleo of ugly, new glass skyscrapers and gorgeous, old brick and brownstone buildings built in Victorian or Colonial Revival style. It had been the home of Mark Twain, would be Katharine Hepburn's final resting place, and contained the oldest public museum in the country, the Wadsworth Atheneum. I found the city a bit gray

and sketchy in terms of safety; it went block to block as in New York, but the actors always traveled in a pack from the theater to our housing, which was on the second floor of a shopping mall, usually stopping off en masse at the Irish bar on the first floor. I had an enormous apartment all to myself, big enough to ride a nonmetaphorical horse around in. It was a very social group—lots of parties, poker games, and barhopping. I had a crush on the guy playing Demetrius, the object of my affection in the play, but luckily he had a serious girlfriend. Bradley Whitford lived down the hall from me and would stop in for a sandwich; everyone at the theater lusted after him, except me. We were just buddies, and I was done with actors.

That didn't mean I wanted to be ignored by them. Since I was running around in little dance tights and a sports bra during most of the play, I joined the YMCA and started doing leg lifts like crazy. Being practically naked in the show put the fear of God in me and my dimply thighs.

Jenny's due date approached; every time I called her house and she didn't answer, I worried that she was giving birth in her car or something. Her son Nathaniel came right on time, but sadly, three weeks later her dad succumbed to cancer. He had been in remission, but then the cancer suddenly and swiftly returned. I was happy he got to see his grandson and hold him, but everyone was devastated by his death. I took the train down on my day off and spent a sad afternoon at Ninety-seventh Street with Jenny and Dave. I wasn't able to go to the memorial service because I had two shows and no understudy. I felt that I was letting them down by not being there, but the show had to go on.

The play was up and running and very physical—the fairies all flew in the production, and I thought that the moment when Bottom flies off with Titania into the night was one of the most beautiful things I'd ever seen. I also learned why Peter Pan is usually played by a woman: if a man wore those harnesses, he could end up with earmuffs made of his own testicles. The lovers ran around and jumped in and out of a large pool of water in the stage floor during the second act. Invariably, the first two rows of the audience got as soaked as if they were watching Shamu at SeaWorld. I had to wear knee pads to prevent carpet burns and accidentally pulled Demetrius's pants off completely one night groveling after him.

Lots of people—friends, roommates, ex-roommates, and family—came to Hartford to see the show. Didi came with her new fiancé, even though she wasn't divorced from her second husband yet. His name was Michael, and he was an actor, an ex-marine with red hair and a salty sense of humor who I thought was a good match for her. Michael appealed to the bawdy, bourbon-drinking broad in her as opposed to the WASPy boarding-school side. My sister, Robin, who had recently moved to New York, came for opening night and quickly developed a crush on my cast-mate Brad Whitford.

"He's so hot!" She giggled and fanned her hand in front of her face.

"His girlfriend just dumped him—want me to introduce you?" I batted my eyes at her, calling her bluff.

"No, thanks. I just like to look."

My sister's track record with men was no better than mine. She had a penchant for difficult, withholding types and bad boys just as I did. So far, that hadn't worked out for either of us.

Being in *Midsummer* felt like the most rewarding experience of my short career; I learned so much from Mark and my fellow actors about pacing, endurance, and the pow-pow-pow of doing Shakespeare and turning on a dime. Performing the play was exhilarating, like running a race and winning every time. But when the play ended, I went back to the city and again took up my place in the registration line at unemployment. My high was over.

I was broke. I had sold my car for $1,000, and the money from my grandfather had run out despite my frugal living. I made ends meet temping for a few agencies for nominal pay, since I didn't know how to type. I worked as a reader at auditions. I got a one-week gig on a soap opera called *One Life to Live*, playing a debutante in a big dress, which paid the bills for a month and let me work with Celeste Holm, the Oscar-winning actress. I got to spend a week with her, laughing and listening to her stories about double-dating with JFK and his older brother, Joe, the one who was killed in World War II. She drove the wardrobe people crazy by taking home parts of her costumes, the Ferragamo shoes especially. "They're mine," she'd declare indignantly. Perhaps she was confusing ABC with RKO or some other movie studio from her glittering Hollywood past. Or perhaps she remembered just how quickly a run can end and where the unemployment line begins. Either way, she was gracious, hilarious, and very kind to me, even though I don't think she even knew my name.

No sooner had I paid up my rent and share of the bills than I had to move. Dave had a new girlfriend, and they were serious. With two jobs and a ridiculously low rent, they didn't need to sublet rooms anymore, and they wanted to be alone—to have a grown-up relationship in an apartment decorated with unbroken furniture and items brought inside on purpose. It was the end of almost a decade of roommates and boarders and of the apartment at Ninety-seventh Street serving as a crossroads or way station between school and real life. I understood, but the timing wasn't great, as I had $75 left in my bank account.

Maybe out of guilt for kicking me out or maybe just because he was a nice guy, Dave helped me get a job hostessing at Bouley. When David Bouley had left Montrachet to start his own restaurant, he had taken Dave and a couple of the other young stars of the kitchen with him. The new restaurant was a huge success and always overbooked; I took reservations over the phone during the day and seated people in the evening—an upgrade from the days of indecipherable sandwich orders. It was a crazy kind of glamorous, getting seriously dressed up every night, putting on heels and standing up to the Masters of the Universe as they foamed at the mouth and threw their platinum cards at me to try to get a table for their supermodel girlfriends or Valentino-jacketed wives. Only in Manhattan can a girl just over five feet tall in borrowed designer clothes and getting paid eight bucks an hour in cash wield so much power. My first night on the job, the waiters took me out after closing to a dive bar a few blocks away called Puffy's to celebrate my survival. After a few too many drinks, I ended up singing on top of—and then drunkenly falling off of—the jukebox. The management asked us to leave, and the thrilled waiters hoisted me up in the air above their heads and carried me out to the street to put me in a taxi home. Apparently, I'd passed the test. The next morning I had a bruise the size of a basketball on my butt.

Just as Dave had helped me out with a job, Didi came to my rescue on the apartment front. Her fiancé, Michael, had a small, dark, dumpy bachelor pad on the interior of a building on Amsterdam Avenue in the Eighties that he wasn't quite ready to give up, so he kindly let me sublet. It was cheap and close to my old neighborhood; I didn't even have to change dry cleaners.

Despite the apartment and the job, I felt despondent and restless. I hadn't had a serious acting job in months and was anxious because my career seemed to be over. I was busy, dashing around the city to pick up scripts, clocking some hours at Bouley, spending a week answering an office phone on the East Side here and there. I continued my sessions with Elaine, who graciously allowed me to pay her when I could. Didi sent me on many auditions—I was the callback queen, but callbacks aren't a job. Then at the end of March 1989, I went down to the Public Theater to try out for a production of Shakespeare's *Cymbeline*. The director, JoAnne Akalaitis, was an avant-garde theater legend who'd been one of the founding members of the experimental theater group Mabou Mines. She had flaming-red hair, cropped short and spiky, wore retro, thick-framed glasses and black pants and jackets like a punky teenager, and had a ghostly pallor that made her look as if she'd never been outside.

The leading-lady role in the play, a princess named Imogen, is the longest woman's speaking part in Shakespeare and quite difficult. After I read one of the speeches, I mumbled thanks and started gathering up my stuff.

"I feel like I've met you before." JoAnne was chewing gum and turned my résumé over in her hand. "Is that possible?"

"I don't think so." I shook my head. She was probably a year or two younger than my mother, but was nothing like her. JoAnne had a warm, maternal, matter-of-fact manner. I guessed she got along well with her kids.

"There's just something very familiar about you." She smiled and asked me to come to the callback on Saturday.

The callback was more of a combat and movement class led by a fight choreographer. Afterward, JoAnne told me she wanted me to be in the play, but she laughed and said she didn't know what I would be doing in it yet. I said great, ecstatic for the chance to work with a director of note and at the Public Theater, too.

She cast me as a lady-in-waiting to Imogen, who was to be played by Joan Cusack. The bonus was that I would get paid a much-needed extra $20 a week to understudy her. I had one line—"The Queen, my lady, desires your highness's company." My character didn't even have a name. But I didn't care, I was working. The company ran the gamut, from actors deeply rooted in the experimental theater, to classically trained ones from Juilliard and Yale, and included Don Cheadle, Wendell Pierce, Peter Francis James, Frederick Neumann, Joan MacIntosh, and Michael Cumpsty.

I could tell that a few of the actors didn't enjoy JoAnne's directing style, but it was so out there, I found it all fascinating. We did a big group warm-up, dancing onstage to African music before each rehearsal, then we'd lie on the floor as she'd read us Artaud. We did mudra exercises—a series of formalized hand and face gestures—and moved around the stage in slow motion. She didn't like doing table reads, so everybody was up on their feet the first day, running scenes. All the movement in the court scenes was stylized, to accentuate all the artifice and intrigue. JoAnne was well-known for having male nudity in her productions; the villain Iachimo's first scene was in the buff in a massive bathhouse, and the young men who lived in the forest, played by Don Cheadle and Jesse Borrego, wore practically nothing—leaping around the stage in loincloths. This might have explained why they were always being followed around by packs of teenage girls. I was so jazzed—me, in a show with hot and legendary actors at a world-famous theater? Even though I had a small part, I felt as if I'd arrived. With so little time onstage, I often sat out in the house watching rehearsals and scribbling down Joan's blocking. JoAnne, who'd started out as an actress, treated everyone in the cast the same and was nurturing and direct; when she'd get mad at someone, or about something, she'd yell—and then it was over. She didn't hold grudges. I admired her style. I felt drawn to her in a mommish way. She seemed so strong, sure, and so much her own person.

One day at rehearsal, she introduced us to the show's composer: "Hey, everyone, this is Phil. He'll be doing the music."

"Phil" turned out to be Philip Glass, arguably the most celebrated living modern composer as well as her ex-husband. For the next few weeks, Phil hung out with us, watching rehearsals and scribbling in a notebook. I was agog, not just because he was famous but because he and JoAnne were divorced and yet working together and enjoying each other's company. Their ex-relationship was more successful than any of my relationship relationships.

Soon after rehearsals began, I started dating a man, Isaac, I had met at one of Didi's parties. A divorced Jewish lawyer with a four-year-old son, he was smart, funny, and nine years older than me. He was a little goofy looking, tall and wiry, with big round eyes and tightly coiled hair that he kept short. He wore expensive suits and had a spacious apartment on the Upper West Side and a beach house on Long Island. I would spend the night at his house but would always move to the guest bedroom early in the morning so as not to confuse his little boy, Eli. Isaac's ex lived in the same building, a few floors below, and Eli moved back and forth between apartments. Having grown up with a ever-changing roster of my mother's boyfriends, I tried to be especially sensitive toward Eli, who was chattery and blond with huge blue eyes. I'd always hated it when some guy my mom was dating tried to muscle in and act as if he were my dad or offered to buy me stuff so I'd like him more. I sort of waited for Eli to come to me; I let him take the lead. And it worked.

"Wanna pway bawl?" He sniffed and ran his sleeve across his nose.

"Sure." I resisted an impulse to grab him and kiss him to death, which would have scared him.

Soon, the maid was doing my laundry and leaving it neatly folded on top of the washing machine, and Isaac would bring me a cup of delicious coffee in a fine china cup on a tray in bed. I'd watch him get dressed for work, and he'd ask me if I needed anything. He knew I was always strapped for cash, so he never hesitated to pick up the check for fancy wine lunches at Café Luxembourg or late-night *steak-frites* at Florent, a greasy-spoon bistro in the Meatpacking District after the show.

"Do you have any money?" He knotted his luscious Italian silk tie expertly one morning before heading off to his law office.

"I have a couple of bucks."

He rolled his eyes comically and took his wallet out of

his jacket breast pocket, pulling out a twenty. "Jesus, take this. I don't want you starving to death. The life of an actress!"

I took the money and thanked him. I didn't feel badly about it, because I knew he didn't care, and it was only twenty bucks. That didn't even qualify as Holly Golightly's $50 for the powder room. Let alone my mother's grand piano or washing machine.

During a long technical rehearsal, I was lying on a table backstage, getting in a little power nap, when JoAnne stopped in the hall next to me. I opened my eyes.

"I just realized where I know you from." She was chewing gum and had her hands on her hips. "I babysat you when you were three or something."

"Really? Wow." I tried to imagine JoAnne in capri pants, little white socks, and Keds. I was having trouble.

"Yeah, it was summer stock in North Carolina—Chapel Hill. I played your dad's daughter in *A Man for All Seasons*, and I used to take you and your sister to the public swimming pool on the day off." She grinned widely at me, clearly happy to have solved the mystery.

Then she asked me how my mother was. I said I didn't really know, that we were sort of estranged.

"Hmm, well, it must be her fault. If a kid isn't speaking to a parent, it's always the parent's fault."

"What did you think of my mother? What was she like back then?"

"Pretty. Thin. She seemed, I don't know, disappointed

by her life. Like she thought it was going to be this fairy tale, and it wasn't. I felt sorry for her, to tell you the truth."

JoAnne's pity surprised me. I had never had any sympathy for my mother. To me, she was this gorgon who suddenly flew out of the darkness to swoop down on me and do her best to make me feel small and unloved. Her mantra was to replay her abandonment by everyone she loved—the most recent escapees being my sister and me. Through therapy, I'd begun to see that I was far stronger, and higher functioning, than I—or she—gave myself credit for. My mother could never overcome her horrific abusive childhood, but perhaps one day I'd be able to look upon my mother with some degree of forgiveness, even compassion for her, as JoAnne seemed to.

The show opened—and it was eviscerated in the press. All the papers said it was a dud, a bomb. The day after the scathing reviews came out, the cast and crew were summoned to the theater a half an hour early. Joe Papp, the founder of the New York Shakespeare Festival and the Public Theater, stood in the house to greet us. He seemed tall, but perhaps that was his towering presence. He was a strikingly grand man, elegantly dressed in a suit, with a wiry head of unruly graying hair, an impressive and handsome nose, and furry, caterpillar eyebrows that framed his energetic, lived-in face. Before he even opened his mouth, I felt as if I'd follow him into a burning building.

JoAnne was nervously chewing gum, arms folded across her chest, pacing a piece of carpet next to Mr. Papp. She cleared her throat. "Hey, everyone, Joe has something to say."

The great man smiled and nodded and then said in a perfect mid-Atlantic accent, "I want you all to know how proud I am of this production. The critics are wrong. They simply do not understand what JoAnne is—what all of you are—trying to do. This is a production of vision, of ideas, and they must be made to see that. And they will. I've invited all of them to come back next week for a special performance. I know that, after they see *Cymbeline* again, they will toss out their reviews and proclaim the show a triumph."

We all clapped, thrilled. Our leader had spoken; with stars in our eyes, we ran backstage to get ready for the evening performance, believing that we weren't in a turkey.

The following week, as the critics from *Time*, *Newsweek*, and the *New York Times* found their seats in the theater and the actors' half hour was called, Joan's makeup table at the end of the row in the ladies' dressing room sat empty. Since I was her understudy, I felt a little nervous, but figured she was just running late. We'd had the day before off, and she'd flown somewhere to meet her boyfriend. She was probably stuck in traffic coming from the airport. But another fifteen minutes went by, and she still hadn't turned up. Suddenly, at five minutes to eight, Mr. Papp strode into the dressing room, surrounded by an entourage. I had my wig on and my long skirt, but no top. Standing there in my bra in front of the artistic director of the Public, I started to have a creeping sense of doom. *Holy shit, I'm going on for Joan.* It all seemed to be happening so fast, but in slow motion, like a car accident—time sort of stopped. I was having trouble breathing.

Mr. Papp regarded me, looking me up and down. "Is this the understudy?" He made a theatrical, sweeping arm gesture in my direction. The entourage nodded yes, heads bobbing up and down in unison, while I felt as if I might faint.

He looked me right in the eye. "Are you ready to go on? Do you know the lines?"

"Um, yes, Mr. Papp," I croaked. "I know the first half but might have to be on book for the second act."

"So you need to carry a book? There's no shame in that. Someone get this girl a book!" he thundered, and a minion scampered away to find one.

"Let's get this young woman into a costume!" he bellowed, and another member of his posse ran to get Joan's clothes.

I nodded weakly as they started pinning me into her costume—a long, voluminous, rose-colored nightgown—for the first scene. Joan was quite a bit bigger and taller than me.

JoAnne, who had been lurking in the corner chewing her nails, walked up to me and took my shoulders in her hands, fixing her steely gaze upon me. "Just do it," my former baby-sitter said solemnly.

Frantic, I shoved quarters at my friend Sharon Washington, who played the other lady-in-waiting, to call Didi from the pay phone in the greenroom and let her know I was going on.

After the terror, I began to feel excited, even eager, to get out there. I was about to go onstage at the Public Theater in a leading role, and I thought suddenly I might even be quite good in it. Maybe this was my big break! As I exited the dressing room, all the women kissed me and patted me on the back. I walked through the greenroom—the other actors cheering me on and applauding. I could feel the adrenaline coursing through my veins. Brilliant and invincible, I would conquer New York and receive the key to the city.

Practically levitating, I turned into the hallway to the stage and ran smack into Joan, who was frantic and jabbering a story of being stuck in traffic on the Grand Central Parkway. As soon as I saw her, water came pouring out of every pore in my body. Drenched in flop sweat, I had an immediate, piercing feeling of disappointment—I was sorry that she'd shown up, I was so convinced that I was ready. It was not my big break, after all.

In June, after we'd been running for a month, my old boyfriend Graham showed up in New York. I hadn't seen him since our last year in acting school—after the sweater incident—where we avoided each other in a civil fashion. I'd heard he and his girlfriend had broken up, and he'd moved to Seattle, where he was acting in local theater and working in a coffee place. He'd recently sent me a letter, care of my friends Jen and John, that cried out for some kind of declaration on my part. I hadn't responded.

I got him a comp to the show, and we walked across the street to Indochine afterward for a drink. Indochine had become the cast hangout, a restaurant that looked like a decadent café in a jungle with palm-frond wallpaper, wicker chairs, and whiffy hostesses who looked like fashion models. I could tell he'd hated the show; almost every one of my friends who'd come to see it thought it was a disaster. But I could also see that he was bothered that my fellow cast members came up to me to say hello after we'd grabbed tall, metal stools at the bar. I'll admit I enjoyed it—not only that I was working as an actor and he was not, but that I was liked and settled while he was still trying to find a place to land. Maybe I had moved on.

"What are you doing in the city?"

"I've moved to New York." He smiled and turned his scotch on the rocks around on the cocktail napkin.

I noted, with some amusement, that he looked out of place in this downtown world, with his quarterback looks and preppy clothes. "Really? What happened to Seattle?"

"Christ, it rained all the time. I'm over it. So whaddya think?" He lit up a Camel Lights.

"About what?"

"Me moving to New York."

I signaled the bartender to bring me another Maker's Mark. "Great. If that's what you want." I was determined to keep things light, whatever game he was playing.

"I found an apartment, and I think I got a gig bartending on the Upper West Side that starts in a few weeks."

I smiled and chewed my lip. There was a silence.

"Are you seeing anyone?"

"Um, yes, actually. A lawyer. He's a really lovely guy."

Graham nodded and fiddled with the little plastic straw in his glass. "Well, maybe when I get settled, we can meet for coffee or a movie sometime."

"Okay, sure." I shrugged, nonplussed.

He walked me to the subway, and we exchanged a chaste hug. Our eyes met briefly before I turned—pretending not to see the baffled look on his face—and walked down the steps. I didn't have time for his games; I was busy working and taking care of myself. I was my new priority, not some old boyfriend.

Cymbeline closed at the end of June after a sold-out run. The show was never re-reviewed, but with the word on the street that it was a stinker, flocks of haters and curious theater folk came to see what all the fuss had been about. So we played to packed houses every night until the end. It was bizarre performing the show to a wall of silent onlookers, who were clearly mystified by JoAnne's interpretation of the play—as if we were in an underwater tableau vivant or a freak show that no one understood.

With the closing, I was once again an unemployed actress. I registered with another temp agency, Rosemary Scott, which had a single-room office in a generic Midtown building where three motor-mouthed women in knockoff Chanel suits barked into phones nonstop all day. Despite my inability to type or even file, they managed to book me into jobs, answering phones mostly. I worked in a posh furniture showroom in Midtown, at a Japanese bank so close to the top of the World Trade Center that I could feel the building sway slightly in the wind, at a supplier of office equipment where they kept me for two weeks just because I made them laugh.

After work I'd meet Isaac for drinks at fancy bars or the University Club, where he was a member. I was staying over at his apartment quite a bit, then going out to his place in Speonk on the weekends. Robin came along one weekend, and we attempted to cook Isaac dinner. We burned the roast chicken, and our risotto was a yellow puddle of goo. We giggled at Isaac when he refused to eat it, and we ended up going out to eat.

One weekend when I'd taken the train out to Speonk, I was sitting by the pool with a friend of Isaac's—a world-weary Italian woman, Gia, who was married to Isaac's business associate. She had incredible taste, looked like a thinner Sophia Loren, and had an adorable little girl who was splashing in the pool with Eli.

"So," she said in her beautifully accented English, "are you going to marry Isaac? He is crazy for you, I think."

"Oh, I don't know. We've never talked about it." Isaac and Luca, Gia's husband, sat out of earshot drinking beers with their pants rolled up and their feet in the water, keeping an eye on the kids.

"He is a good man and he cares for you. You should marry him."

"Well, first, he hasn't asked me, and second, I'm not in love with him."

"So what if you do not love him? You will be rich!" She dismissed me with a wave of her hand.

Isaac was a good boyfriend, someone who treated me well, appreciated me for me. I was determined to just enjoy an even-keeled relationship for a change. We had no great passion, but we were fond of each other and made each other laugh. And the sex was great. Slowly, I had begun to wonder if Isaac was it—the one for me. I had been around, slept with a lot of guys, broken some hearts, and been dumped big-time. I was twenty-eight, and Isaac felt like my first adult relationship, in which I wasn't constantly putting my ego on the line. He liked me the way I was and saw me in a way that many other men hadn't. He respected me and treated me with concern and kindness. We were perfect . . . except that I wasn't in love with him. But maybe true romance wasn't in the cards for me. If I married him, I'd be very comfortable—like my actress girlfriends who could afford to work for lousy money or not to have day jobs because they had trust funds or rich husbands. And I'd be a stepmom to Eli, whom I loved. I had never thought about having a child before, but maybe we could have one together and give Eli a little brother or sister.

The summer was winding down; the weekends in the Hamptons ended when Isaac closed up the house and started a new, high-profile job at a firm in Midtown. He was still slipping me an occasional twenty for lunch and subway money and had kindly paid my rent one month when I was completely skint.

"Don't worry about it," he'd shushed me when I told him I felt guilty taking the $300. "You can pay me back . . . someday, okay? Or you know, we can work it out in sexual favors." He grinned and wiggled his eyebrows.

"All right. Thanks." I felt like a loser. A grateful loser, but a loser nonetheless.

"And cheer up! I'll take you out to dinner someplace tonight. All right?"

I nodded.

Even Robbie asked me why I didn't marry him. She thought he was sweet and that his helplessness in practical matters and in the kitchen was endearing. "He's crazy about you. And think of all those guys Mother went out with. The ones we dreamed she'd marry."

It was true. Our mother had had a seemingly endless line of suitors—admen, TV writers, heirs to industrial fortunes and patrician estates—who always wanted to marry her. As little girls being tossed about in her wake through New York and London and the rest of Europe, we'd dreamed of settling down with any number of them into a "normal" and "secure" family life. We'd even sing "If Mama Was Married" from *Gypsy* to each other. But she never said yes. The only great romance of her life seemed to have been with our ex-stepfather, Pop, Didi's dad, and the best years of that relationship occurred after their divorce and with an ocean between them. As for all the others, I was beginning to wonder now if the answer had been simple all along: she wasn't in love with them.

So despite Isaac's kindness and sense of humor and generosity, I broke up with him. Sitting in plush, powder-blue velvet armchairs at his club, nursing old-fashioneds, I told him that I thought we should break up.

"What?" He sputtered. "Why?"

"Because we're not in love."

"But, we have fantastic sex." He reached over and squeezed my knee.

"I want to be in love. I want that in my life."

"Okay." He looked a trifle deflated but certainly not devastated. "I think you're making a mistake. You'll miss me," he said slyly.

"I know. It's been wonderful. I'm just ready for . . . something else."

After the breakup and bereft of easy twenties from Isaac, I picked up a coat-check-girl job at a French bistro near my apartment, a place called Poiret. I worked for tips and could make a $100 on a good night. But I found the job humiliating—coat check felt even more invisible than a hostess. I would stand in front of the coatrack and hand out numbers to the customers, take their perfumed furs or camel Aquascutums or Burberry raincoats, then watch them eat at white-linen-covered tables and drink too much. One evening ICM mega-agent Sam Cohn came in with his client/lover Dianne Wiest. He was so drunk he fell right on top of me as I was helping him with his coat. Mortified, he gave me a $50 tip before dashing out into the night. But I was just as embarrassed to be in the coat check instead of acting, and to need the fifty so badly, and to have to spend some of it on new stockings because his fall had caused a big run in mine.

I was still auditioning, but I hadn't landed even a one-day spot on a soap in months. I would trudge back to my illegal sublet after tryouts, temping, or standing in the Kafkaesque lines at unemployment, the post office, or the grocery store and go to sleep, even if it was only five thirty in the afternoon. The city made me so tired—even a small thing, like an errand to pick up sides or drop off my laundry, took it out of me. I felt that New York was winning, and I wasn't getting anywhere.

Then early one evening when I wasn't checking coats, I came home—sleep on my mind—to find David, my summer romance from three years before, sitting on my front stoop with his bicycle.

"What are you doing here?" I was a bit cranky after another fruitless day fighting the city. My feet hurt, and I just wanted to veg and watch some TV, not be visited by ghosts of broken hearts past.

"I got your address from Dave and I was in the neighborhood, so I thought I'd stop by," he said as if it were no big deal.

I didn't believe him, he wasn't that good an actor. He looked like a runaway extra from an Evelyn Waugh novel with the bicycle, a book bag, and a lit cigarette in his hand. He was wearing a thrift-store tweed jacket and a bow tie. All that was missing was the teddy bear, but he was rather dashing, I had to admit—and seemed to have grown up a little. He was now twenty-six—the age I had been when I'd first met him.

He next announced that he'd moved to New York to attend the graduate writing program at Columbia. As I stood there listening, I tried to seem cool and slightly indifferent to him and his news, but that unusual gravitational pull still existed between us. I wondered if he felt it also.

In the three years since we'd parted, he had called and written to me periodically. It annoyed the hell out of me at first—I mean, he'd dumped me and now he wanted to be my "friend"? *Well, I have enough friends, thank you very much,* I'd thought. Then, as more time went by, and he kept writing, I slowly started to respond. So we had kept in touch through the mail, even as we were both moving around quite a bit. His letters to me were filled with carefully wrought details of his travels and surroundings and longing romantic insinuations; I wrote back, chatty and off the cuff, careful to keep my distance. I had heard through a mutual friend that things hadn't worked out between him and the girlfriend he'd gone back to.

"I actually came to ask you if you'll have dinner with me Friday night?" he asked after a few minutes of catch-up.

I considered turning him down, but "Um, okay" came out of my mouth instead.

"Great!"

We stood there on the sidewalk, looking at each other, not speaking for a few moments. It was as if we were in a play, and we'd both forgotten our lines. I thought about the letters he'd written me, which were upstairs in my apartment in an old, frayed Tiffany's box, bound with a white ribbon. I didn't know what he was thinking. We said our good-byes; he went off on his bicycle and I trudged up the steps to my flat to sleep the evening away.

We met a few days later at one of the Ethiopian restaurants popular with the African cabdrivers on Amsterdam Avenue above 121st Street. I took my sister along with me for protection. The three of us made small talk about the writing program, his travels to Southeast Asia working as a recruiter for his dad's small Midwestern college, and living in the city. After dinner, David suggested we come back to his place around the corner for a nightcap.

"Sure," I said, but kicked Robin under the table, indicating that she couldn't possibly desert me. She looked annoyed but forced a smile and nodded.

We walked a few blocks to Butler Hall, a rather grand, old brick building on Morningside Drive, where his graduate-student housing was. The lobby had a little tinkling fountain, Persian carpets, dark-wood paneling, and a doorman. The roof of the building even had an elegant restaurant, called La Terrace. David took us up there first to see the view from the restaurant's outdoor patio. We could see from the lights on the George Washington Bridge to Midtown, and below, the streetlamps that lined the walkways of Morningside Park and Harlem. It was spectacular.

When we went down to his apartment, David poured

us each a bourbon and popped a Django Reinhardt cassette into his boom box. It was the same tape I'd made for him years before, with a gorgeous rendition of "September Song," which was "our song"—or one of them, anyway. When you are so in love, every song seems to belong to you. I smiled nervously.

My sister rolled her eyes at us and placed her glass down on the little wooden table pushed up against the wall. "You two need to get over yourselves." She smirked as she walked out the front door.

So David and I were alone, sipping our drinks in a semi-lit apartment overlooking the night sky, as a whoosh of pigeons circled the tops of the buildings, and the gunshots went crack every now and then in the park across the way.

"There's something I want to tell you," he said.

I thought I should sit down, whatever it was. I perched myself on a light green sofa that looked as if it had been lifted from a seventies motel lobby. "Yes?"

"Show you, actually." He went to his bedroom, returned with a small, thin book, and sat down next to me. "Two years ago, when I was in Asia doing recruiting for my dad's college, I had an epiphany. I was sitting by the pool at our hotel in Hong Kong listening to this guy from Black and Decker talk about how hard it was to find a location for their new factory. He was going on and on, and the sun was glinting off the water and the skyscrapers, and suddenly, it hit me. . . ." He looked at me but was clearly seeing, reliving, the moment. "I'd made a terrible mistake letting you go. And I knew that if I ever got the chance to make it up, to do it over, I had to. So, this is it."

He handed me the book. The epiphany was written inside and dated from Hong Kong two years before: ". . . woke to a blinding sun and this nightmare: That I love you and that I was wrong to spend this entire year apart from you and that I will never make a worse mistake and that without you I am truly alone."

I was stunned into silence, didn't know what to say.

"When I found out you were back in the city and I was moving here, I knew it was my chance. So, I'm taking it."

Overwhelming, unbelievably arrogant, and romantic, his declaration was also risky. All his chips were on the table—and he was no actor.

So I kissed him.

We drank too much. We made love. I left in the morning feeling as if I'd been hit by a big wave—thrilling, dark, and disorienting all at once.

Desperate for work and still checking coats, I started going out for shows anywhere: George Bernard Shaw in Florida and *Amadeus* at Missouri Rep. I came close to getting the role of St. Joan at a theater in Utah, but ended up not booking it. Discouraged and depressed as I went to auditions for shows in Philadelphia, Baltimore, and Montgomery, Alabama, I wanted to run away but couldn't find a job that would take me. I started sleeping a lot and crying too much, despite my happiness at David's and my reunion. Elaine told me that relationships don't make your life, they only enhance it.

In our next session, she expressed some concern over my mental state. "Wendy, I've been thinking that you might benefit from medication. A predisposition toward depression runs in your family. Have you ever considered going on something that might help you function a bit better?"

She was right. My dad had struggled with depression, my mom was certifiably crazy, and I had a cousin who'd committed suicide in his twenties. Still, taking pills seemed cowardly. I should be able to handle it all on my own, right?

"I'm not depressed. I have a boyfriend! And I can still make jokes!" I chortled grimly.

"Look at it this way, if you had a headache, wouldn't you take something for the pain?"

"I suppose so. . . ."

"There's a new drug on the market called Prozac. I'm going to write you a prescription. It takes about two weeks to take effect, and I'll monitor you in case we need to adjust the dosage."

She scribbled on a prescription pad and handed it to me. I figured I might as well give it a shot.

Ten days after I started the meds, I was walking down the street on my way to an understudy audition for a play on Broadway called *The Heidi Chronicles* that had just won the Pulitzer. I began to whistle as I felt this surge of, well . . . happiness. I felt like dancing; my anxiety about the tryout actually evaporated, and I walked into the room feeling confident and relaxed. The audition was at Playwrights Horizons, where the show had originated before moving to the Plymouth Theatre on Forty-fifth Street. I read for the playwright, Wendy Wasserstein, a giggly, zaftig woman with a bevy of dark, corkscrew-curly hair, and the head casting director of Playwrights Horizons, Daniel Swee, who resembled a small boy in grown-up clothes and wire-rimmed glasses. The job covered ten roles—I had seen the show the night before, after Didi had told me the producers would comp me. The play, about a woman's struggle to find love and happiness without compromising her identity, resonated with me.

After I'd finished reading, Wendy picked up my résumé off the table in front of her. She and Daniel leaned their heads together and seemed to have a little powwow, then looked up at me, smiling.

"That was wonderful, Wendy, and of course I love your name." Wendy laughed like a little girl, which made me laugh, too.

"Thank you."

I made my way down the stairs to the street and walked along Forty-second Street. I knew I'd nailed it; I even had this weird feeling that I might actually get the job. When I got home, there was a message from Didi on my service to call her right away.

"They loved you. They don't even want to do a callback. They want you to start immediately!"

We both screamed and jumped up and down like demented cheerleaders, she in her office and me in my small, dark bedroom. I was a coat-check girl no longer.

"So, you need to go to the show every night so you can learn it. Your wig and costume fittings will be in a few days, and you'll rehearse with the stage manager."

"Oh my God!"

"And there's one more thing. You'll definitely go on for one of the actresses, who has to go to a wedding in January. You did it, girl! I knew you could. You are going to be on fucking Broadway!"

"I couldn't have done it without you. Thanks for believing in me, Didi."

"Sure, Gwendolyn. Let's go out and celebrate!"

When I met her at the bar at Café des Artistes, she'd ordered a bottle of champagne. We drank the whole thing and toasted to the future and each other and Broadway. In some ways it felt like the end of a long journey begun by our parents' crazy elopement more than twenty years before. The unlikeliness of our friendship made the moment all the sweeter.

David was thrilled for me. Like Isaac, and unlike so many of my other boyfriends, success didn't threaten him. He had been made nonfiction editor of the Columbia literary magazine and, since they had little office space, would meet with writers or interview subjects at bars in Midtown after work and classes. Afterward he'd stop by the Plymouth and watch the second act of the show or wait for me in the greenroom.

He made fast friends with Peter Mumford, the stage manager, who called him my "stage-door johnny." If David was
working late, I'd call the pay phones at the West Bank Cafe
or Mulligan's or Rudy's to see where he was and meet him
there—their numbers were scrawled on the back page of my
little black address book. At Christmas, he rented a car and
drove to Ohio to spend it with his family while I worked—
the holidays are a busy season for Broadway and being a part
of it was exhilarating.

Robbie and I spent Christmas Day together at my apartment, eating roast chicken, drinking champagne, and watching one of our favorite movies, *High Society*. We were having
a blast—free of the past, guilt, and expectations, we made
our own fun and had one of our best Christmases yet. The
phone rang and for a second I feared it was Mother, but it
was David. He regaled me with stories of his visit with his
Norman Rockwell–esque family, who went to midnight
Mass on Christmas Eve and then came home to drink
mulled wine by the fire. On Christmas Day, they'd gone ice-
skating on the pond and drunk hot chocolate.

Seriously? I thought. *It's so corny.* "Call me when you get
back." I quickly hung up and went back to my sister and the
movie.

"I can't believe she'd pick Bing Crosby over Frank
Sinatra!" Robs shook her head in disbelief.

"I know, it's just wrong. I mean, Frank is so much sexier."
I nodded, twirling a drumstick in my hand.

A few days later, David called again. He was in a phone

booth outside the car-rental place a few blocks away. "I'm back."

Behind his voice, I could hear the car horns and bus engines, loud voices, and tinny Christmas music coming from bodega speakers—the perpetual roar of the city where I'd grown up. It all sounded so familiar to me—his voice and the loud but lulling sounds of New York: home.

"Come over."

I hung up the phone, and at the precise moment I placed the receiver down in the cradle, I knew, in a thunderclap, that we would get married, have kids, and grow old together.

But I didn't tell him yet.

I couldn't say why at first. It wasn't that I was afraid or doubtful after his having left me once before, or that my experiences or my mother's history made me worry. It actually felt the opposite: for once, I wasn't worried, and I wanted to hold on to that feeling. For the first time in my life I felt as if I had the map, could see the future—what I wanted and where I was going—which was comforting and exciting and empowering.

In January I went on for the other actress in *Heidi* and made my Broadway debut, a dream come true. Then in February I replaced the same actress, who was leaving to do a film. I moved downstairs from the understudies' dressing room and into a new one with one of the cast members, Julie White—a brash Texan with a throaty laugh and dirty mouth. And the Plymouth Theatre became another theater home—just as the Guthrie had been for my dad. The smells of wood and paint, burned coffee, and cigarettes were the same as in every other theater, but doing eight shows a week made them mine. Julie and I would laugh and shout across Forty-fifth Street at the dressing rooms of the boys doing *A Few Good Men.* Sometimes David would meet me for drinks at McHale's with the cast—the same bar I'd first been to with Michael, but now somehow different, somehow mine. It was like a New York fairy tale come to life.

One freezing-cold night in March, David and I were out after the show and found ourselves above the dark skating rink at Rockefeller Center. I mentioned I'd learned to ice-skate there and probably hadn't ice-skated since.

"Well, then there's only one thing to do," he said, and grabbed my hand. We ran down the stairs and, jumping the rope, onto the ice. Our shoes slipped easily across the surface and we danced together on the deserted rink. I can't remember the song we sang, but I do remember its abrupt end as we crashed down onto the hard surface in our long coats, laughing. We lay there with our heads together, flat on our backs, looking up at the buildings and the night sky.

"I am not seeing this," a voice said from the dark.

We looked up to see a security guard staring down over the railing high above us.

"Man, I am really not seeing this." He laughed and turned his back on us.

"What should we do now?" I asked David.

"Let's move in together."

I looked at him, my lost-and-found love lying next to me on the ice, and we kissed.

So on April 1, I packed up a taxi with Bloomingdale's bags, a couple of milk crates of shoes, and my trusty Ciao! suitcase and moved into his tiny apartment in Butler Hall. We decorated with plants and trinkets we found on the street and still lifes of fruit. In our closet-sized kitchen, David made spectacular dinners, like *boeuf en daube*, inspired by parties in Fitzgerald and Woolf. I introduced him to opera, which I'd continued to listen to and love since that long-ago, never-to-happen date with Ben. The Met offered a marathon performance of the entire *Ring Cycle* that spring, and we spent Saturdays until my call time lying in bed eating Chinese takeout from the Cottage and watching the Valkyries and Rhinemaidens on our rabbit-eared TV. He introduced me to Led Zeppelin, whose first boxed set came out that year. I'd missed Zeppelin living in London and preferring glam, but they had been the sound track to David's all-American high school years and, along with Wagner, Mozart, and, of course, Django, became part of ours at Butler Hall. I'd never been in a relationship or with the right person long enough to reach this phase of sharing and discovery, but I soaked it all in, along with the newfound routines of home.

After the show closed, I was once again an unemployed actress, and David was finishing a collection of stories for his thesis. Even though we were scraping money together for chickens to roast and cheap wine, we still had shared a sense of surprise—making every day exciting and different. New York was still its old brutal self, but now we were in it together.

A blissful year later, on my thirtieth birthday, David asked me to meet him at the Rainbow Room bar after a day of auditions. I took the express elevator up and found him in a booth looking out over Manhattan, the Empire State Building, and all the way down to the World Trade Center, the water, and Staten Island beyond. I had barely sat down when I caught the look on his face. His eyes were filled with tears. *Oh my God*, I thought, *he's going to propose.*

Choked up with emotion, he barely croaked out "Will ya?" before I grabbed him and kissed him, staining his jacket with my mascara tears.

He pulled a ring from his pocket—emerald and diamonds. I suddenly realized the waiter was there with a bottle of Dom Pérignon. He, too, was crying, as was the bartender.

"She said yes!" the waiter shouted, and applause broke out all over the bar.

postscript

They say it's good luck when it rains on your wedding day—
and it did on mine.

We were married in front of all our friends and family in September in a small French Catholic church on
Morningside Drive a few blocks from Butler Hall. The mon-
signor who interviewed us for Pre-Cana was a card-carrying
member of Actors' Equity, and the priest who married us
drove a Harley. Robin and David's sister, Ellen, were bridesmaids, his brother Stephen was his best man, and Didi's
daughter, Ali, was our flower girl. My stepsister Mary, umbrella grasped firmly in her hands, stood guard at the church
door in case of a surprise appearance by my mother. My dad
walked me down the aisle and read a Shakespeare sonnet.

After the ceremony the entire wedding party walked a
lovely three blocks over to my friends and old NTC classmates John and Jen's apartment on Riverside Drive for the

reception. Django Reinhardt and Frank Sinatra played as speeches were made and laughter rolled through the beautiful rooms overlooking the park and the Hudson. A lifetime of searching seemed to begin and end here as the families that I had lost, found, and made merged with David's, and for a few hours everyone we loved was all together. I may not have known exactly what I was looking for when I'd first come to New York or for most of the time since, but I knew then, in that apartment on 112th Street, that I'd found it.

We spent that night at the hotel in the World Trade Center and our honeymoon in Ireland.

And we lived happily ever after.

acknowledgments

Is it easy to write yet another book about yourself? No, it is not!

I couldn't have done it without a dedicated crew of people—friends and family—who took time out of their busy lives to answer my questions, offer help, advice, and invaluable support.

A huge shout-out to my National Theater Conservatory classmates Anna Miller, Art Manke, Jeffrey Baumgartner, Jennifer Dorr White, John Eisner, and Leslie Hendrix, for sharing their remembrances of our years together as well as their photographs and scrapbooks from that time.

My dear friend Jenny Ott, who saved every letter I wrote her and kindly allowed me to borrow them back when I began this book. Amy Wachtel, for her scrupulous rock 'n' roll journal keeping.

My sister, Robin Lawless, and my stepmother, Sarah Lawless, for the unique and important insights they provided.

Thanks to my marvelous agent, Robert Guinsler, whose care of and belief in me and my work goes beyond the pale. I am fortunate to have him in my corner.

The fantastic team at my second home, Gallery Books, especially my savvy publishers Louise Burke and Jennifer Bergstrom. I am grateful for my editor Kate Dresser's wonderful girl Friday smarts and her persistence in coaxing the deeper truth out of me, particularly when I didn't want to go there.

Finally, to my amazing children, Harry and Grace, who've been so understanding while I neglected them to write this book. I love you more.